METHODS OF TEACHING INFORMATION TECHNOLOGY

Foreword

Teacher education is quantitatively marching ahead towards quality education. The central and state governments through the NCTE and the Directorates of School/Higher Education are rendering their legitimate service in improving the quality of teacher education by formulating and implementing various academic policies and educational programmes. Along with these policies and programmes, the teacher educators and the prospective teachers teaching and studying in teacher education institutions need good curriculum and quality books.

The methods of teaching each subject play a pivotal role in enhancing the efficiency of their practitioners. Identifying the very importance of the methods of teaching and the quality of books, a series of books on the methods of teaching different subjects have been developed by experienced teacher educators for the benefit of teachers in making in teacher education institutions. Thanks to the authors.

Valuable suggestions for the improvement of these books are welcome from fellow teacher educators, prospective teachers and other academicians involved in the arena of teacher education.

The authors and the editor dedicate this series of books on the methodology of teaching to Mr. Tilak Raj Wasan, Proprietor, Discovery Publishing House, New Delhi, for taking up this commendable task of publication to meet the felt needs of teacher education faculty and clientele.

Dr. Digumarti Bhaskara Rao

Research Director in Education

Nagarjuna University

br_digumarti@rediffmail.com

Preface

The movement of modern education in India is almost two century old. It has come of age now. Over the decades, great educationists have contributed towards the development and evolution of education, as a discipline. Thus, education in India has been enriched a lot.

As a result, the Indian education system can be placed at par with any advanced education system in the modern world. In fact, education is a vast sea and Teachers' Training is a stream in it. So, it makes it essential that the responsibilities of the faculty members are focused on the task of providing better training to the future teachers, for their better learning and proper development. And this responsible exercise can only be undertaken, if the trainers are equipped with all the needed skill and knowledge of the subject, they are supposed to teach. Hence, it becomes essential for making adequate provisions, for each course to the teacher-trainees. Methods of Teaching are very important for the successful training of teachers and for their career in future.

In order to provide all related material in one cover, here is this book, on this important subject. Of course there are several books on the subject in the market, but, every book has its own style and way of presentation. Similarly, the present one, too has its own merits and advantages.

During the course of the preparation of this book, the undersigned has done his best for the accomplishment of the job. He would be pleased and feel contented, if this book is acknowledged, as a textbook and a reference tool for the teachers and students, alike.

Author

Contents

1 Introduction

Information is one of those misunderstood concepts. Yet it is at the same time one of the most used. We go to the bus station to seek information from timetables. We obtain information from government offices such as the DSS and the DVLC. Banks, supermarkets, leisure centres, libraries and even the police ply us with more. Newspapers, television and the radio present us with their own ideas of what information should be. In many instances, however, we may not agree with their conclusions. McLeod termed its subjectivity as being one person's junk and another's treasure.

We all understand and deal with this accordingly when extracting news from the media, for example. Yet many of our Organisations consider information to be something more. They see it as a vital resource, to be managed like any other valuable resource. How it is used and disseminated through the available technology can determine how efficient, and indeed effective, an Organisation is. Peter Drucker sees information acquired in a systematic and purposeful way as enhancing an Organisation's productivity.

Information is important, we cannot operate without it. But more than this, we are discovering that our ability to process it by increasingly sophisticated technological means is fundamentally changing the way that employees perceive their Organisational environment. The consequences of this could be either to break down established functional controls or indeed to enhance them by becoming super-efficient. Much will depend upon the characteristics of the Organisation before implementation.

As firms become increasingly 'information dependent' we need to identify the perceptual relationship between ourselves and the information we use. How, for instance, can we possibly design an adequate information system if we do not understand the nature of information? The answer to this lies, in part, with the conventional wisdom of the day. Managers, like everybody else, develop their views through exposure to established ideas. Thus, the way in which they understand information will influence the way in which they treat it. Such conventional wisdom is coloured by the technicians, on the one hand, and the user's own experience on the other.

Anecdotal prescriptions abound as guidelines to the way presented for all who care to listen. These arise from a blanket of professional and academic thinking which surrounds the business environment and provides remedies for action. We could categorize all these ideas into two bodies of thought, two paradigms. The first could be termed the resource-driven paradigm. This is because its central theme in understanding information is the continuity and consistency of the information itself. It is very much in vogue at present.

The second body of thought is the perception-driven paradigm. Information is seen as an abstract concept, the product of individual perception. It is a temporary phenomenon and as such belongs only to the receiver. The difference is not merely one of academic debate. Managements adopting one or the other can affect the design of their Organisations. If information is considered to be a resource then resulting systems are usually more centrally controlled, the assumption being that all information is corporate property. Whereas information considered to be personally owned is seen as being outside the formal structure.

Within the framework of this paradigm the view of information is coloured by its use as a resource. Like any other resource it can be tapped at any time with the certainty of achieving a predictable value from it. Information is regarded as unchanging, and therefore can be easily accommodated into a firm's formal procedure. There are a range of propositions available which seeks to explain information. Each proposition has a consequence for Organisational design. Listed below are those major themes and what their implications might be on business.

Herbert A. Simon took the view that information, along with energy, constitute the two basic currencies of our society. We need energy to breathe, to move, to think, to live. But this alone is not enough. We need to know when to breathe, when to move and how to think. Information provides us with that knowledge. To adopt this perspective is to interpret information as an independent entity. It is all about us waiting to be picked up and used. There may be minor variations in its interpretation by different individuals, but consistency can be easily achieved through better training.

Specific sets of information, such as finance information, are given a unique value by Organisations which are usually based upon departmental rather than individual needs. Particular information is thus attached to particular departments. This allows information to be generally accessible because perceptions of it are bound by the formal departmental framework. Information is then tied into that framework and cannot be used legitimately within any other context, thus guarding its consistency. What is excluded, therefore, is an important role for the individual receiver. This is not to suggest that information cannot be perceived by individuals. Psychologists such as Anderson and Bower have long been aware of the importance of information reception in determining an individual's behaviour.

However, information can be received automatically without an individual having to understand it. For example, through training an employee could process production statistics without knowing what they mean. In this case it is the functional process (through its formal procedure) that is acting as the receiver rather than the individual. An accounting process, for instance, responds to specific inputs without anyone having to understand them. A motor car responds to certain information transmitted through mechanisms such as the throttle, steering wheel or brake. Both of these examples are designed to act as receivers to specific information.

By implication, information can be transmitted to any receiver that logs into the particular transmission. In the same way as a radio picks up a station when it is switched on, the right form will pick up the right information. And like radio waves, information is omnipresent, only needing the correct tuning. Such a view allows information the continuity and consistency required to be regarded as a resource. It also allows a further proposition.

The design of any formal information system must assume that information does not change during transmission. It can, however, be transformed from data or other information sets before transmission. Within such a framework it is the transmitting functions (departments, processes, etc.) which are considered to be the main determinants. The information receiving functions (also departments, processes, etc.) are designed to link into the operational needs of the transmitter functions.

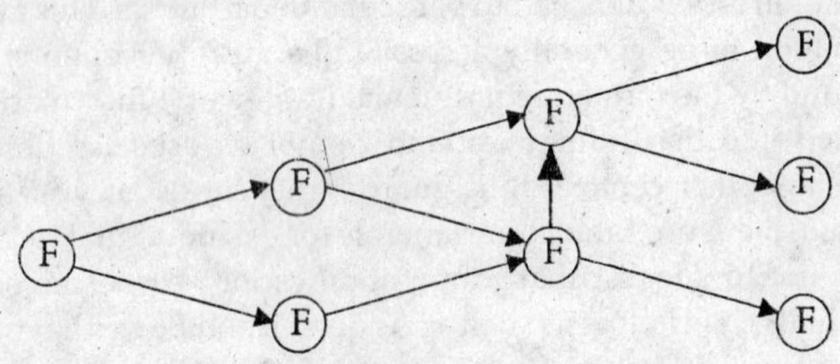

F = functions

Fig. 1. An information network between functions

Each function, however, can be both transmitter and receiver of information, and together with other functions will form part of an integrated network (Figure 1). The functions are tied by their simultaneous roles as information receivers and transmitters, thereby being prevented as much as possible from deviancy in their information usage.

Consequently, business Organisations are driven by those functions which transmit information. The higher the value that a particular set of information is given, the more important will be its relating transmitter function. For example, the finance department could both transmit and receive information. Indeed, each job function within that department could also do the same. A cost clerk, for instance, receives information from the factory floor which he then processes into other information and transmits to some other source, perhaps management. The value of the information he processes will depend upon the utility his Organisation has placed upon it. If the utility is high, then the prestige attached to the transmitting function will also be high irrespective of job complexity. In the same way, if a department has a great number of important information transmitters within its control, then it too will be prestigious and possess influence. Why certain sets of information are prestigious and others are not will depend, amongst other things, upon the Organisation's political processes.

The perception-driven paradigm does not consider information to be a resource. Individuals or groups are seen to own their information. What belongs to the Organisation are the data sets, the facts and figures specific to certain functions. For instance, data on how an Organisation is performing in its market quite obviously belong to that firm. How well that data is used is dependent upon the individual's own competence in interpreting it. Management can control this indirectly through training, but they cannot directly control the thought processes which turns data into information. Once again, there is a collection of propositions or ideas about information which formulate a general approach.

Adherence to this paradigm, as in the previous paradigm, may not necessarily be by conviction but rather by default because people not treating information as a resource automatically form part of this group. However, there are others who are members by conviction. Information is said to be receiver-dependent, in that, any set of information can be considered to be information only if it is recognised as having value by a particular individual. Thus, a river flooding may be information to someone who lives on its banks but of no consequence to someone living several miles away.

It would be difficult, therefore, to understand information as a group or Organisations property since its determination is subjective. Management teams have implemented computer technology and in so doing also developed their information sets into a resource. They experience problems, usually some time after a successful launch, and then abandon using their technology in an integrative manner, returning to the 'islands' approach (that is, a computer system, perhaps physically integrated through networks, etc., but perceptually segregated into different functional areas). Information is no longer seen as a resource; indeed its treatment as such is often seen as the culprit and not the technology itself.

Both paradigms recognize a difference between data and information. Computer personnel, for example, have long known of the distinction. Information is seen by them as processed data. The two are interrelated, data being the input to a process, and information the output. In the same way that an output of one system can form the input of another, information from one system can form the data of another. This is consistent with treating information as a resource. Perceptually-conceived information on the other hand is not the consequence of a formalized process. Data are a factor, but then so are other aspects such as individual traits, culture, structure and political processes.

The relationship between data and information is, therefore, not so strong. This contradicts the objectives implied by the creation of management information systems and data processing. The former allows the individual access to established information, whilst the latter converts data into information. Since the production of information cannot be formalized there is no point in trying to achieve it. Systems should, therefore, be designed to produce the most accurate and readable data in order to enhance easy conversion into information.

When Ligomenides describes information as a fundamental force, he should be referring to data. Levitan, on the other hand, is correct in claiming information to be dynamic and continuously evolving. The logic of these two views can be seen when data and information are differentiated. It is only data which is time-independent, and therefore unchanging and static – a fundamental force. By this we mean that data retains a constant empirical value: a fact is a fact and cannot be altered. Information, on the other hand, can be altered and changed. It is time-dependent and thus its value can alter from one moment to the next. It is dynamic and evolving because it is determined by an individual's perception.

It is, indeed, time and utility which transform data into information. If at a particular time a set of data is useful to an individual then it can be described as information. Equally, at another time the same set of data may not have utility and therefore not be information. The data themselves have not changed in any way, remaining always constant. What has changed is the individual's perception of those data. Information is in reality the consequence of a complex psychological process which transforms perceived data, into usable thought inputs.

It is, therefore, data which the individual receives from the environment, the brain which transforms these data into information. No formal system can directly pre-empt this stage; thus no formal system can transform data into information.

Data can be transformed into different data, transmitted and received. For example, production data submitted to the cost department and processed into second generation costed production data, which are in turn submitted to the financial director. Information is transformed, in part, from data; it can only be received and never transmitted. The financial director may attach value to costed production data and thus receive it as information. If he/she passes it on, it will once again be as data, perhaps refined into third generation data. There cannot be information systems because information is so transient.

The individual's subjectivity, which can be developed by training and formal procedure, determines what is information. At another time that perception may be different. Information systems cannot work in this way. Their assumption must be that information is not transient but consistent.

Quite obviously information systems do exist in one form or

another. They may not be what they claim to be but they are nevertheless working. Is it worth arguing the difference? The answer to that lies within ourselves. Our actions and behaviour, and consequently our Organisations, are governed by our perceptions. If, therefore, we understand information to be permanent rather than transient then how we organize ourselves will be coloured by that. We will design systems which use information as a resource and expect it to be totally consistent.

The difference between these two paradigms may seem subtle, and in terms of information usage it may well be. However, NBS research indicates that the effects upon Organisational design can be major. Structural characteristics consequent upon individually-owned information, for instance, can adopt two extremes. On the one hand they can be organic and informal (adhocracies) whereby all members are seen as contributing equally, each possessing a particular range of techniques to interpret data, whilst at the other extreme there are formal and mechanistic Organisations (bureaucracies). The rigidities of structure stifle any use of information as a resource, so by default such processes are left to the individual. These contrast with the resource-driven paradigm in which the structural characteristics of Organisations are seen to be centrally orientated, with spheres of influence at the periphery, their importance dependent upon the perceived value of particular sets of information.

The development of an Organisation oriented toward the resource-driven concept of information is well known, and many large firms are aligned in that direction. A sophisticated network is established, more than likely computerized, accessing and distributing information. Particular attention is paid to ensuring standardization of information sets. For example, a piece of costing information is so devised that it can be used by accounts, marketing and production. These Organisations treat all information as their property, attaching to it a value like any other asset. This denies the employee any sense of ownership and tends to detach them from the work process with consequential inefficiencies evolving. It is asserted, that a motivated staff is a contented and efficient staff.

One important way to motivate is to give the individual responsibility within their job. Such responsibility is manifest in how much ability a person will be given to determine the information need of their particular function. To standardize information in the way that many corporate systems do, takes away that fundamental element of responsibility. Levitan, on the other hand, would claim this to be an inevitable consequence of increasingly sophisticated corporate structures. In addition, Karen Levitan and others imply that information which is not used as a resource is inferior. On the contrary, one could argue that giving the individual ownership could result in a greater entrepreneurial drive.

Standardization is the killer of innovation. It is difficult to conceive of any substantial Organisation, however, where such a degree of individuality could be tolerated. Their size demands a need for cohesion through standardized practice. Therefore it is only in the smaller establishments where such freedom would work. Large Organisations which do not treat their information as a resource still exist. Their mechanisms of control, however, are not informal or organic. Indeed, the realities are the converse. Individuality is stifled by greater control, rather than less. No-one is trusted to use information for the Organisation's good without formal control procedures. Classic examples of such Organisations are to be found within the civil service or large quasi-government institutions such as the post office.

It has been suggested that there is a relationship between the way in which a firm uses its information and its structure. A matrix can be established differentiating Organisations in terms of how they treat their information and the consequential structural characteristics. If, for example, information is plotted against size (another important contingent of Organisation) four major structural types could be identified. Each is the outcome of the way a particular firm uses its information.

On the vertical axis of the matrix are the two extremes of information. On the horizontal axis are the two extremes of Organisational size (Figure 2). Both information and size are considered to be contingents, that is variables which affect the characteristics of an Organisation. The four possible combinations of these two variables determine four Organisational structures. Thus, each structure is an ideal for each of the four combinations. For example, a managerial structure is the appropriate structure for a large firm using information as a resource.

Resource	Managerial	Technical/ Professional
Treatment of information	Bureaucratic	Entrepreneurial
Perception	Large	Small

Structure parameters

Managerial	:	larger in size with central/top control but with more departmental integration
Bureaucratic	:	larger in size with formal structure and a diversified control
Technical/professional	:	smaller in size with a professional body and formal structure
Entrepreneurial	:	centrally controlled but with less formal structure and smaller in size

Figure 2: Information/structure matrix

Research into the validity of such a matrix is by no means complete. There is evidence from the NBS regional survey, for example, that such a correlation does indeed exist. In general, the more successful managerial-style firms tend to treat their information as a resource, whilst the more successful entrepreneurial Organisations tend to treat their information as a perceptual phenomenon, and so on. It is not yet certain whether the matrix is predictive, that is implying combinations which are not successful. There is sufficient evidence, however, to support the claim that information usage affects Organisational structure.

The issue of information is much more than whether or not it is a resource. Information is indeed the essence of an Organisation, shaping and determining its structure.

For example, bureaucratic Organisations could hot effectively treat information as a resource because their mechanisms could not control it that way. A technical/ professional Organisation, on the other hand, is better able to handle its information as a resource because of its structural characteristics.

The implication is that there should be a natural balance between the design of an Organisation and its information structure. Where this has not been achieved it is because managers are not matching the structure of their Organisations with an appropriate usage of information. NBS research has also shown that the implementation of computer technology can worsen any potential for imbalance. This is perhaps because of two factors.

Firstly, the characteristics of the technology itself do tend to enhance resource-driven rather than perception-driven information. Secondly, the greater volume of information generated makes the problem more apparent.

If the matrix in Figure 2 is valid then there is neither a right nor a wrong way to control information: much depends upon the individual circumstances. Resource-driven information and perception-driven information are opposite extremes of one continuum.

Management teams were grasping eagerly at the new computer technology as a solution to their efficiency problems. There were at that time forces in the environment—market, political, social or economic—with which the traditional methods of Organisation could not cope; it was believed that the computer would provide all the answers. In the space of that time many colleagues began to discover that the impact of computer technology seemed to be contradictory. On the one hand, it did tend to improve efficiency, whilst on the other it was not always so certain that an improvement in effectiveness followed. It seemed that underlying, and as yet not understood, forces were at work.

Departments employing the same technology were more or less successful than others. Business Organisations with all the ingredients of success and implementing computers to further fuel their growth quite often experienced failure a few years later. Since those early days there has been considerable discussion and research on the impact of information technology. It seemed that the perceptual aspects of Organisation were not merely misunderstood but often ignored, and thus we were not able to understand fully the implications of introducing information technology. We now realize that not only does it have an impact on the way we run Organisations, it also has an impact on our behaviour. There is a readily understood physical aspect of any firm and a more abstract, perceptual aspect which arises from the way that people behave as a collective. Information technology is not the only agent in this process, but because of its particular characteristics it can have an extraordinarily powerful effect on both these aspects. One of the two main objectives of this book, therefore, is to underline the importance of the relationship between, information technology (and to a lesser extent general technology) and its Organisational structure.

The two are inseparable. Models that seek to understand either technology or Organisation must do so within the framework created by this relationship. Otherwise an essential factor leading to an appropriate analysis will be missed. The other main objective is to produce a model which can do this. Unlike many of its predecessors, the model will not concentrate on the functional or hierarchical nature of Organisations but rather on the dichotomy between the physical and perceptual aspects. This exists whether or not there is information technology present, but in many cases the implementation of such technology can exacerbate potential dysfunctional forces existing between the two. In effect there are two Organisations—a physical Organisation and a perceptual or virtual Organisation.

The impact that information technology can have on the sometimes tenuous relationship existing between the two can be quite profound. The model explores thoroughly this relationship. It proposes virtual Organisation as the antithesis of physical Organisation. That is abstract, unseeing and existing within the minds of those who form a particular Organisation. The point being that because the framework of virtual Organisation is often subjective and open to many different perceptual interpretations, it is difficult for anyone to establish an appropriate response to it. This makes it no less real; nor does it reduce the need to respond to it. Left unattended the effects of virtual Organisation can be quite catastrophic, especially if stimulated by the impact of information technology. This has considerable significance for the practitioner, especially those who have introduced, or are thinking of introducing, information technology. The model suggests that for a firm to survive there would ideally exist a dynamic equilibrium between the two Organisations which has been termed the Organisational balance. Anything which upsets this balance, such as the introduction of information technology, has to be compensated for by proactive action of management. If managers do not understand, nor indeed perceive the existence of virtual Organisation, then they will not be able to take the appropriate measures. Long-term structural weaknesses or even total failure of the business can result.

Demonstrating the existence of virtual Organisation can be problematic. By definition it cannot be observed directly since it exists only in the mind. At best one could ask a selection of staff for their impressions and make certain deductions, but these are likely to be dubious and tainted with the researcher's own perceptions. As such there has deliberately been no direct empirical research to establish the foundations of this model. Support for its validity has been sought in three other areas. Firstly, there is indirect empirical data gained from several research projects conducted at the Newcastle Business School. This comprises a study over two years by Stuart Maguire and myself into eighty-five small to large firms in all sectors of the North East. We examined particularly the strategy that firms employed to implement and control their information technology.

The data were gathered through a series of observations, interviews and involvement in the process. Other data were obtained from one or two firm studies on the impact of information technology by a group within the Newcastle Business School called AMBIS (Advanced Manufacturing and Business Information Systems). The argument for using these data rather than dedicated data is that they should be less contrived. Secondly, there is support to be gained from relevant personal experience. Although many would find this approach invalid because it does not comply with traditional or conventional ideas about research data, there is an increasing acceptance that such data can prove useful. In the social sciences, for example, Duke argued that such an approach (amongst others) would make a valuable contribution to the understanding of social experience. It is accepted that it cannot provide the only data, but the data that it does provide should be considered no less valid than any other.

We return to a more traditional style in support of the main arguments. That is, rather than gathering empirical evidence first and then developing a model, we should develop the model first from experiential instincts and then support it with data. This is put forward in the belief that to pursue the traditional methods of data-first research would not produce the generic model necessary to achieve the objectives set above. We have become unimaginative in our ideas about Organisation because we have been blinkered by too many sets of data.

How the book is structured in terms of presenting a logical argument takes on a greater significance than if it were based merely upon direct empirical data. It requires presentation of basic argument, counter-argument and a compromise position which leads the reader forward to the logical conclusion. This is the dialectic which involves thesis, antithesis and synthesis.

This overview, therefore, should not only cover the background to the book's major arguments and supportive material, but also provide the reader with a basic chapter plan.

To explain the impact of information technology we must look beyond the functional aspects of business Organisations. The importance of information is reflected in its ability, through the appropriate technology, to corrupt departmental boundaries. This chapter, therefore, proposes that it is better to understand an Organisation as a network of information flows, which is itself set within other network flows of region, market, industry, and so on. Such a perspective is underlined by many firms accessing information beyond their established functional boundaries. Within the Organisation, this could involve different departments accessing a common pool of information from the company database.

Externally, employees can gain entrance to public databases such as Prestel, which are run by autonomous bodies. The drive is towards centralization and hence better management control. Paradoxically, the opposite is being encouraged, whereby every user has the potential to access information which enables them to operate more efficiently, and also to do so outside the control of their manager. Under these conditions it is difficult for managers to control not only who reads and writes what but also, and perhaps more importantly, who knows what.

Large amounts of information can be processed and communicated via a network without managers ever being able to determine whether it runs contrary to their own policy. Security has, as a consequence, become an extremely important issue. The more the dissemination of information is allowed, the more likely control mechanisms will become corrupted.

In simple terms, data are facts, whilst information is the consequence of interpretation. What is information to some is not to others, and it is the subjective interpretation of what is and is not valuable which has caused managements considerable problems. The control parameters on the Organisation's database are based upon managers' own perceptions of its value as information which may not coincide with that of a potential intruder or misuser. But more than this, individual employees' perception of their information stock widens because of their greater accessibility to the information network. As a consequence, their perception of their own job parameters also widens beyond what management might think desirable.

2

Fundamental Issues

While mankind has developed myriad ways of applying and controlling power to dominate and shape our environment, through the use of — tools, weapons, machines, fuels, vehicles, instruments, clothing, buildings and roads, metals, plastics and drugs, agriculture, and electricity — the handling of information has lagged considerably, perhaps because the human brain is itself so remarkably powerful.

Until recently, there have been only three major developments in this area: the invention of written (or painted or carved) language, some five or six thousand years ago; that of simple arithmetic operations, using what would now be called a digital representation of numbers, about a thousand years later; and that of printing, about five hundred years ago. With written language, we get the capacity to make a permanent record of information and also to convey messages across space and time: storage, retrieval, and communication.

With digital arithmetic, we get the ability to perform accurate, repeatable manipulations of quantitative data. With printing, we can make many identical copies of the same record and so broadcast a single message to a wide and continuing audience.

Beyond these outstanding advances, until the last hundred years or so, the only progress has been in the engineering department with increasingly plentiful production of more powerful and reliable and efficient, faster and cheaper devices to implement these concepts. In the last hundred years, we have seen the rapidly accelerating advent of a technology so powerful, novel, widespread, and influential that we may indeed call it the Second Industrial Revolution. Its basis is electromagnetic, in many interconnected forms: photography, photocopying, cinematography, and holography; telegraphy, telephony, radio communication, radar, sonar, and telemetry; sound and video recording and reproduction; vacuum tubes, transistors, printed circuits, masers, lasers, fiber optics, and (in rapid succession) integrated circuits (IC), large-scale integration (LSI), and very large-scale integration (VLSI) of circuitry on a tiny semi-conducting 'chip'; and, finally, the bewildering variety of electronic digital computers.

Revolution by Computer

The progress has been truly amazing. In only about 40 years, electronic communications and news media have become commonplace and indispensable. Computers have proliferated, becoming increasingly fast, powerful, small, and cheap, so that now there is scarcely a human activity in which they are not to be found, bearing an increasing share of the burden of repetitive information processing, just as the machines of the First Industrial Revolution have taken over the majority of heavy and unpleasant physical labour. Now, information can not only be stored, retrieved, communicated, and broadcast in enormous quantities and at phenomenal speeds; but it can also be rearranged, selected, marshalled, and transformed.

Until recently, these activities were the sole domain of the human brain. While creative, judicious, moral, and aesthetic choices are still best left to people, all the tedious and mechanical mental processes can now be relegated to the accurate, fast, and tireless machines. Any sequence of operations on information that can be precisely specified can be carried out without further human intervention or supervision.

At first, computers were the experimental toys of university researchers; then they became the tools of government establishments and giant corporations, huge, expensive, individually designed and manufactured, and beyond the reach of any but the wealthiest Organisations.

People thought of the future in terms of machines of ever-greater speed and capacity; centralized behemoths would hold all the world's information in gigantic data banks, whence major decisions would issue to be imposed upon the populations at their mercy.

With the emergence of powerful, cheap, mass-produced computers-on-a-chip, the picture has changed radically. Now we see tiny computers everywhere: in wrist-watches, microwave ovens, electronic games, pocket calculators, cameras, typewriters, musical instruments, etc.

What used to be done, with few options, by intricate mechanical devices is now performed, with great flexibility and convenience and at much less expense, by the ubiquitous preprogrammed microcomputer.

The probable future has become one of millions of small yet powerful computers, controlling virtually every machine and appliance. These are distributed in every home, on every desk, in every workshop; many of them connected in a maze of small and large networks, much like the present telephone network. This enables individual computers to communicate, sharing information in a gigantic distributed data-base, and gaining, through distributed processing, computational power whose extent is yet difficult to gauge; all this following the individual requirements and choices of the owner or operator of each machine. Increasingly, we are confronted, not only with the results of the use of computers throughout industry, commerce, banking, advertising, science, the communications industry, newspapers, airlines, and hospitals; but with the realistic possibility of purchasing computer power for our own small enterprises, offices, and homes. This may be done in a variety of ways; but in all of them, the real cost of computation is constantly diminishing.

It is probably fair to say that the question of computerization is not "whether," but "when" and "how." We must choose whether to lease equipment or to buy it; whether to install terminals, connected to a computerized "service bureau," or a complete local computer system; whether to get a package of standard programs directed towards our kind of work, to commission new programs tailored to our special needs, or to learn programming and write our own; whether to go it alone or to share a system with a number of similar users (especially if they are in the same building); how far to take our first efforts at computerization; what to include and what to continue doing by hand. Computer programming is likely to become the literacy medium of the third millennium AD.

Elementary schools may well be teaching it before long, and we might be well advised to gain at least a smattering of knowledge of computers and of programming competence, especially since computer languages and programming environments are becoming increasingly helpful and friendly to the uninitiated user.

A computer is a machine for the automatic processing of information. Historically, this information was numerical, and computers were machines for doing arithmetic.

Unlike the simpler calculating machines, which can perform only one elementary arithmetic operation at a time, they need to be told what to do next (usually by suitable button-pushes); computers can be given a list of operations to perform (often with branching and repetitions, depending on tests of sign or value included among the operations), which they will then execute in proper sequence without further intervention. This sequence of instructions is called a *program*.

A digital computer stores its information in the form of words, finite ordered sets of digits, each of which can have only one of a finite set of values.

Considerations of simplicity, reliability and economy dictate that electrical engineers should design computers to consist of a great number of similar pieces of circuitry, each of which can only be in one of two states, usually denoted by 0 and 1.

Such *binary digits* (or bits) are the elements of which computer digital representation is built. A row of eight bits is called a *byte*, and the majority of computers have their storage of information organized in words of one, two, four, or eight bytes (8, 16, 32, or 64 bits).

The number of bits in a word is termed its *length;* if this is *k,* then the number of possible distinct pieces of information that can be stored in such a word is 2. In particular, four bits together can have 16 different contents, and these are standard binary representations of the numbers 0-15:

0000 = 0 0001 = 1 0010 = 2 0011 = 3

0100 = 4 0101 = 5 0110 = 6 0111 = 7

1000 = 8 1001 = 9 1010 = A 1011 = B

1100 = C 1101 = D 1110 E 1111 = F

with A = 10, B = 11, C = 12, D = 13, E = 14, and F = 15. These may now be viewed as the 16 possible digits of a representation (the hexadecimal, or hex), which is much more compact and humanly intelligible than a long string of zeroes and ones. For example, the byte 10110010 becomes "132," and the four-byte computer word 01001100011100101101000110001110 becomes the eight-digit hex word "4C72D18E."

The following are various parts of which any computer is composed. These are, essentially,

1. a *central processing unit* (CPU), which is the controlling and computing centre of the machine;

2. a *memory,* possibly of different levels, in which both *data* and *instructions* are stored;

3. a variety of *input* and *output (I/O) devices,* through which the machine communicates with the world outside it.

The CPU consists of an operation control unit (OCU), an arithmetic/logical unit (ALU), and a relatively small, very-fast accessible local memory (LM). The OCU keeps track of the memory location of the next instruction to be executed, and analyzes the current instruction, so as to activate the proper operation of a memory transfer, nonsequential jump (by appropriately changing the address of the next instruction), input or output of information, or computation (performed by the ALU), as is indicated by the instruction code.

The ALU actually carries out the elementary arithmetic operations (addition, subtraction or negation, multiplication, division or reciprocation) and logical operations (these being bit-by-bit operations, without carry' such as not, and, and xor; eg., not 1010= 0010, 1100 and 0101 =0100, 0110 xor 1010 = 1100) on the data given to it by the OCU. The LM receives the operands called for by the OCU and also the results of the ALU'S operations upon them. For example, the OCU may retrieve the factors of a multiplication from the main memory into a pair Of LM registers and instruct the ALU to multiply them and place their product in another LM register. Such registers are usually called accumulators, and they are normally double-length (since the product of two k-bit numbers is a 2k-bit number). Other LM registers are used for counting (eg. repetitions) and are called index registers; others hold intermediate values and are called buffers; and, finally, there are one-bit or two-bit registers which reflect the information on which tests are made by the OCU (for example, the occurrence of a carry, the vanishing or positivity of an answer, or the occurrence of an arithmetic overflow): these are termed flags.

Originally, the CPU was a sizable piece of electronics, hand-assembled and highly complex. With the advent of micro-miniaturization of circuitry, printing, and photographic techniques, and the mass production of components only the largest computers (mainframes) are built in the old way. Smaller systems generally have the entire CPU on a single chip. Among these, the name microcomputer is now applied to those with less than a million words of memory and a word length of one or two bytes; the name minicomputer applies to the larger machines, with two to four-byte words and one to a hundred million words of memory. (The smallest micro is probably more powerful than the big computers used by universities and industry in the 1950s.)

The *main memory* (mm) consists of magnetic or electronic components which store the information (both data and instructions) needed by the computer. The individual words are directly addressable from the CPU by number (rather like houses in a street), and their contents are retrievable in very short times, of the order of the operation time of the CPU (ranging from fractions of a *nanosecond*, 10^{-9} or one billionth of a second, for the fastest main-frames to several *microseconds,* 10^{-6} or millionths of a second, for the slower micros). This is often referred to as high-speed storage or random-access memory (RAM). While most of the mm is erasable and may be changed at will, some memory is used to store constants and often-used utility programs and is not erasable by the CPU: such memory is called *read-only memory* (ROM). Sometimes this is optional and can be plugged into the computer : this is called *firmware.*

Note that a computer with one-byte-long addresses can have at most 28= 256 words of mm; a two-byte address can reach 256^2 = 65536 words; a three-byte address can select any of 16777216 words of mm; and so on. In practice, most micros and minis have mm ranging in size from 2 14= 16384 to 218= 262144 words. It should be noted that 10^3= 1000 and 2^{10}= 1024. Because computers are so heavily slanted towards base-2 representation, it has become almost universal computer parlance to use the prefix *kilo* or K (which usually denotes a thousand units) to denote 1024 and the prefix *mega* or M (which usually denotes a million units) to denote $2^{20} = 1024^2$ = 1048576. Thus, we write 16K for 2^U and V4M for 2^{18}. Perhaps the commonest size of MM consists of 64K = 65536 words.

Almost all computer instructions comprise an operation code (usually one byte long, allowing 256 possible operations to be specified), followed by an operand reference (number, index, or address) of variable length (since some operations require more data than others; for instance, the STOP instruction needs no operand, so it is one byte long).

The *extended memory* (EM) is sometimes considered under I/O devices, both because it is often physically located outside the computer (while the CPU and the mm are usually in the same enclosure), and because its speed of access is much slower than the speed of operation of the CPU and is comparable with the range of speeds of I/O devices. Most read/write memory is magnetic (optical memory is read-only, and fast RAM is either magnetic or electronic), either in the form of tape, drum, or disk, coated with magnetic material, much like sound recording equipment; it is similarly erased, read, and recorded upon by "heads" which contain electromagnetic sensors/ polarizers. The cheapest (and most limited, in both speed and capacity) device is a common portable cassette recorder, with 1/4" tape cassettes. From this, one moves to specially engineered cassettes and recorders, and thence to high-speed 1/2" or I" reel-to-reel drives carrying thousands of feet of tape at very high speeds. Access times can be quite good for sequential access, along the tape, but random access time is poor at best, running to seconds or even minutes. Economy and a virtually unlimited total storage capacity (on numerous cassettes or reels; but only as many units as one has on-line tape-drives are actually accessible without human intervention) are the only advantages.

Memory Power

When we wish for practically useful EM, combining large capacity with relative economy and speed of random access, we must turn to drum or disk memory; and, nowadays, the former have been practically replaced by the latter. Disk memory is of two types: floppy disk and hard disk, the first being the cheaper, slower, smaller-capacity option. Floppy disks are flexible, have diameters of 51/4" or 8", generally, and are removable from the disk-drive, so allowing one to build up an unlimited library of stored data. The information is stored on concentric circular tracks (not on a single spiral track, as on a sound record), on one or both sides of the disk. The number of tracks and the number of bytes per track vary (the density increasing with precision of engineering, and so with cost of the drive), but the total capacity of a floppy disk is in the range of 50KB to 1MB. The disks rotate at, typically, 300 rpm, and access time is governed by the time required to place the movable head on the right track, a fraction of a second, plus the fifth of a second taken by the head to traverse the circumference of the track, in search of a record; thereafter, consecutive bytes are accessed at some thousands per second.

Hard disks are rigid and have larger diameters. There are drives which range from anything from one to a dozen disks, rotating at about ten times the speed of floppy-disk drives (and so diminishing the access time of records in a track) with one or several heads.

Fixed-head drives naturally must have a head for each track (which costs more), but save head-movement time in random access. Winchester disks are movable-head drives with sealed-in disks, where the heads ride very close to the disk, cushioned by the layer of air between. In floppy-disk drives, the head actually rides on the disk, eventually wearing it out.

The capacity of hard-disk drive ranges from 10 MB to 100 MB in a single drive. Some movable-head hard-disk drives have removable disks or disk-packs, allowing for greater library storage.

The I/O devices are the computer's link with the outside world. In large mainframe computers, we see *paper card* (as in Hollerith or "IBM" cards) and paper tape readers and punches: the perforations in the paper carry the information. Increasingly in large computers, and almost universally in small ones, the main input is from the keyboard of a terminal. This is much like a typewriter keyboard, and depressing any key sends an 8-bit code to the computer.

When the computer is waiting for input from this terminal, it reads the code and interprets it as a datum; when it is busy, either the message is lost or it is held in a "buffer" for subsequent input (this depends on how the connection is made and what the computer is made to do). It is quite common for the computer to be connected to several terminals, all competing for its attention. This is called time-sharing. The computer cycles around the terminals, look for their several inputs while dividing its CPU time among them. The main output of the computer is to the display devices of the terminals; these are either video displays (cathode ray tubes, CRT, just like the screens of black-and-white or color TV sets; indeed, simple micros sometimes use ordinary television sets as display devices) or printers (in so-called hard-copy terminals). Of course, the computer may be connected to additional video displays and printers, of different qualities, as well as to plotters, a kind of printer for drawing graphs and diagrams. Many types and speeds of printers exist. Other input devices, such as audio amplifiers (receiving signals from radio tuners, record players, etc), video receivers and recorders, laser disk drives and a variety of scientific instruments, can all be classified as transducers (devices that transform physical quantities, such as position, conductivity, pressure, temperature, vibration frequency, or amplitude, into electromagnetic impulses) linked to digitizers (which convert such impulses into sequences of zero/one pulses). Output from the computer can similarly follow the reverse process, yielding visible or audible results, or the control of mechanical or electrical equipment. Thus, computers can draw pictures (often, moving pictures), make music and other sounds, and can control appliances, machinery, and whole manufacturing processes.

In order to connect remote terminals to a computer, use is often made of telephone lines; and, for this purpose one employs a device called a modem (for "Modulator/DeModulator"), which converts the computer's digital signals to and from telephone audio signals. This has a cradle shaped to hold the ear and mouth pieces of a telephone's hand-set. It is also possible to connect several computers in this way. This is called the formation of a computer network. Of course, computers may also be connected by cable, fibre-optics, or microwave link. It should be noted that terminals usually, and other I/O devices often, themselves contain computers of varying degrees of power and complexity; so that even a multiuser computer with a central CPU may still be seen as a kind of computer network in its own right. The computers in I/O devices such as terminals or printers are often referred to as peripheral processors (PP).

Many networks do not have a central computer at all; but are simply a collection of independent computers linked for the sharing of information and, sometimes, computing capabilities. Often, they permit the exchange of messages *(computer mail)* and the pooling of data *(distributed data-base)*. They may also share a common bank of memory, accessible to all.

Finally, since the invention of computer networks, designers have been investigating the possibilities of computers made up of an array of CPUs *(multicomputer, parallel processors, distributed processing)*. These new ideas are very powerful and farreaching: they will probably revolutionize our ideas of computers, and of their applications, in the next few years.

The various peripheral devices are connected to the CPU without examining how. In fact, this may be done in several ways. We can simply have a separate connection (or port) for each device, but this limits rather severely the number of devices that may be connected to the CPU. Another way is to have a single bus (or connection) to which any number of devices may be attached.

The information signal must then carry an appropriate address. The bus receives all signals, and individual devices (including the CPU) seek out and decode only those addressed to them. It is also possible to have a switching device, which receives addressed data and directs them to the appropriate recipient device, rather like a central post office.

The decision on what communication arrangements to adopt is made on the basis of considerations of cost, capacity, and speed. It is often the case that the several devices forming a computer or a computer network have their data coded in different ways.

It is then the job of the CPU(s) and PPs to share the work of interpreting signals into appropriate codes for each machine. This is broadly termed the problem of interfacing devices. Sometimes, the solution is to have a standard code or structure for the communications device (one meets the s-100 bus, the rs-232 serial port, the ASCII character-code, and so on).

Another interfacing problem arises from the difference in the rate at which different devices can send and receive information (this is measured by the baud rate, named after Baudot, the inventor of the first five-hole paper-tape code; one baud is one bit transferred per second; hence kilobaud, kb, and megabaud, Mb typical rates range from 200 baud to 200 kb). One solution is to send each piece of information (usually one character at a time, which takes 8 to 10 bits) only when the last has been acknowledged (this is referred to as a handshake); this is sure, but slow. Another way is to use a storage buffer in which a large batch of information is accumulated for fast transmission, thus not wasting the time of the faster device.

One last kind of choice must be mentioned: some channels of communication are serial (they transmit one bit at a time), while others are parallel (they can transmit a byte or a whole word at a time); the latter are obviously faster, more complex, and more expensive. When devices are connected by cable, the degree of parallel communication is exhibited in the width of a flat ribbon cable, carrying several wires, side by side, and in the number of pins in the plugs and sockets by which they are connected to the machines. Parallel transmission is a variation on multiplexing. What we have described is generally referred to as the hardware of a computer. By contrast, the programs that make the computer work, the "soul" of the machine, as opposed to the hardware "body," are collectively called its software. Inevitably, there came to be programs that were hard-wired (in the now outdated phrase) into the computer, in the form of ROM. These are termed firmware.

A computer without software is a helpless set-of circuits, and the expertise required to create the basic software that will bring the machine to useful life is comparable to that required to design the machine itself. Indeed, these days, computers are designed in cooperation between computer architects, who design what the computer will do, hardware engineers, who design how it will be constructed to be able to do it, and software engineers, who design and program the operating system that will run the machine. Beyond this, the computer will also need application software of many kinds, to enable it to do a variety of jobs, such as file-handling, accounting, statistics, payrolls, inventories, complex graphic displays, games, and so on. Typically, the application software is written (i.e. programmed) by the endusers (if they are sophisticated enough) or firms of consultants and programmers and system analysts, often called software houses. Sometimes, a software house will produce part or all of an alternative operating system, or an addition to an operating system, to make a computer more flexible or more efficient than the manufacturer's own software system allows it to be.

Computer's Own Language

The CPU of any computer is designed to accept and execute a specific set of *operation codes (op-codes),* ranging in number from a dozen or so to several hundred. Different makes and models of computers and microprocessors may have entirely dissimilar op-codes; but the operations that they represent are much more alike than different, both through functional necessity and historical development.

The interpretation of the op-codes is built into the hardware of the OCU (though sometimes the details of interpretation may be modified by the user through what is called *microcoding),* and it is part of this interpretation that the complete instruction being decoded contains a certain amount of further information (such as parameters, indices, and one or more memory addresses).

The "length" of a computer instruction (the number of consecutive memory words, or of bytes, occupied by it) may vary, but the OCU automatically adjusts to this. An executable program (sometimes called "object code") consists of a sequence of machine instructions, consecutively stored in the computer's memory and (with the exception of "jump" instructions) executed in the order in which they are stored.

The aggregate of possible machine instructions is called the machine language. In the computer, a program consists of a long string of binary digits (bits), usually written as 0's and 1's; and, of course, the same program would be interpreted quite differently (usually as nonsense) by any computer for which it is not designed. Indeed, the slightest error in a program almost always leads to an error in its output (usually a fatal error!). This state of affairs is sometimes expressed by the computer adage, "Garbage in; garbage out," or just "GIGO." Errors in programs are called bugs; and the tedious, odious process of finding and correcting such errors is termed debugging. It is estimated that, in the production of a working program, the debugging time may be two to four times as long as the time it takes to plan and write the program initially.

To give the reader a feeling for the nature of machine language, we present a simplified, fictitious, but typical, machine language specification. Our computer has two 16-bit accumulator registers (acc), X and Y, which may be coupled into a single 32-bit ace XY, with X holding the more and Y the less significant digits; these are attached to the ALU; and a program control register (pc) Z, also of 16 bits, attached to the OCU, which contains the address of the next instruction to be executed. Instructions will contain a 2-bit acc code a, with a = 0 referring to X, a = 1 to Y, a = 2 to XY, and a

= 3 to Z. The memory consists of 216 = 65536 16-bit words, directly addressable with a 16-bit address, n.

There are four addressing modes, denoted by a 2-bit mode code d, with d = 0 referring to absolute address (address *n*\0 refers to the actual number "*n*"), *d* = I to direct address (address *n*\1 refers to word n in the memory), *d* = 2 to indirect address (*n*\2 refers to the memory address which is the content of the memory word with address *n*), and *d* = 3 to relative address (n\3 refers to the memory address that is the sum of *n* and the content of the pc register Z, with any carry to the seventeenth bit ignored). We will write {{*a*}} for the acc denoted by a, (*n**d*) for the memory word with address *n* in mode *d*, and C[*x*] for the content of word or acc *x* (so, e.g., C[{n]2}]=C[C[n]], while C[{n\3}]=C(n+C[Z]). *A port code p* selects one of 8 *output ports* (*p*=*0*, 1, . . ., 7) and 8 *input ports* (*p* = *8*, 9, . . . , 15), these ports transmitting 16 bits at once and having to be reactivated before each function (i.e., each output instruction sends out one 16-bit number, and the machine must wait for the output to be acknowledged before making another output; while each input instruction reads one 16-bit number, if an input is available, and the machine must wait for a new input each time). Finally, a bit code b refers to each of the 16 bits in a word (bit 0 being the least significant-rightmost and bit 15 the most significant-leftmost). In some cases, the codes a, d, p, and b are interpreted somewhat differently, depending on the particular op-code c.

As an example of a very simple computer program, we consider the solution to the following computer problem. Our computer is to be fed a sequence of one thousand 16-bit numbers at input port #9 (these may be keyed in by hand or fed in by a digitizer connected to some experiment). They are to be stored in memory words with addresses 5000, 5001, 5002, . . . , 5999. Their sum is to be computed and stored in address 6000 and output to a printer through output port #2. The program is to be stored beginning at address 0 in the memory.

Again, what is important about this example is not its detailed form, but the difficulty of its interpretation, and therefore also the difficulty of verification and debugging.

The programmer must deal with a mass of details that are of a purely mechanical nature and have no relevance to the problem being solved. "Higher-level languages" are attempts at making the computer understand the programmer's way of thinking, rather than forcing the programmer to think like a machine.

Advanced Stage

After some introductory description of an imaginary computer, and especially of its CPU, and the establishment of some essential notation. Presented with a set of arithmetic and other transformations required by potential users of a proposed new computer, the electronic and logical design engineers seek the simplest circuitry that will execute operations sufficient to generate all the required transformations. Circuits must be simple to be fast, efficient, reliable, and cheap. However, when an instruction has 16 or more bits, most of which should for the sake of efficiency, have some significant effect; the exact and complete specification or the action induced by it may well be somewhat forbiddingly intricate! And indeed, simplicity of circuitry does not usually lead to simplicity of use.

An ample of a program in this machine language, which takes 16 instructions and 28 16-bit words of memory storage, to read in one thousand numbers, store them in consecutive memory locations, sum them, and print out the sum. However, please note that the English description of what the program does (though much easier to say and comprehend) itself requires 103 characters, each equivalent to 8 bits; so that it is almost twice as long as the machine-language program. Indeed, the difficulty of the latter lies not in its length, but in its alien and opaque form of expression of what it does. The first improvement on machine language was assembly language. This is not very different from machine language, but removes the most glaring and trivial irritations. First, instructions may be labelled, so that one no longer needs to count lines to address jump instructions; one jumps to the label. This is also a great help when one wishes to insert additional instructions, either to correct or modify a program (every jump need not be changed). Second, memory may be labelled, so that numbers may be stored in symbolic addresses and retrieved therefrom, leaving it to a computer program to assign actual storage. Third, the entire program becomes relocatable anywhere in the computer memory. Finally, and perhaps more trivially, the op-codes may be replaced by abbreviated mnemonics, and the instruction layout may be relaxed, using punctuation marks. Of course, a program written in assembly language is no longer directly intelligible to the computer or executable by it. It becomes a piece of textual input, to a "translator program" called the assembler. Naturally, the program may be stored in the computer's memory, like any other piece of text; but, before it can be executed, it must be "assembled." The assembler finds appropriate space for the object code (i.e. the machine language equivalent of the input program) and for its needed storage space (often called variables). The assembly language instructions correspond, one-to-one, to machine-language instructions.

For example, we may denote memory locations by one, two, or three lower-case letters (both for labelling instructions and naming variables). A numerical address will still be allowed. Absolute addresses (i.e. actual numbers; d=O) will correspond to quoted numbers (e.g. "6000"); direct addresses (d=l) to variables named as stated; indirect addresses (d=2) to variable names placed in parentheses; and relative addresses will not be used. With relocatable programs and symbolic addresses, they are no longer useful). Accumulators (X, Y, XY, or Z) will not be referred to symbolically, but only by these names. Instruction labels will precede the instruction and will be terminated by a colon (:). Spaces will be ignored. Op-codes will be denoted by strings of capital letters and terminated by a comma (,), which will also separate multiple arguments.

A sample specification of assembly language op-codes is shown in Figure1. In the assembly language notation, A denotes X (a=0), Y (a= 1), XY (a=2), or Z (a=3). Italic letters (p, x, or b) denote numbers (possibly in quotes, to denote absolutes) or variables names (possibly in parentheses, to denote indirect addressing), and are interpreted according to the op-code (e.g. A cannot be XY in IN and OUT instructions; if A is XY in instructions with c = 1, 2, and 4 (with p > 5), the operand must be 32 bits long-either a double-length number, or an address referring to the first of two consecutive 16-bit memory words. Again, the reader must remember that it is not the particular details of our specifications that are important or memorable but the kind and degree of detail occurring.

Assembly language mnemonic	*Machine language instruction*
IN A, (p-8)	c = 0, a ** 2, p >8
OUT A, p	c = 0, a ** 2, p < 7
TO A, x	c= 1
FROM A, x	c = 2, d > 1
FROMA, B	c = 2, d = 0 -
CL, A	c = 3, d = 0
NEG A	c = 3, d = 1
NOT A	c = 3, d = 2
RNDx	c = 3, d = 3, a = 2
ADD A, x	c = 4, p = 0
SUB A, x	c = 4, p = 1
AND A, x	c = 4, p = 2
OR A, x	c = 4, p = 3
XOR A, x	c = 4, p = 4
LADD, x	c = 4, p = 5
LSUB, x	c = 4, p = 6
LAND, x	c = 4, p = 7
LOR, x	c = 4, p = 8
LXOR, x	c = 4, p = 9
CSHL A, P	c = 5, d = 0
CSHR A, P	c = 5, d = 1
ASHL A, P	c = 5, d = 2
ASHR A, P	c = 5, d = 3
JMP, x	c = 6, p = 0
JPCZ A, x	c = 6, p = 1
JPCNN A, x	c = 6, p = 2
JPCNZ A, x	c = 6, p = 3
JPCP A, x	c = 6, p = 4
JPCB A, 0, b, x	c = 6, p = 5
BIT A, 0, b	c = 6, p = 6

(contd.)

Assembly language mnemonic	*Machine language instruction*
BIT A, 1, *b*	c = 7, *d* = 1
BITNOT A, *b*	*c* = 7, d = 2
STOP	c = 8
INTER	c = 9

Figure 1: Typical assembly language mnemonics

Consider Figure 2. Here, numbers are given in decimal notation. Note the tremendous improvement in direct legibility of the program in comparison with the binary strings. The assembler is left to figure out where to store the sum (the variable "sum" which the machine language program put into address 6000) and the current address of the listed numbers (the variable "w," which the machine language program puts at location 28 if the program begins at location 0, necessitating counting the words occupied by the program; if the program were to be modified or relocated, this would have to be changed, and would be an unnecessary source of programming errors); and similarly, there is no need to count words to determine the addresses of "ret" and "out" (placed by the machine language program at 5 and 24 ' as it happens). As an exercise, the readers may wish to try to modify the program so as to allow for the possibility that the sum of the 1000 numbers might occupy more than 16 bits. In machine language this requires no less than 12 changes and seven shifts of memory location.

```
        CL X; FROM X, SUM; TOX, '5000'
ret:    FROM X, W; SUB X '6000'; JPCZX, out
        INX, 1; FROM X, (W); ADD X, sum
        FROM X, sum
        TO X, W; ADD X, T; JP, ret
out:    TO X, sum; OUT X, 2; STOP
```

Figure 2: The summation program in assembly language

In assembly language only the substantive changes (from the programmer's point of view) need be made. The amended program is given in Figure 3. Here we note that only seven changes are needed; but observe that "sum" becomes a double-length address-just another piece of bookkeeping handled automatically by the assembler.

```
      CL XY; FROM XY, SUM; TOX, '5000'
ret:  FROM X, W; SUB X '6000'; JPCZX, out IN X, 1; FROM X, (W);
      TO XY. sum ADD XY. (w);
      FROM XY, sum TO X,W; ADD X, T; JMP, ret
out:  TO XY. sum; OUT X, 2; OUT Y. 2: STOP
```

(Underlined material represents changes from previous program). Alternative version would have third line replaced by:

```
      CLX: IN Y 1, FROM Y (W); LADD, sum FROM XY sum
```

Figure 3: The summation program modified for long sums

Of course, a program in assembly language still represents, instruction-by-instruction, a program in machine language, and therefore still has the defects of "walking the road in extremely short steps," as we put it earlier.

All that shuffling of numbers in and out of the accumulators, counting and restricted testing, is not natural to us, and its mechanical nature suggests that an improvement is still possible. Thus it was not long before programmers devised much more humanly natural languages, which are generically called *higher-level* (or *algebraic) languages.* Some of the more common ones are ADA, ALGOL, APL, BASIC, C, COBOL, FORTRAN, LISP, PASCAL, PL/I, RPG-II, SNOBOL, SPITBOL, WATFOR, and WATFIV. There are more; and all come with a variety of versions and dialects.

The characteristic that puts a language into this class is that one higher-level instruction translates into several assembly or machine language instructions. Beyond this, the languages differ according to the kind of program they are intended for.

While most languages will perform most tasks, FORTRAN was clearly intended to do scientific and engineering computations, COBOL to perform business data-processing, LISP to manipulate lists, and SNOBOL, strings of text. As a final illustration of the power and intelligibility of such languages, we present higher-level versions of our summation program in BASIC, WATFIV, and PASCAL. Once more, note that the details of the individual languages do not matter to us at this point (though, if the reader ever intends to program, then some language will have to be thoroughly understood; but assume that many of my readers have no such intention); it is their general flavor and appearance that is noteworthy; and the casual readability of the samples presented is their salient characteristic.

Of all the hundreds of programming languages devised, it is safe to say that more lines of program have been written in FORTRAN or COBOL than in all others combined, though this reflects their age rather than their desirability. The fast-gaining runner-up must surely be BASIC, which comes with every micro and most minicomputers; though some would say that BASIC, which perpetuates the style of FORTRAN, spoils any chances of producing really good programs and should be replaced by PASCAL. Fashions come and go in programming languages, not always fully based on rational arguments, and personal preferences vigorously touted.

Given a higher-level language, it is necessary to have a translator program to turn it into machine (or more frequently assembly) language. Such translators are of two kinds.

An interpreter operates at execution time: beginning with the first instruction of the stored higher-level program, it translates it into one or more machine language instructions, which it proceeds to execute; then it reads and translates the next higher-level instruction and executes that; and so on. If a jump is encountered in the source program (as the higher-level language program is often called), the interpreter goes to the next instruction in accordance with the jump and proceeds to read, translate, and execute it, without taking into account whether it has already encountered it. Thus, the same source instructions will have to be passed and translated a thousand times (a very time-consuming and wasteful procedure). But the (usually much longer) object program need not be stored, and interpreters themselves tend to be shorter and simpler programs. This is why a BASIC interpreter is a natural adjunct to a microcomputer, which tends to be a little cramped for space; especially since many microcomputer users are riot interested in extremely lengthy computations.

By contrast, a *compiler* is a program that translates a source program into an object program, the former being in higher-level language and the latter in machine or assembly language.

The program is translated as it sits in memory, not during execution; so that the problem of repeated translation is avoided. Indeed, there are many so-called "optimizing compilers" which pass through the compiled object code several times, eliminating redundancies and inefficiencies to produce faster object programs (something that would be impossible for an interpreter to do). Speed is greatly increased, in general, at the expense of space in the computer memory. Of course, once a program has been compiled and proven to be free of bugs (debugging is far easier in source code than in object code), the source program may be stored for future use and only the object program kept in main memory. Compilers are available for almost all higher-level languages on almost all machines, and are essential for extensive applications.

Information Mechanism

The programs, or software, available for computers fall into two classes, *system software* and *application software*. The system software comprises those programs that are considered indispensable to the general operation of a given computer system, forming what is often termed the operating system of the computer, and generally are supplied by the manufacturer, though alternative operating systems are sometimes available from software houses. The applications software includes all those programs that are needed by one computer user but not by another, even if such programs are widely required, and while some manufacturers will sell applications software (as optional additions to their systems), more often this is obtained from software specialists.

We begin with the *operating system*. This may be divided into a kernel of absolutely indispensable programs and a shell of almost indispensable, so-called utility programs. The kernel (or nucleus) is also sometimes termed the monitor. To understand why this kernel program is needed, we consider what happens when we type a character (say an "A") on our keyboard, as part of a message to the computer. Because our timescale recognizes perhaps 1/20 second, while the computer may deal in units of 1/1,000,000 second, if we want to type an "A" we may find ourselves actually trans-mitting some 50,000 A's to the computer, before our finger leaves the key! If the keyboard mechanism were to transmit the A for only one microsecond, on the other hand, the computer might will be busy elsewhere and miss it altogether. Therefore, it is necessary to establish a protocol (in the usual diplomatic sense, a formal structure for the orderly passage of information) or "handshaking" procedure. This is often done by sending the A on one line (or lines) and simultaneously sending a pulse along an auxiliary line, which sets a "flag" bit in the CPU. When the computer is ready to receive a new character, it checks the appropriate flag bit over and over, until it detects that it has been set. Then it reads the character, resets the flag to its "null" state, and sends a signal pulse back to the keyboard (or its controlling circuitry), telling it that the character has been received. The flag is always open, so the transmit pulse need only be sent once by the keyboard; but the character continues to be sent until it is acknowledged by the computer. Thus a keyboard character will neither be missed nor read repeatedly. In addition, either the CPU or the keyboard controller should send the "A" to whatever device displays the typed characters.

If the particular keyboard were to be the only input device ever to be connected to the CPU, it would be best to incorporate all this in the circuitry of the CPU; but since there may be several different inputs to the CPU, and several types of terminals may be used, coming from different manufacturers, it is found preferable to have the I/O procedures made part of the operating system. In addition to the keyboard input already described, there will be short machine language programs for input from any other devices attached to the computer and corresponding programs for output to display screens, printers, and so on. The orderly operation of a computer is subject to interruptions (or *interrupts,* as they are known in Computer jargon), either because a program contains an instruction that at some point, is not executable (such as a division by zero or a reference to a nonexistent memory location), or because someone needs to terminate execution for some overriding reason (such as the decision that a program is in error and is generating garbage or is in an infinite loop). Handling errors and interrupts is another function of the kernel of the operating system, as is the start-up (or "bootstrap") procedure which initializes operation. If, as is often the case, several users are connected to the computer, then the operating system must handle the tasks of Job-scheduling (and Job accounting and billing, if this is appropriate), and the allocation of storage, in main and extended memory, and of other resources (such as printers or communication lines), and the management of *time-sharing* (as between several terminals). Another task that is handled by the operating system is the management of *user files*, and their transfer between main memory and extended memory (such as disk). Indeed, one sees frequent reference to *disk operating systems,* such is the importance of this function of the operating system.

Another function of the kernel is to provide protection and security to users and to itself, both from authorized users encroaching on forbidden territory and from unauthorized users attempting to use the computer.

Ideally, each user should, on giving the correct access code (such as a "password")—this feature did not exist on the first computers, and is still absent in personal microcomputers with only one user/owner-who has access strictly limited to the parts of the computer allocated to him or her by the operating system, but in such a way that the impression is maintained that he or she is the only user present.

Another very congenial aspect of this concept is that some operating systems conduct their memory management function in such a way that the user need make no distinction between main and extended memory; this is referred to as a virtual memory system. The kernel program has to be able to display, move, modify, and search, at least the main memory, and to initiate execution at any given address, or activate any of the peripheral devices. Using these functions, by means of appropriate commands in the "operating system language," together with its file-handling capabilities, the system can load, compile, or execute any program stored in its memory (main or extended) written in machine, assembly, or higher-level language, provided that a suitable compiler or other translator is available to it.

We now turn to the utilities provided by most operating systems. First, we have an assembler (and perhaps also a *disassembler,* which translates a program written in machine language into the more intelligible assembly language; as well as a *macroassembler,* which allows the user to define his own macroinstructions in machine or assembly language), together with a selection of translation programs, either interpreters or compilers, for the higher-level languages that the user wishes to employ.

The smaller microcomputers will provide an interpreter for some dialect of BASIC, since this a relatively simple language to learn and to interpret into machine or assembly language; beyond this, one must pay for additional languages. There may also be a variety of TRACING and DEBUGGING utilities, according to the cost, size, and sophistication of the computer and its operating system.

There will be facilities for linking or chaining programs together. While the kernel will contain the rudiments of a file-handling system (to create, destroy, list, locate, and transfer files), there will also be utilities for further management of these. Such programs will sort, find (among other files), search (in a given file, for information specified), transform, edit, and combine files. Indeed, a good program editor can enormously facilitate the rapid and painless creation and modification of files, which include both text and programs.

The line separating the kernel from the shell of utilities is purely conceptual and far from sharp. Similarly, the boundary of the entire operating system is far from definite. What is available beyond the essentials mentioned above will be called part of any decent system by some, part of a compiled language by others, and just applications software by still others, depending on their point of view. The ability to handle a variety of data structures (such as arrays, lists, strings of characters, trees, queues, and stacks) may come from the use of a suitable higher-level language or from an extended "system development" utility package.

Similarly, languages intended for scientific and engineering applications usually handle floating-point and multiple-precision arithmetic, though this may be provided even in computer hardware. The same applies to routines for computing, for example, sines, cosines, logarithms, etc., and pseudorandom numbers (the last beloved of, computer games inventors!).

A *data-base management system* (DBMS) may be just a glorified file-handling utility; or may be an elaborate program, cross-indexed and relational, with its own language of special commands, for answering any conceivable question about a large amount of intricately structured data.

As is often the case, you get what you pay for, both in money and in memory space; and vendors' claims have to be carefully scrutinized and verified. It is advisable not to overbuy one's capabilities beyond one's needs.

Similarly, a graphics package may simply allow one to produce passable graphs, histograms (i.e. bar-graphs), pie-charts, and perhaps games, with a resolution of some 200 by 300 delightfully named pixels; or it may allow you to resolve perhaps 2000 by 3000 pixels, in a variety of colors, with the ability to draw complex three-dimensional shapes, properly shaded, illuminated, and textured, and move them by commands in a special language. The latter systems are a lot of fun to operate, and can be most helpful to draughtsmen, animators, film designers, and simulator-trainer designers; but they cost a bundle, and they require quite powerful computers to hold and run them.

Another offshoot of the file handier is a cluster of programs for generating reports, journal ledgers, and accounts of all kinds, as well as forms and mailing' lists (the latter leading to a kind of DBMS in which mailing lists are matched to interests and characteristics of the individuals itemized).

Again, there are statistical packages of various degrees of sophistication, from a mean-variance-covariance calculator, to systems able to analyse very complex sets of data by elaborate techniques, using a whole statistical computer language. What has been described as "the most popular program ever written" is usually given the generic name of an *electronic worksheet,* though the trade name of the first such program, Visi-Calc, like Kleenex and Vaseline, has become almost generic.

A table is presented on the video screen and each entry is allocated either a numerical value or a formula relating it to other entries. When the data are sufficient, the resulting numbers are displayed. When an entry is changed, it and all entries depending on it are altered accordingly at once. This provides a representation of a given situation surpassed only by a graph in its impact, and a first-class planning aid. Finally, among the borderline system/ applications software utilities, will put what is usually called a word-processing package (though would prefer either character or text processor). This is an extension of an editing utility, in which the text may by "scrolled" up and down on the screen, edited in the usual ways, but also more specifically for producing letters, articles, reports, and other written copy.

Margins may be set and the text right, left, or double justified, or set up in multi-column pages, with page numbering, indexing, and even the use of different sizes and styles of typeface, in the most sophisticated systems. Here again, cost rises steeply, and one should buy only what one will need.

Beyond these programs, there lies an endless variety of unquestionable applications programs. There are programs for ballistics, boat design, analysis of molecular structure from x-ray diffraction data, tabulation of Bessel functions, simulation of naval battles and economic cycles, etc.

Most of these are not in the market and only work on one machine; but there are very many programs available in the open market, produced or distributed by software houses, with various levels of efficiency, and sophistication. *Programming* is a fascinating, intricate, rewarding, but unforgiving and at times infuriating occupation. We will encourage all of you who have the time to try it. If you have a computer at your disposal, it would be a shame not to learn a simple language, such as BASIC or PASCAL and try your hand at writing a simple program or two. The sense of achievement when you have a working program is great; perhaps because the process is addictive and consumes much more time than you would believe possible.

3

Contribution to Education

Private data networks, academic and research networks have been a major influence on the development of information applications in wide area networking, since they offer a venue for experimen-tation and co-operative activity less constrained by strict commer-cial viability; the network is normally funded at a national level, by institutional subscription, or through co-operative arrangements, and thus access appears to be free at the point of use. The 1980s saw a steady broadening both of those able to access research networks and in the range of information services and facilities available, as the network infrastructure has developed.

In some cases, it appears that the research network may form the basis of a new generation of high capacity, fast broadband networks offering widespread public access.

Research networks, by their nature, are mostly composed of a collection of co-operating autonomous institutions: Organisations involved in higher education and research institutes. The management of research networks tends to reflect this structure by the way in which control is distributed amongst the participants.

Technical control lies with the network 'hubs', those institutions which provide the basic backbone of the network and the major routing facilities, or with a management group specifically set up to control the development and standardization of facilities. This kind of group may exercise control over Organisa-tions which can attach to the network, but will not control the registration of individual users, and will not at present maintain any central directory of all users.

Similarly, services which are available over the network are the responsibility of the individual institutions which offer them, as is local control over which types of user are allowed access to these. Although the degree of decentralization will vary across different networks, in relation to the primary source of funding, there is generally no single central locus of control which determines all aspects of network use. There are, therefore, no centrally maintained directories or lists of all the services which might be available; it is up to the individual user to discover this information for themselves, perhaps aided by information or resource tools created through the initiative of other users, often on a rather *ad hoc* basis.

Navigating, through a research network is, at the moment, a matter of individual learning and initiative, presenting a steep learning curve to novice users. This barrier extends not only to knowledge of the specific facilities which might be available, but also to the way in which these facilities can be used on different computers and software systems, which may vary tremendously from one site to another.

The basic information services which are offered by research networks fall into three main categories. *Information exchange* services allow individuals and groups to communicate with each other across time zones and geographical space much more quickly than postal delivery would allow, and has proved the most popular and heavily used end-user application on networks by linking together people who would otherwise find it hard to meet face to face.

- *Electronic mail* facilities enable the exchange of messages and ideas on a one-to-one basis, whether more formally as in the sharing of notes and drafts of work-in-progress, or informally for general social contact.
- *Discussion groups* which use electronic mail in conjunction with mailing lists support the exchange of information and messages between all members of a group at the same

time. This is popular for ongoing debates and the exchange of news items in discipline-specific areas, allowing members to share ideas and experiences in an informal setting, to 'meet' new contacts, and to follow and influence the development of new ideas in their field.

- *Bulletin boards* are used in discipline-specific settings, but require a positive action from the user in connecting to the service, and reading or downloading items of interest, rather than depending on the blanket distribution of material through mailing lists.
- *Computer conferencing* and interactive videoconferencing are still quite rare activities on such networks, but will become increasingly common as the technical infrastructure becomes capable of real-time interactive and multimedia services, and are likely to have substantial implications for distance learning education.

File and document distribution support the distribution of items such as text documents, image files, and software programs on an individual search and retrieve basis.

File transfer is permitted by the use of standard protocols so that data files can quickly be moved from one machine to another under the control of the end-user. As more electronic material is becoming available within the public domain, certain computer network sites offer an 'archive' service, in which data files can be stored on open access for retrieval by all network users.

Mail servers are commonly used as primitive database systems, returning files in response to commands received within electronic mail messages, as an automatic process with no manual intervention. This is often the method used for distribution of the composite articles within an electronic journal, for example—the user will request a particular file by name by placing the appropriate commands and filename within a mail message addressed to the mail server.

Information services are available through remote log-in protocols, which allow the user to link to a remote system and use it as though there were a direct connection between the two, within the constraints set by the host system. The service may be on a different network, as long as both end systems (user and host) are able to run the same protocols, and the networks and gateway used will support this.

Online public access catalogues available for remote searching from outside the library or campus site are a common use for this facility, as long as the OPAC allows for a remote connection. There is, of course, no common standard interface for the various online catalogues and so the user must know, or be able to learn, the functions and abilities of each different system.

Non-bibliographic databases are increasingly becoming available across research networks, particularly those which contain information within the public domain, or government-sponsored public information. Once again there is no standard searching approach, and the format and content of the databases may be very different.

The full range of academic and research networks worldwide includes both large and small-scale networks at differing stages in their development, and is too numerous to list here. Most research networks are organized on a national basis, or as a cooperative endeavour between smaller countries, as for example in the Gulf states. A comprehensive directory of networks is given in the books by Quarterman and LaQuey, together with a summary of protocols used, and a description of network interconnections.

The European academic and research networks are brought together in RARE (Reseaux Associes pour la Recherche Europeenne), the association for European research networking Organisations and their users. This aims to overcome national boundaries in research networking by creating a harmonized computer communications infrastructure for the whole European research community. Based in Amsterdam, RARE has over 40 national and international research networking Organisations as members, which are listed and described in the RARE 'State of the union' report.

The RARE association also sponsors a number of working groups which initiate and co-ordinate advances in network technology and services; these include, for example, work on user support issues, information retrieval across the networks, and developing multimedia services. The academic network for the United Kingdom is called *JANET* (Joint Academic Network). Similar networks exist for nearly all the other European countries, including Eastern Europe, although the range of facilities which each is able to offer can vary widely; in some former Communist countries, such as Romania, access is very difficult and services are unreliable. Others are far more highly developed, with extensive experience and expertise, and are moving towards a strategic position of greater independence from government support and self-sufficiency.

The Dutch academic network, *SURFnet,* is an example within this category. SURFnet networks together institutes of higher education, and scientific and industrial research Organisations in the Netherlands, and has maintained a close involvement with the Dutch bibliographic utilities, taking a proactive approach to the development of information services.

In 1989 SURFnet became a private company, with a 49% share held by the Dutch telecommunications company PTT Telecom, and was required to become self-supporting in the near future. This has led it into substantial development in services and user support, working on-site with institutions and with individual discipline-based groups of users between institutions, to encourage and develop new users and uses for the network. There are several other major influences and initiatives which affect the shape of European academic networking at a transnational level, both outside and within the EC. These include:

Organisations which are co-operative efforts between countries grouped together by geography. *NORDUnet* is a collaborative effort between the Scandinavian group of national research networks: Denmark, Finland, Norway, Sweden, and Iceland aiming to enable an efficient connection to the rest of Europe. A similar arrangement has been proposed for the countries in the area of the former Yugoslavia.

EUnet is a large subscription-funded network, which serves European users from Scandinavia and the CIS (former Soviet

Union) to North Africa. Founded by the European Forum for Open Systems, EUnet connects 6000 individual sites and networks together as Unix system users.

International treaty Organisations which are established as European-wide enterprises, with funding from a number of countries. The most influential of these is CERN, the European Laboratory for Particle Physics, which has constructed *HEPnet* as a dedicated network serving research centre in high energy physics.

Ebone is the European backbone network, which provides a neutral interconnection between the backbone research networks which form part of the global TCP/IP based Internet described later in this chapter. The backbone provides a high capacity 'highway' between the major first-level nodes in Europe (Stockholm, Amsterdam, Geneva, Paris, and London) to which other sites connect.

EuropaNet has developed from an EC-funded project conducted by COSINE (Co-operation for Open Systems Interconnection Networking), intended to develop a coordinated approach to networking the European research community, and provide an international infrastructure accessible by academic Organisations, research institutes, and Organisations co-operating with EC research and development. A pilot International X.25 Infrastructure (IXI) network commenced in 1990, forming a backbone which linked research networks in many countries, both inside and outside the EC itself. This has now been replaced by EuropaNet as a high capacity multi-protocol backbone which will handle both OSI (open system) and TCP/IP Internet-style protocols.

The *EARN* (European Academic Research Networks) association provides networking services for researchers and academics in Europe, the Middle East and Africa, as a store and forward network based on IBM computers. EARN is closely integrated with the US-based BITNET network, and is in fact almost indistinguishable from this in use, effectively acting as its European arm. In some countries EARN forms the major research network, while in others there is a gateway connection between EARN and the national network.

There are three main international research networks with worldwide coverage, which are normally accessible from national-based networks, and which are based in or emanate from the United States.

The *Internet* described later in this chapter, is the largest of these; based in the US, it now has extensive worldwide coverage. The Internet is beginning to assume a quasi-public status, and is currently the subject of wide-ranging legislative attention.

BITNET is a major US-based co-operative computer network interconnecting over 3000 academic and research institutions in more than 35 countries, as far apart as Eastern Europe, Latin America and the Far East; the network encompasses a number of more local networks within its structure. BITNET was originally funded by the IBM corporation in the early 1980s, and was free to the academic community; this support is now terminated, and access is through institutional subscription. BITNET has close links with the Internet, and many sites are accessible through both networks, almost indistinguishably.

Usenet is a loose assemblage of Unix-based sites, including many thousands of computers, from large systems to personal workstations. It is strongly associated with the Unix world, and has an independent and co-operative spirit, with no central management or control, depending on allegiance to a code of good practice; the nature of Unix systems tends to limit the appeal of Usenet to a fairly specialist community.

The main feature of Usenet is the large number of discussion and newsgroups which exist within it, known as *Network News*, amounting to almost 30 Megabytes of 'news' daily. Essentially Usenet is not a technical data network, and does not have separate fixed lines between sites; it is more of an informal, agreement for the exchange and passing on of 'news' achieved by a variety of means, including dial-up over the public data network. Much of Usenet activity is now carried out via the Internet.

JANET, the Joint Academic Network, is an X.25 packet-switched service which provides inter-site access for and on behalf of the UK higher education and research community. Initially formed to support scientific data processing, JANET has since expanded to encompass a fundamental role as a communications medium for the academic and research communities as a whole, and now includes a broad range of information services and resources.

JANET was formed in 1984 through a rationalization of the existing academic and research networks which were established at that time in the UK. These included the two national research networks which belonged to the Science and Engineering Research Council and the Natural Environment Research Council, together with eight regional university-based networks.

Since these networks did not all work to the same standards, the introduction of an overall team for management and development of the network was required. The management and control of JANET is currently based at the SERC Rutherford Appleton laboratory in Oxfordshire: the joint network team deals with policy and development matters, and with management of the network infrastructure. Control of the local site facilities and their use of JANET, and administration of the physical connections to the JANET network, is the responsibility of the local representatives; however, these responsibilities must be fulfilled as a condition of connection to the network.

JANET provides the infrastructure which connects the facilities of its users together, rather than determining day to day use of the network. JANET is funded by the joint information systems committee of the UK Higher, Education Funding Councils on behalf of the research and educational institutions, by top-slicing a part of the overall national budget for higher education before it is devolved to institutions.

The network is thereby provided as a general educational and research facility, essentially funded through government agency. Organisations which have been permitted to connect to JANET but which do not fall within this category pay an annual subscription fee. It is expected that in the near future, the management of JANET will be taken over by UKERNA, the UK Educational and Research Networking Association; this represents a move away from direct central government funding. Restrictions on the type of Organisation which can connect to JANET have been slowly relaxed over time, as the needs of JANET's primary users demand a wider range of networking contacts.

Within the 'guidelines for acceptable use' which require that network usage is related to educational and research purposes, rather than to a directly profit-making enterprise, institutions with primary connections can now allow local secondary users to connect to JANET using their primary connection as an entry node. At the present time, the guidelines allow the following kinds of Organisations to directly connect to the network:

- universities and other higher education and research institutes which are funded by a central government agency;
- government research establishments not directly funded;
- not-for-profit Organisations engaged in collaborative research with higher education institutes;
- libraries and related Organisations, including the national libraries and the UK bibliographic utilities;
- educational councils and research institutes;
- learned societies,
- commercial Organisations involved in collaborative research, or providing a service or support to higher education (for example Blackwell's periodicals service).

The JANET network developed as an X.25 (84) packet switching technology as the underlying data transmission scheme. The recent upgrading of data lines has increased the bandwidth capacity to 2 Mbps on most sites, by the use of leased lines from Mercury Communications.

At the inception of a formal JANET service in 1984, X.25 was the only realistic, choice within the European market which was able to offer wide connectivity and reasonable performance, and which was compatible with public telecommunications, while avoiding the pitfalls of proprietary protocols. Since this time, however, the alternative approach of TCP/IP has emerged as a strongly supported protocol within the research community, affecting forward planning of JANET services.

The higher level network functions were originally provided by the proprietary *Coloured Book Software* protocols, designed as an interim measure. This set of protocols provide the basic network services; the Grey Book defines an electronic mail service, for example, and the Blue Book deals with file transfer. The network administration has had the long-term goal of making a transition to the use of OSI protocols; some services, such as X.400 mail, are already available. The development of a Domain Name Server provides a name to address translation to make network connections more transparent for the end user. This is made possible by a Name Registration Scheme (NRS) which maintains a directory of the individual systems which are JANET-accessible on all the 200 or so UK sites (and some others); these have both a network address (a string of numerals prefixed by 0000) and a more usable network name.

The naming scheme can be used by local nodes to distinguish between different machines at the same site by progressively structuring the address into smaller sub-domains. Thus, a full JANET address name will identify the *uk* geographical area, followed by an *ac* to denote the academic network, a single word name for the institution as a whole, and any necessary sub-units in the Organisation, until an actual machine name is identified (for example, the address *uk. ac. oxbridge, cc. vaxe)*. All network node names are registered on the central database, which can be downloaded into local data storage and used by name servers at individual sites.

Individual users are registered on their local machines, and any others to which they have log-in rights, by the naming convention chosen by the individual site. Information objects addressed to a specific username (for example *user@uk. ac. oxbridge, cc. vaxe)* will be delivered to the site by the network; the local system is then responsible for delivering the data to the workspace of the local user.

The basic services of electronic mail, remote log-in and file transfer have given rise to a wide range of different specialized services and access to information resources which are available to all JANET users.

The academic community which JANET serves includes a wide variety of disciplines, many of which are not traditionally linked with computer and information usage. Electronic mail, as well as serving for one to one interpersonal messaging, is often used to support group communication and as a simple interface to online information services.

The Networked Information Services Project (NISP), based at Newcastle University, was set up to explore the possibilities for enhancing, group communication and information dissemination facilities on JANET, with a particular emphasis on drawing in those groups not yet familiar with computer networking. This has led to the development, from 1989 onwards, of a mail server service known as *Mailbase.* Working with groups of academics and researchers from areas as diverse as music, history and library management, Mailbase aims to provide groups with the ability to participate in focused discussions by joining e-mail based discussion lists, each limited to a narrow topic; and for groups to run these information services themselves. Each list has an owner, responsible for managing it, and may be 'open' to public access, or 'closed' to all except invited participants; the degree of access to archived discussion can also be controlled.

Contact with the service is through the sending and receipt of electronic mail messages to the mail server based at Newcastle, and can be done from any JANET site. Some of the lists are working on specific tasks—the development of network training materials, for example—the results of which are made publicly available as retrievable documents from the Mailbase service.

As of 1992, the project reported some 6,000 users of this service, with a total of 12,000 subscriptions to the 200 existing lists. Membership of lists varies from several hundred to single figures. One of the most enthusiastic users of this service has been the academic library community, which formed a number of lists on specific topics, most of which have now merged together under the name of *lis-link*. This generates some 5-10 messages per day, providing a forum for sharing ideas and experiences, seeking answers to specific reference questions, and testing opinion on library-related issues; with the advantage of fast response from other users.

The interchange on discussion lists is normally carried out from within the familiar mail package of local systems, with no requirement for the user to be aware of delivery and connection details. Remote log in is available by invoking the calling facilities of the JANET PAD (the local link into the X.25 packet switching system), and using the local workstation as though it were a terminal with direct connection to a distant system.

In many cases, the called computer will require the caller to have a registered username and password before making any facilities accessible. Some services, however, have been set up for general access by JANET users and do not require a caller to declare an identity.

Bulletin boards require the user to connect to the systems and choose items of interest typically organized under a multi-level menu structure; documents can be read on-screen, or dispatched to the user's home system. Examples of successful bulletin boards on JANET are the Joint Network Team news service, *JANET.news; HUMBUL,* a bulletin board for users in humanities disciplines; *History .news;* and the Bulletin Board for Libraries, BUBL. This latter is a library-oriented information service, containing news, events, announcements, current information on networking issues, and network training materials. The bulletin board also offers a current awareness service, by listing the contents pages of relevant periodicals, and acts as a forum for the sharing of ideas and expertise on a range of LIS topics. Although still used by a relatively low proportion of the library community, BUBL achieved a usage rate of 2400 per month in January 1993.

Online public access catalogues (OPACs) of the educational member institutions are normally available to anonymous remote users through a JANET connection, which enables access to the system as though from within the library itself, though this may entail some degradation in the quality of the user interface. At least 60 UK library catalogues are available in this way, and these include those of the larger research libraries; details are listed in a directory by Peter Stone. Access to the new British Library online catalogue is likely to be available from late 1993.

A recent development is the mounting of the Institute for Scientific Information Citation Indexes for science, social sciences, and the humanities, and the Excerpta Medica database, as a JANET resource. This is accessible under the name of BIDS (Bath Information and Data Services). BIDS provides unlimited access to these indexes to all members of academic institutions which have paid an annual subscription fee. For the individual institution, the service is an interesting alternative to offering equivalent access through CD-ROM databases mounted on a local area network.

An added advantage of the JANET access method is that it will be able to extend the service to include document delivery as well as citation retrieval options as these become available. The British Library intends to offer a new table of contents database, and Inside Information, through the BIDS service containing article descriptions from the 10,000 most requested titles from the Document Supply Centre, linked to online ordering facilities. There are a number of other databases available through the network, containing various types of non-bibliographic information: for example, the Biron database contains information on datasets held by the ESRC (Economic and Social Science Research Council), and the HENSA archive gives access to public domain software.

Several fee-charging databases and electronic resources are also available, including access to the British Library *BLAISE* service and to major online bibliographic databases. This has the advantage to the user of saving on telecommunications' costs, since use of JANET as a carrier is effectively free to the end-user. The JANET User Group for Libraries (JUGL), one of the user groups which advises the network management, has overseen the development of a library-oriented guide describing many of the resources available over JANET through *Project Jupiter,* and has contributed to network training initiatives in this area. This has helped with the navigational problems in pointing to the existence and location of useful resources, and has helped to firmly establish JANET as a medium for reference of information resources within the library environment.

The JUGL user group has also initiated the *Plan for Library Action on NETworks* (PLANET) in an attempt to encourage library and information workers to become actively involved in developing and exploiting network resources and services through an awareness of and involvement in existing projects, and the encouragement of discussion and debate on future developments.

Interactive gateways allow a user to connect to a service on a different network, and to perform searches within these services interactively, by translating from JANET into the protocols running on the other network. This is particularly attractive for JANET users who wish to make use of Internet facilities, and are otherwise unable to do so. These gateways act as guest intermediate systems, which are connected to both networks; to search an Internet database, for example, a JANET user first contacts the appropriate gateway, and from there initiates a second link, which is controlled by the gateway computer, to the destination--the information exchange between the two end systems is conducted in two stages.

JANET gateways enable the use of remote log-in and file transfer with Internet systems in this way; the user is able to nominate the desired destination through the addressing scheme. The *NISS gateway* (National Information on Software and Services) is a more specific service offering links to specified information systems, both commercial and non-commercial, through hierarchical menus listed on sets of screens. Some of these services are freely available to all users, and others require previous registration and the use of a password and identifier.

The advantage of the gateway is that several popular services are brought together under one umbrella, without the need for special knowledge on methods of connection on the part of the user; some of the physical connections offered include services outside the UK which may not otherwise be available from all user sites. In the section on bibliographic services, the NISS gateway offers links to Datastar and Dialog bibliographic hosts; to the German DIMDI biosciences online and STN scientific and technical network; to the OCLC EPIC reference databases in Ohio, and the US Research Libraries Group Citadel system; to the ARTTel system of the British Library Document Supply Centre; to the MELVYL catalogue of the University of California, and the CARL database in Colorado; and to the Data Distribution Network of the European Space Agency. Neither research nor educational work is limited by national boundaries, and it is desirable to extend the communicative abilities networking offers beyond these geographic limits. JANET achieves this by the use of public gateways to other major networks, falling into two principal groups.

The *public data network* (known as the PSS) gateway enables stations on JANET to link into systems that are only available in this way, without the need to reconnect to a different network at the user end. This also offers a route into JANET for those who do not belong to one of the member institutions. As a part of a public telecommunications system, use of the gateway itself is charged for by British Telecom, although activity within JANET itself is not.

Relay gateways provide links with other major research networks in Europe and the United States. These do not offer a direct connection to services on the other network, but electronic messages and files can be passed from one network to the other, performing any necessary translation in the process, in a store and forward manner. This allows JANET users to exchange information with network users worldwide, and with relative case, although the addressing system is more complicated.

– The *Earn-Relay* gateway exchanges information packets with BITNET and EARN network services;

– The *Nsfnet-Relay* gateway performs a similar service for destinations on the Internet;

– *MHS-Relay* is an X.400 gateway giving access to Telecom Gold 400 for electronic mail messages in this format, and to an IBM Mail exchange with employees and customers of that corporation worldwide;

As pressure for direct access to the wealth of information and personal contacts on the Internet increased during the early 1990s, the JANET management team initiated a project to develop a JANET IP Service (JIPS), to enable JANET sites to behave as though directly connected to the Internet -network. This enabled sites to run the TCP/ IP protocols necessary for interworking with Internet sites, through a so-called IP 'tunnel', by carrying IP traffic as X.25 data—in effect running one protocol on top of the other, disguised as data packets. Implicitly, this development has recognized the importance of TCP/IP at the present time for the research community, and recognizes the value in allowing the existence of alternative standard protocols on the same network for the benefit of global connectivity.

A JANET site must have the appropriate hardware— an IP router—and software installed to use the service, and must develop an Internet compatible naming scheme for directly linked users. Parallel running of protocols requires a user to launch the correct application for a particular need (and to know which this is), and so is not a transparent process to the user. For those with networking skills, however, the JIPS development opens out an enormously wider range of information and communication possibilities, and is a step within the UK towards greater international connectivity, as well as opening up access to more advanced information applications. A UK researcher can, from an office desktop, log in to the catalogue of the New York Public Library, retrieve copies of archived files from Sydney, and communicate with colleagues on the Pacific Rim, unconstrained by distance and time differences. By September 1992, over half the data traffic carried on JANET was IP traffic.

The introduction of multiple protocols does, however, introduce network management problems in relation to the end-user: everything must have two names—a JANET name and an Internet name and there are often duplicate applications for the same task, confusing the user. There are pressures within JANET to move to the use of the TCP/IP protocol suite as the underlying native mode, and it seems likely that this will occur in some parts, so that X.25 traffic is carried on top of an IP-based network, reversing the current position.

From 1993, parts of the JANET network are to be upgraded to a substantially higher speed and capacity in the SuperJANET project, to be installed by British Telecom. This project is intended to make use of advanced communications technology to provide research and education within the UK with a high speed, high performance broadband network capable of transmitting voice, data, and image together. This new network, using optical fibre, will upgrade the bandwidth available to a maximum of 140 Mbps using ATM packet switching techniques.

Working at a speed some 1000 times faster than the present JANET, this will enable the development of a range of applications and information services previously unfeasible. It is anticipated that early applications will include the use of distance learning courseware, electronic publishing, library document distribution, medical imaging, and multimedia information services.

The SuperJANET project intends to link into the existing Livenet network of the University of London, at present used to transmit live video images of medical surgery in operating theatres to classes of medical students, for teaching purposes. There is a two-way audio link with the theatre, so that students may ask questions from the surgeon, and an image base of still and video images as background material is also available. Super JANET will extend this link to a wider audience of medical schools. Within the library field, a number of projects have been proposed, indicating a recognition of the importance of networking in this area.

1 Seven university libraries will co-operate in a resource sharing project on the delivery of journal articles in electronic form, with a much faster response than normal interlibrary loan methods.

2 A need has been identified amongst researchers who require access to high quality images of rare documentary material and archives, such as illustrated manu-scripts, at different locations; a project will use ancient Persian manuscripts held at Manchester University to investigate this area.

3 A number of publishers are co-operating in the creation of a body of material to build an experimental electronic journal, covering a broad subject area which tests a variety of information needs—colour maps, graphics, half-tones, and scientific notation, for example.

The history of the JANET network shows that in a few short years, the available facilities are being used for applications never imagined in the early stages, and it is likely that a similar turn of events will overtake these initial ideas for SuperJANET. While it is certain that this round of development will result in unanticipated services as needs and understanding develop, it is less certain that the future funding and access mechanisms will remain as at present.

The Internet is an extensive academic and research-based network linking a very large number of broadly educational, research, and other related Organisations across the United States and worldwide. It has a very large number of users and makes accessible a wide range of information services and resources. The Internet proper, in technical terms, refers to the relatively small number of machines which constitute nodes on the main network in the United States. Most people use the term, however, to refer to the vast range of networks, which may emanate from other countries as far apart as Canada, Israel, Germany, Mexico, New Zealand, and Australia. Within the United States, the enormous success of the Internet over the last five years is moving the network away from its beginnings as a traditional academic orientation towards a new and radical direction as a major national educational and community resource for economic development.

The Internet originally developed as a military network from projects funded by the Advanced Research Projects Agency of the US Department of Defence from 1969 onwards, and was known originally as ARPANET. In 1989, ARPANET was finally completely decommissioned from military service, and devoted to educational and research purposes. Along with other emerging state and national network elements, this began to become interlinked through a major data communications backbone established by the National Science Foundation between six new supercomputer sites in 1985. In the late 1980s, the National Science Foundation developed a high speed network backbone called *NSFnet* from the existing infrastructure, linking-some 16 main sites around the United States with data rates of 1.5 Mbits per second (known as the T1 standard).

The NSFnet forms the main data highway for the Internet, providing links via the 16 main sites to regional networks, and thence onwards to local networks and individual Organisations. These main nodes may also provide gateways through to many other national and international networks, such as Earn (the European counterpart of BITNET) and CA net in Canada. The regional networks cover broad geographical areas, although with some overlap as a result of recent growth, and are run by a variety of Organisations from commercial enterprises to government funded groups. Parts of the NSFnet backbone are also provided by commercial enterprise, and this mix of public and private characterizes the Internet situation.

In principle, an Organisation which has an Internet connection, or 'feed', from a local or regional node, and which has the required equipment capacity, may itself provide any number of feeds to other Organisations and individuals who are looking for an Internet account, relaying the network traffic back and forth on their behalf. In this way, the network is able to grow organically and, since one system user may have more than one feed available to it, can provide multiple communication pathways between sites, and therefore a more robust and reliable service.

By November 1992 nearly 8561 foreign, regional, state, and local networks constituted the Internet, connecting more than 700,000 host computers with an estimated 4 to 5 million users in 44 countries. In anticipation of serving a more widely expanded role, the NSFnet is currently being upgraded to support a much higher data transmission speed (45 Mbits per second, known as T3 standard), providing the bandwidth which will enable the development of a range of interactive services in multimedia telecommunications This strengthened backbone is now referred to as a 'cloud' to emphasize its non-linear, interconnected, nature. The glue which binds all these diverse systems and machines together is the use of the TCP/IP communication protocols suite.

Most of the machines which constitute the Internet proper, and many of those which communicate with it, use this rather old, but widely used and constantly developing set of protocols; their widespread use in the Internet is part of its inheritance from the ARPANET, and is a major reason why TCP/IP usage is seen as the main rival to the open-systems movement.

Control of the network is distributed through various levels, with (at the moment) no overall control imposed from a central point. The main backbone NSFnet is currently managed by a not-for-profit consortium consisting of IBM, MCI (an important commercial network provider), and the Merit Organisation, based in Ann Arbor, Michigan.

The network uses a Domain Name System, similar to that of JANET, so that IP address numbers (long strings of digits) can be replaced by more explanatory structured domain names; the main difference from the JANET method is that these names are structured in reverse order, progressing from the narrower to the broader domain: from Organisation on the left to country on the right. New system users register with regional co-ordinators, who have the responsibility for mapping connection points, in order to make their existence known to other network users. This gives the Internet a much more informal flavour compared with JANET, making it difficult to say exactly how many Internet users exist, since there is no one point at which they are all counted.

There are agreed conventions on the use of the Internet to which all users are expected to conform: that it is intended for educational use and should not be used for purposes of commercial gain. This restriction is commonly quite broadly interpreted, and by no means all of the traffic between educational and other institutions is strictly educational in content; although it does preclude the offering of straightforward commercial services across the network, even though many Organisations with Internet connections are commercial in nature. Some believe that this restriction will be relaxed in the near future.

The main decision-making body for the Internet is the Internet Society, a voluntary Organisation which aims to promote Internet technology and developments. A sub-group of this, the Internet

Architecture Board, is responsible, for approving new and upgraded standards and for allocating resources such as IP addresses.

The Internet Engineering Task Force (IETF) is another voluntary body with open membership, which represents the user voice in Internet debates. The, IETF holds regular meetings—in Europe in 1993—and has a number of working groups developing specific issues. The Internet, then, depends to a large extent for its success on willing co-operation among its participants, and conformity to the spirit of network culture and etiquette. For example, an unwritten rule is that users who are established on the network through the benevolence of a host Organisation supplying their feed are ethically bound to consider similar requests made to them in the future. The cost of these connections is normally born as a part of the network overhead; by this means the overall cost is spread among the participants, so that network use often appears to the individual user as free, or at least providing unlimited usage for minimal cost.

There is a stronger tradition of more widespread public access to the Internet in the United States, with the availability of low cost dial-in lines as an alternative to full peer connection. Within the UK, there are a number of private Organisations which provide Internet access as a commercial enterprise, for those who do not have an entry through the JANET network. This approach has been very successful, with a phenomenal growth in network activity from 1989 onwards, since then network traffic has grown, on average, by 20% per month. In the year up to October 1992, the total amount of network traffic in bytes almost doubled to about 3000 gigabytes per month. This phenomenal growth has catalysed the discussion on the future development of the Internet, and its methods of funding and management may change dramatically in the future.

Internet provides electronic mail services based on the Simple Mail Transfer Protocol (SMTP) mail convention. Electronic mail has also given rise to a variety of alternative uses beyond the simple exchange of messages between individuals to a greater extent than in the UK. A large number of news groups and discussion groups have grown up over the Internet based on the use of mail servers; within BITNET, which has become identical to the Internet for many practical purposes, these are known by the name of the Listserv software used on IBM machines.

These function as automatic distribution lists for subscribers interested in an individual topic, which rebroadcast messages from individuals to the entire group. The Usenet newsgroups are also distributed over the Internet, and are available in a similar way. Listserver-type systems are present on numerous sites, rather than being centralized as in the UK Mailbase project, and there are hundreds of interest groups, ranging from technical discussions on aspects of computer science, through topics based on subject disciplines and educational and research issues, to social and recreational groups.

An example of one of the more active, for library and information workers, is PACS-L, dedicated to the discussion of public access computer systems; this has about 2000 members in several countries, and generates some 10-15 messages per day. Within the LIS field, there are groups centred around specific information service types, library systems suppliers, and broader social issues. There are estimated to be over 3500 conferences active, in addition to the Usenet newsgroups. Electronic mail is also used for the distribution of several electronic journals which are available over the Internet, most with free subscriptions. Once edited and compiled by human intervention, the journal may be distributed either in its entirety as a long e-mail message, or in the more sophisticated cases only as a contents page; subscribers can then receive individual articles as an e-mail message by sending a command which is automatically processed. Over 100 electronic journals, newsletters, and digests exist in the Internet environment. In this case, the listserver can be seen to function as a primitive database system. This practice saves on the use of network bandwidth by not transmitting unwanted information in the shape of unused articles; but also allows users to gather the information in the format most appropriate to their needs. Journals may also include graphics files, and text files may be available as plain ASCII or Postscript (laser printable) versions.

For sites with a direct Internet connection, real-time interactive access with public online information systems is available to remote sites. As with JANET, a common use is for access to online library catalogues. Since most of the main educational sites in the US are connected, a wide variety of catalogues are available, some with major collections – for example the Melvyl catalogue at the University of California, and that of the New York Public Library. An estimated 337 library catalogues are available through use of the Telnet remote access protocol. The Library of Congress files are accessible over the Internet, indicating the extent to which it is being used for formal purposes by library institutions. These files offer access to 28 million catalogue records included in the LCMARC files, together with copyright files, public policy citations and federal bill status files.

The Library also allows Internet access to its technical processing and cataloguing system, and to its SCORPIO reference and retrieval system. A wide spectrum of non-library sources of information are also available. Many of the government agencies attached to Internet make information resources openly available; these include, for instance, databases mounted by NASA in space science and astronomy and the CIA World Factbook. This kind of access is likely to increase in the future as the Internet develops: recent legislation colloquially known as the GPO Access Bill, for example, to require the US Government Printing Office to provide online public access to the Federal Register and the Congressional Record, as well as other material. A range of resources are listed in *The whole Internet* by Ed Kroll.

Sites with direct Internet access have the ability to transfer files directly from one machine to another in their original format, using the FTP protocol. The practice of 'anonymous ftp' has arisen in the Internet community, by which ftp archives are established on a host machine at a particular network site, with named directories which contain archives of files available for transfer.

Although computer system users would normally have to be registered with the site system administration in order to connect to a particular machine, these hosts have allowed free access to these specified ftp archives without the necessity to register a username or password beforehand; although it is normal practice to enter the caller's network address as the password information. This practice of 'anonymous ftp' is widely used to transfer entire documents, saving on the time-consuming necessity to view and save on-screen copies, and retaining any original formatting included with the file. The file can then be downloaded to a user's own machine, and used in whatever way is appropriate; the archive is able to distribute image as well as text-based information. Many ftp sites allow remote users to deposit files in the archive for others to retrieve.

A recent OCLC report estimated that there are about 3 million such files at more than a thousand ftp sites on the network, although the 20 largest sites account for more than half of these. Much of the material is source code for public domain computer programs, although the method is increasingly being used for the distribution of text files between specific groups or more widely. A major problem is that, as the report states 'the ability for network users to share information surpasses by far their ability to discover information on the Internet'.

As with JANET, a main problem with resources on the Internet lies in the difficulty of finding out what information is available. Since there is no central administration of the network which controls all uses of it, there is no central directory of resources, although distributed network information centres are emerging.

The problem is of a much greater magnitude than that faced by JANET, however, due to the much larger number of individual connections, and consequently the larger number of services and resources potentially available. It is also the case that resources are often duplicated in different network sites, and may exist in varying and incomplete versions and formats.

A number of resource guides have been drawn up by enthusiasts, covering both library-based databases, and those offered by other Organisations, as well as lists of discussion and news groups which are known to exist. These text documents may themselves be available in ftp archives, or retrievable as mail messages. None of these, however, are fully comprehensive, and all are subject to swift outdating in the climate of rapid change.

Long-term answers to the problem are the subject of debate, especially among some sections of the library community.

From 1992, the Internet is poised on the brink of a further phase of development. A concept sponsored by Vice-President Albert Gore for many years, and now enacted in the High Performance Computing Act of 1991, promises to continue national development in the existing interconnected array of networks to upgrade and expand the system, opening it out to more colleges, schools, and public libraries as a national research and educational resource. This 'information superhighway', to be known as the National Research and Education Network (NREN), was aimed at the development of a national 3 gigabit per second (a gigabit = one thousand million bits of data) network capacity by 1996. This represents an increase of approximately 2000 times over the current bandwidth, and as a rough guide enabled the network to carry 100,000 pages of text or 1000 bit-mapped photographic images each second.

As with SuperJANET, this supported a vast expansion in the number and range of services possible, and has made multimedia communications such as desktop videoconferencing feasible as an everyday reality. Another major goal for NREN was the standardization of protocols across the existing patchwork of networks, and the integration of TCP/IP with OSI protocols to enable both to be used in parallel. This is not an isolated development, but is indicative of a number of initiatives within this vein in the United States.

The Pacific Bell corporation, for example, is building a broadband network (CalREN) in California to link participating universities, research laboratories, major hospitals, and leading high technology firms in the Los Angeles and Bay Area to develop innovative applications for education, healthcare, and business. These include projects such as the use of tele-seminars for remote educational programmes, medical image processing, remote patient monitoring, and specialist diagnosis, and the development of collaborative precompetitive research with industry and commerce.

Proponents of the NREN argue that the United States is falling behind in economic competitiveness because government, business, industry, and education cannot access the information resources which it needs so as to maintain international competitiveness and economic strength. Another school of thought argues that such needs would be best met by. market forces in the shape of existing commercial networks such as MCI, funded by charging market prices for services. This argument has raised serious issues on future policies for the NREN on the issue of charging of services, which at the moment appear as though free to many end-users; and the use of NREN by commercial service providers.

Network in Educational Institutions

As the wider area networking scene has been undergoing substantial development, the local focus of higher educational networking has also seen significant developments. Concepts such as the 'electronic library', in which larger proportions of educational support material are delivered in electronic form to users who are more geographically dispersed, have raised the profile of local networking as a means of integrating access to the diverse range and types of information available from all sources within the campus environment. In recent years, such developments have been carried out under the name of Campus-Wide Information Systems (CWIS), which are intended to bring together this variety of local information within a single framework.

Access to this information should be simplified by an easy to use interface, which does not present barriers to the casual user, and is potentially available from all points of the local network. In many ways, this parallels some of the forms of community information systems which have emerged as civic facilities, but is more localized upon and targeted at a smaller and more easily identifiable community. The concept of a CWIS as a broad umbrella encompassing diverse information types precludes too strict a set of conditions on the structure and format of the information; in this sense, the CWIS forms an information base of both structured and less structured information, rather than a database in the precise sense of the term. A typical CWIS might include:

- staff and student directory information, including telephone, postal and e-mail addresses;
- a diary of local events and university calendars;
- course information, administrative details and time-tables;
- a listing of research projects and interests;
- university rules and regulations;
- newsletters related to the local campus;
- community and travel information;
- library catalogues and library service information;
- locally produced indexes and databases;
- links to other CWIS, catalogues etc., located at different campuses.

By bringing this information together in one access structure, a CWIS can help to integrate a campus community which is split between different sites or spread over a wide area and develop a sense of community. There is also some interest in developing this approach as a method for inter-university communication at the campus level to encourage collaborative endeavours and cooperation, rather than through formal administrative structures. There are about 20 different campus wide information systems in the UK at the present time, although these can take very different forms, and a formal categorization is difficult; and there seems to be extensive interest in exploring the potential of the idea further.

The information system can be developed as an extension of a library online catalogue, and be included within the same framework as an available network resource, or be developed as a general computer-support facility. The direction from which the impetus for development comes is likely to influence the shape of the outcome, and the underlying objectives it is intended to achieve.

The CWIS may be centralized onto a single machine from which remote access is possible, or act as a gateway to other local systems, calling the information up as needed. Whether the CWIS takes a centralized or more distributed approach, the task of maintaining and updating the information is normally the responsibility of the information providers. This may be either by submitting updated files to the operators of a centralized system, or by directly maintaining the data in one of the nodes which constitute a distributed system, to which the CWIS offers gatewayed access. In either case, the CWIS is essentially acting as a framework for the presentation of data, rather than determining the content too precisely.

4 Teaching Methods

In order to achieve the aims and objectives of the teaching of a particular subject certain maxims are laid down. The teaching of the subject is then planned and carried out keeping these maxims as the guiding principles. No doubt, teaching is an art but the success of a teacher lies in making his subject so simple as to make it intelligible for his students. The moment a teacher fails in this task he ceases to be a teacher. A geography teacher has to take greater pains as he has to act both as a science teacher as also a social science teacher.

Teaching is thus a most difficult task and everybody is not fit to be a teacher. Some persons may have a 'flair' for teaching and some other can improve their teaching if they are fully aware of different methods of teaching. In order to make children learn effectively, the teacher has to adopt the right method of teaching. In this chapter an attempt will be made to discuss some common methods of teaching of geography.

Before taking up the discussion of various methods of teaching of geography it would be better to know about the maxims of the teaching of geography because to be successful in his task, the geography teacher shall have to fall back upon these maxims. Given below are the maxims on the basis, of which geography teaching is conducted and carried out.

Proceed from simple to complex. It is a well-known maxim of teaching and this is the natural process of mind. It is also psychologically successful method. For imparting the knowledge of sea and ocean a geography teacher can show a pond or a tank to his students. Similarly, a model of mountain can be used to explain various things about a mountain.

Proceed from known to unknown. It is always better to proceed from known to unknown. It demands that the teacher should make efforts to establish some association with the previous knowledge of the students while imparting them any knew knowledge. For example while teaching about forests and their qualities the geography teacher can establish association with gardens that the students have seen. Due to this the regional geography is quite important.

Proceed from concrete to abstract. Though it is desirable to proceed from concrete to abstract but it is difficult in teaching of geography. Geographical factors, that are abstract in nature, cannot be displayed in concrete form. However, teacher should try his best to act according to this maxim. The teacher should make use of pictures, maps, sketches and diagrams and try to establish the abstract facts in the minds of the students.

From whole to part. Such a method is more scientific and psychological. Since quite, long we have been teaching the geography of different countries separately and after teaching them geography of a particular country an attempt was made to take them towards whole. This made the lerning of geography quite difficult and now we lay more stress on proceeding from whole to part. In this approach the whole of the region is taken for study first and then its various sub-divisions are explained. This makes the education scientific. The knowledge acquired in this way is more stable.

Proceed from definite to indefinite. Through concrete and definite examples we can have a better idea of abstract and indefinite things. Teacher of geography should take full advantage of the knowledge of students about certain natural things in proceeding from definite to indefinite. He can make use of maps, charts, etc. and give the students proper foundation.

Proceed from particular to general. It is always better to cite some specific example before proceeding to general principles of a phenomenon. It helps the students to follow things easily and properly. The geography teacher should proceed from the Geography of region and then go over to the Geography of the general principles of the whole world.

Proceed from psychological to scientific. In the beginning the geography teacher should teach his students in a psychological manner. He should also keep in mind the mental development of his students. Slowly and slowly he should shift from psychological to scientific method. He should make an effort to divide the syllabus in such a manner that the curiosity of the students be satisfied as well as accentuated. In present age geography is taught on the basis of cause and effect which is a scientific basis. This scientific basis has to be reached through psychological manner.

With the development of the subject-matter and knowledge of geography, various methods have evolved and are used for teaching of geography. The methodological revolution in geography commenced with the introduction of statistical techniques and since then development of different methods has been on the increase. In recent years we have witnessed the great innovation in the field of teaching methods. The four important aspects of geography teaching are:

(i) A point of view built on a distinct method.

(ii) Its philosophy and motivation : know your neighbour and know yourself.

(iii) Its synthetic approach.

(iv) Its regional concept.

The methods of teaching of geography should be one of the chief concerns of the geography teacher. Teacher has to employ these methods keeping in view the psychological requirements of the students. The psychological requirements of students of different ages are different and so we have to modify the method of teaching accordingly. Some of the important methods of teaching geography are:

(i) Socratic Method or Question-Answer Method.

(ii) Inductive Method.

(iii) Deductive Method.

(iv) Lecture Method.

(v) Textbook Method.

(vi) Descriptive Method.

(vii) Observation Method.

(viii) Story-Telling Method.

(ix) Political Method of Teaching of Geography.

(x) Regional Method of Teaching of Geography

(xi) Human Method of Teaching of Geography.

(xii) Comparative Method.

(xiii) Project Method.

(xiv) Dalton Plan Method

(xv) Laboratory Method.

(xvi) Excursion Method.

Some of these methods of teaching of geography are described in details.

Observation Method

Students travel from one place to another during tours and while going about from one place to another they get an opportunity to observe and see things for themselves. A real impression of an object or a place can best be gained through personal observation. Direct experience is an essential step to right understanding. If the students are given an opportunity to acquire knowledge of geography by observing things themselves, the knowledge shall be stable and shall have a practical value. The knowledge acquired through this method is clear, complete and perfect.

It is most desirable that observational work of the pupils be carefully directed and guided by the teacher. The students in lower classes may be asked to observe geographical things in their environment, near their homes, village and such other localities. They may be told to collect the geographical data. This data will help them understand similar conditions in their own provinces extending to other countries of the world. The 'observation method has a very wide range and can be very conveniently employed. It is a very popular method of teaching of geography. This method is found to be more useful in teaching the following branches of geography:

(i) Natural or physical geography.

(ii) Commercial geography.

Some of the important requirements of this method are as under:

(i) The teacher himself should have properly observed and seen those things which he expects his students to see and observe. It is important because in the absence of a thorough knowledge of such a thing/place he will not be able to impart a scientific knowledge to his students.

(ii) Necessary data must be collected during observation.

Difficulties of the Method

(i) While on trips/tours the teacher sometimes has to face the problem of discipline.

(ii) The tours/trips cannot be planned to observe things that are situated far away.

(iii) Some times guardians are reluctant to permit their wards to go out for observation.

Excursion Method

Excursion occupies an important place in teaching of geography. An excursion arranged for the study of a part of the country on the spot is the most useful method of teaching of geography. In excursions and travels students get an opportunity to observe and see things by themselves. Truely-speaking excursions are part and parcel of observartion method. Keeping in view of this educationists have laid down that excursions should form a part of the teaching of geography. Excursions present the object in its natural colours. These excursions also serve a useful purpose of character formation of the student so that he may not be a misfit in society.

In lower classes students have ample time and so it is possible to plan excursions. A good teacher can arrange a number of excursions and can encourage his students to observe carefully the phenomenon (physical, social, industrial, economic, etc.). The excursions should begin from the observation of hills and valleys that are situated in the neighbourhood of school. The easiest and most important thing to observe is the natural objects like landscapes, land formations and different types of soils.

In the higher classes when the students have developed mentally and physically, they may be taken out on long excursions. The importance of excursion method for teaching of geography has been summed up in the following words *by fames Fairgrieve.*

"More Geography is learned by feet rather than head."

To develop the power of expression of his students it is desirable that while an excursion, teacher provides his students with opportunity for expressing their view about places and things seen by them. The excursion should be planned in such a way that they are not very long and an effort be made to make maximum utilisation of time. However this utility of time should not spoil the interest of students in the subject-matter.

For proper utilisation of time the whole class be divided into groups and each group be asked to make observation of a particular aspect of the nature of geographical environment. Then these groups may be asked to exchange notes.

After the excursion the outdoor observation work be closely related with in-door work. The students should be encouraged to study all those things in the maps. This would strengthen their knowledge and encourges them to proceed from concrete to abstract.

This method of teaching geography fosters such social virtues as cooperation, give and take and group feeling. The importance of this method of teaching has been given in the following words by Prof. *E. A.Macnee*, "It is essential that the foundation of geographical knowledge shall be laid in the field. No amount of reading from books can make up for a prctical knowledge gained by looking at earth which the child is studying. It follows that from very early stages expedition should from part ofgeograpgy."

For the success of this method it is essential that teacher himself is very fond of excursions and is willing to arrange such excursions. Teacher should be willing to face the problems and inconveniences likely to come up during such excursions.

A substitute of the journey is to have talks with travellers of other lands like Japanese,English and the Americans.

Still another alternative is to read a book on travels.

Laboratory Method

In this method of teaching of geography subject is taught like a science subject. Certain experiments are carried out in the laboratory like Geography room. The teacher may demonstrate any experiment and the students shall try to follow it. By this method it is possible to easily impart concrete experiences to students during the course of a lesson when the teacher wants to explain some abstract points. This method combines the instructional strategy of'information imparting' and 'showing how'. This method combines the advantages of both the lecture method and the demonstration method.

In this method of teaching teacher performs experiment before the class and simultaneously explains what he is doing. He also asks relevant questions from the class and students are compelled to observe carefully because they have to describe each and every step of experiment accurately and draw inferences. After thorough questioning and cross-questioning the inferences drawn by the students are discussed in the class. In this way the students remain active participants in the process of teaching. The teacher also relates the outcome of experiment to the content of the on-going lesson. The student may be asked to observe the experiment carefully and respect it. The students may also be encouraged to do the work independently.

The knowledge that has been acquired by drawing out conclusions and finding out results is very stable and useful in future life. Students may also be asked to draw charts, maps, prepare models, etc. It is also possible to explain the revolution and rotation of the earth with the help of demonstration.

This method is based on the principle 'truth is that which works' Requirements for a Good Demonstration

For success of any demonstration following points be always kept in mind:

(i) It should be planned and rehearsed by the teacher beforehand.

(ii) The apparatus used for demonstration should be big enough to be seen by the whole class. It would be much better if a large mirror is placed at a suitable angle above the teacher's table which will enable the pupils to have a view of everything that the teacher is doing while performing the experiment.

Alternately, if the class is well disciplined the teacher may allow the students to sit on the stools placed on the benches to enable them to have a better view.

(iii) Adequate lighting arrangements be made on demonstration table and a proper background be provided.

(iv) All the pieces of apparatus be placed in order before starting the demonstration. The apparatus likely to be used should be placed on the left-hand side of the table and it should be arranged in the same order in which it is likely to be used. After an apparatus is used it should be transferred to right-hand side. Only things relevant to the lesson be placed on demonstration table.

(v) Before actually starting the demonstration, a clear statement about the purpose of demonstration be made to the students.

(vi) The teacher must make sure that the demonstration-cum-lecture method leads to active participation of the students in the process of learning. This he can achieve by putting well-structured questions.

(vii) The demonstration should be quick and slick and should not appear to linger on unnecessarily.

(viii) The demonstration should be interesting so that it captures the attention of the students.

(ix) The teacher must be sure of success of the experiment to be demonstrated and for this he should rehears the experiment under the conditions prevailing in the class-room. However even after all the necessary precaution the experiment fails in the class-room due to one reason or the other, the teacher should not get nervous, instead he should make an effort to find the reasons for the failure of the experiment. Sometimes in this process a good teacher may draw very useful conclusions.

(x) No complaints about inadequate and faulty apparatus be made by the teacher. In such a situation a good teacher finds an opportunity to show his skill.

(xi) It would be much better if the teacher demonstrates those experiments which are connected with common things which are seen and handled by students in their every-day life.

(xii) There should be a correlation between the demonstrations and the sequence of experiments performed by the students in their practical classes.

(xiii) For active participation of students, the teacher may call individual student, in turn, to help him in demonstration work.

(xiv) During lecture-cum-demonstration session, teacher must act like a 'showman' and a 'performer'. He should know different ways of arresting the attention of the students.

(xv) He should write a summary of the principles arrived at because of demonstration, on the blackboard. The blackboard can also be used for drawing necessary diagrams.

Demonstration Method

We commonly find science teachers making use of

demonstration method for teaching of geography. The conduct of a demonstration lesson is very difficult and here we will try to discuss some of the essential steps that should be followed in a demonstration lesson.

Planning and Preparation. A great care be taken by the teacher while planning and preparing his demonstration lesson. He should keep the following points in mind while preparing his lesson:

(a) subject matter,

(b) questions to be asked;

(c) apparatus required for the experiment

To achieve the above-stated objective the teacher should thoroughly go through the pages of the test book, relevant to the lesson. After this he should prepare his lesson plan in which he should essentially include the principles to be explained, a list of experiments to be demonstrated and the type of questions to be asked from the students. These questions be arranged in a systematic order that has to be followed in the class. Before actually demonstrating the experiment to a class the experiment be rehearsed under the conditions prevailing in the class-room. In spite of this, something may go wrong at the actual lesson, so reserve apparatus is often useful. The apparatus should be arranged in a systematic order on the demonstration table. Thus for the success of demonstration method a teacher has to prepare himself as thoroughly as a bride prepares herself for the marriage.

Introduction of the Lesson. As in every other subject so also in case of geography the lesson should start with proper motivation of the students. It is always considered more useful to introduce the lesson in a problematic way which would make students realise the importance of the topic. The usual ways in which a teacher could easily introduce his lesson is by telling some personal experience or incident, a simple and interesting experiment, a familiar anecdote or by telling a story.

A good experiment when carefully demonstrated is likely to leave an everlasting impression on the young mind of the pupil and it would set his pupils talking in school and out of it, about the interesting experiment that had been demonstrated to them in the geography class. This should be kept in mind not only to start the lesson but be used, on every suitable occasion, during the lesson.

Presentation. The method of presenting the subject-matter is very important. A good teacher should present his lesson in an interesting manner and not in a boring way. To make the lesson interesting the teacher may not be very rigid to remain within the prescribed course rather he should make the lesson as much broad-based as is possible. For widening of his lesson the teacher may think of various useful applications of the principle taught by him. He is also at liberty to take examples and illustrations from other allied branches to make his lesson interesting. The life history and some interesting facts from the life of the great geographer whose name is associated with the topic under discussion can also be cited/to make the lesson interesting. Thus, every effort be made to present the matter in a lively and interesting manner and a lesson should never be presented as 'dry bones' of an academic course. It is also advisable to make use of pictures, posters, diagrams, slides, films, etc. in addition to experiments to illustrate the topic in hand.

Constant questions and answers should form part of every demonstration lesson. Questions and cross questions are essential for properly illuminating the topic being discussed. Questions be arranged in such a way that their answers form a complete teaching unit. Though an effort be made to encourage the students to answer a large number of questions, if students fails to answer some questions teacher should provide the answers to such questions. It is unwise to expect all the answers from the pupil and a teacher should feel satisfied if he has been able to create a desire in a student to know what he does not know.

The lesson be presented in a clear voice and the teacher should speak slowly and with correct pronunciation. He should avoid the use of any bombastic and ambiguous terms. The continuous talk is likely to lead to monotony and to avoid it experiments be well spaced throughout the lesson.

Performance of Experiments. A good observer has been described as a person who has learned to use his senses of touch, sight, smell and hearing in an intelligent and alert manner. We want children to observe what happens in experiments and to have ample opportunities to state their observations carefully. We also want them to try to explain what happens in reference to their problem, but we want to make certain. There is separation between observations and generalization and conclusions.

The following steps are generally accepted as valuable in developing and concluding science experiments with the children;

1. Write the problems to be solved in simple words so that every one understands.
2. Make a list of activities that will be used to solve problems.
3. Gather material for conducting experiments.
4. Work out a format of the steps in the order of procedure so that every one knows what is to be done.
5. The teacher should always try the experiment himself to become acquainted with the equipment and procedure.
6. Record the findings in ways commensurate with the maturity level and purposes of the student.
7. Assist students in making generalisations from conclusions only after sufficient evidence and experiences.

The demonstration experiment be presented by the teacher in a model way. He should work in a tidy, clean and orderly manner while demonstrating an experiment. Some of the important points to be kept in mind while demonstrating an experiment are as under:

(i) Experiments should be simple and speedy

(ii) The experiments must work and their results should be clear and striking.

(iii) Experiments be properly spaced throughout the lesson.

(iv) Keep some reserve apparatus on the demonstration table.

(v) Keep the demonstration apparatus intact till it has to be used again.

Black-board Summary. A summary of important results and principles be written on the blackboard. Use of blackboard should also be frequently made for drawing necessary sketches and diagrams. The blackboard summary should be written in neat, clean and legible way. Since black board summary is an index to a teacher's ability he should keep the following points in mind while writing on black board.

(i) Proper space be left between different letters and words.

(ii) Always start Writing from left hand corner of the black board.

(iii) Start a new line only when the first one has extended across the black board.

(iv) Take care not to divide the words at the end of a time.

(v) Make all efforts to keep all the paragraphs and similar signs in calculations under one another.

(vi) While drawing sketches and diagrams preferably use 'single lined' diagrams.

(vii) All the diagrams drawn on the board be properly labelled.

Supervision. Students be asked to take the complete notes of the blackboard summary including the sketches and diagrams drawn. Such a record will be quite helpful to the student for learning his lesson. Such a summary will prove beneficial only if it has been copied correctly from the blackboard and to make sure that students are copying the blackboard summary properly the teacher should check it by frequently going to the seats of the students.

A summary of commcn errors committed while delivering a demonstration lesson is given below:

(i) The apparatus may not be ready for use

(ii) There may not be an apparent relation between the demonstration experiment and the topic under discussion.

(iii) Black-board summary is not upto the mark.

(iv) Teacher may be in a hurry to arrive at generalisation without allowing sufficient time to arrive at these generalisation from facts.

(v) Teacher may sometimes fail to ask right type of questions.

(vi) Teacher sometimes may use a difficult language.

(vii) Teacher sometimes takes to talking more which may mar the enthusiasm of the students.

(viii) Teacher may not have allowed sufficient time for recording data, etc.

(ix) Teacher has not given proper attention to supervision.

Following are the merits of this method

(i) It is an economical method as compared to purely student-centred approaches.

(ii) It is a psychological method and students take active interest in teaching-learning process.

(iii) It leads students from concrete to abstract situations and thus is more psychological.

(iv) It is a suitable method if the apparatus to be handled is costly and sensitive. Such an apparatus is likely to damage if handled by students.

(v) This method is safe.

(vi) In comparison to Heuristic method, project, etc. it is time saving but lecture method is too speedy.

(vii) It can be used successfully for all types of students.

(viii) In this method such experiments which are difficult for students can be included.

(ix) This method can be used to impart manual and manipulative skills to students.

Some of the disadvantages of this method are as under:

(i) It provides no scope for 'learning by doing' for students, as students just observe what the teacher is performing. Thus students fail to relish the joys of direct personal experience.

(ii) Since the teacher performs the experiment in his own pace, many students cannot comprehend the concept being clarified.

(iii) Since the method is not child-centred it makes no provision for individual differences. All types of students including slow leaners and genius have to proceed with the same speed.

(iv) It fails to develop laboratory skills in the students. It cannot work as a substitute for laboratory work by students in which they are required to handle the apparatus themselves.

(v) In this method students many a time fail to observe many finer details of apparatus because they observe it from a distance.

It is thoroughly accepted that success is greater with experiments in elementary schools if they start with real purpose, are simple done with uncomplicated apparatus, are done by children under careful direction of the teacher, and help the children think and draw valid tentative conclusion.

This method is considered to be one of the good methods for teaching of geography to secondary classes.

Lecture Method

Lecture method is the most commonly used method of teaching geography. This method is most commonly followed in colleges and in schools in big classes. This method is not quite suitable to realise the real aim of teaching geography. In lecture method only the teacher talks and students are passive listners. Since the students do not actively participate in this method of teaching so this method is a teacher-controlled and information-centred and in this method teacher works as a sole resource in class-room instructions. Due to lack of participation students get bored and some of them sometimes may go to sleep. In this method students is provided with ready-made knowledge by the teacher and due to this spoon feeding the students loses interest and his power of reasoning and observation get no stimulus.

In this method the teacher goes ahead with the subject matter at his own speed. The teacher may make use of black board at times may also dictate notes. This teacher oriented method in its extreme fqrm does not expect any question or response from the students.

It has the following advantages:

(i) It is quite economical method. It is possible to handle a large number of students at a time and no laboratory, equipment, aids, materials are required.

(ii) Using this method the knowledge can be imparted to the students quickly and the prescribed syllabus can be coverd in a short time.

(iii) It is quite attractive and easy to follow. Using this method teacher feels secure and satisfied.

(iv) It simplifies the task of the teacher as he dominates the lesson for 70-85% of the lesson time and students just listen to him.

(v) Using this method it is quite easy to impart factual information and historical anecdotes.

(vi) By following this method teacher can develop his own style of teaching and exposition.

(vii) In this method teacher can easily maintain the logical sequence of the subject by planning his lectures in advance. It minimises the chances of any gaps or overlappings.

(viii) Some good lectures delivered by the teacher may motivate, instigate, inspire a student for some creative thinking.

The disadvantages of lecture method can be as under:

(i) In this method the students participation is negligible and students become passive recipients of information.

(ii) In this method we are never sure if the students are concentrating and understanding the subject-matter being taught to them by the teacher.

(iii) In this method knowledge is imparted so rapidly that weak students develop a hatred for learning.

(iv) It does not allow all the faculties of the student to develop.

(v) In this method there is no place of 'learning by doing'.

(vi) It does not take into account the previous knowledge of the student.

(vii) It does not provide for corrective feedback and remedial help to slow learners.

(viii) It does not cater to the individual needs and differences of students.

(ix) It does not keep to inculcate scientific attitudes and training in scientific method among the pupils.

(x) It is an undemocratic and authoritarian method in which students depend only on the authority of the teacher. They cannot challenge or question the verdict of the teacher. This checks the development of power of critical thinking and proper reasoning in the student.

After considering various merits and demerits of method it may be concluded that this method may be suitable for teaching in higher classes (XI,XII) where we aim to cover the prescribed syllabus quickly. In these classes this method can be used successfully for imparting factual knowledge, introducing some new and difficult topics, make generalisation from the facts already known to the students, revision of lessons already learnt, etc.

Teaching by this method these students of classes XI and XII will also help those students who intend to join college so that they can prepare themselves for college where lecture method of teaching is a dominant method of imparting instruction.

This method of teaching can be made more beneficial if the teacher encourages his students to take notes during the lesson. After the lesson teacher can give his students some time for asking questions and answer their queries without any hesitation. While delivering his lesson the teacher may see that the lesson is delivered in good tone, loudly and clearly. He should use only simple and understandable words for delivering his lesson. If teacher can introduce some humour in his lesson, it would keep students interested in his lesson.

Project Method

This method was given by Dewey. The American philospher, psychologist and practical teacher. The project method is a direct outcome of his philosophy. According to Dr. Kilpatrick, "A project is a unit of whole-hearted purposeful activity carried on preferably, in its natural setting." According to Stevenson, "A project is a problematic act carried to" its completion in its natural setting." According to Ballard, "A project is a bit of real life that has been incorporated into the school.

The project method is not totally new. Project equivalents are advocated for the adolescent period by Rousseau in Emile (BK-III). A project plan is a modified form of an old method called "concen-tration-of-studies." The main features of "concentration-of-studies plan" is that some subject is takpn as the core or the centre and all other school subjects as they arise are studied in connection with it.

Project method is based on the following principles:

(i) learning by doing.

(ii) learning by living.

(iii) children learn better through association, cooperation and activity.

Various definitions of project have already been considered. A modified definition of project is given by Tomas and Long. They define it as "a voluntary undertaking which involves constructive effort or thought and eventuates into objective results".

Considering various definitions of project we may consider it as a kind of life experience which is an outcome of a craving or desire of the pupils. This is a method of spontaneous and incidental teaching. "Learning by living" may be a better meaning of project method, because life is full of projects and individuals carry out these projects in their every-day life.

The projects may broadly be classified as:

(i) Individual projects, and

(ii) Social projects.

Individual projects are to be carried out by individuals whereas social projects are carried out by a group of individuals.

For completing a project we have five stages in actual practice. These are

(i) Providing a situation

(ii) Choosing and proposing.

(iii) Planning of the project.

(iv) Executing the project.

(v) Judging the project. Recording the project is also essential.

Providing a situation. A project should arise out of a need felt by pupils and it should never be forced on them. It should be purposeful and significant. It should look important and must be interesting. For this the teacher should always be on the look-out to find situation that arise and discuss them with students to discover their interests. Situations may be provided by different methods. Some such methods may include talking to students on the topics of common interest e.g. how did they spend their holidays, what did they see in Delhi, etc.

Choosing and proposing. From various definitions of an educational project we get the same underlying ideas (a) school tasks are to be as real and as purposeful as the tasks of wider life beyond the school walls (b) they ' are of such a nature that the pupil is genuinely eager to carry them out in order to achieve a desirable and clearly realised aim.

According to Kilpatrick, "the part of the pupil and the part of the teacher, in most of the school work, depends largely on who does the proposing". The teacher should refrain from proposing any project otherwise the whole purpose of the method would be defeated. Teacher should only tempt the students for a particular project by providing a situation but the proposal for the project should finally come from students. The teacher must exercise guidance in selection of the project and if the students make an unwise choice, the teacher should tactfully guide them for a better project. The essentials of a good project are:

(i) It should have evident worth for the individual or the group that undertakes them.

(ii) The project must have a bearing on a great number of subjects and the knowledge acquired through it may be applicable in a variety of ways.

(iii) The project should be timely.

(iv) The project should be challenging.

(v) The project should be feasible.

It is for the teacher to see that the purpose of the project is learly defined and understood.

Planning. The students be encouraged by the teacher to plan out the details of the project. In the process of planning teacher has to act only as a guide and he should give suggestions at times but actual planning be left to the students.

Execution. Once the project has been chosen and the details of the project have been planned, the teacher should help the students in executing the project according to the plan. Since execution of a project is the longest step in the project method so it needs a lot of patience on the part of the students and the teacher. During this step the teacher should carefully supervise the pupils in manipulative skills to prevent waste of materials and to guard accidents. The teacher should assign work to different students in accordance with their tastes, interests aptitudes and capabilities. Teacher should see that every member of the group gets a chance to do something. Teacher should constantly check up the relation between the chalkedout plans and the developing project and as far as possible 'at the spot' changes and modification be avoided. However if such changes become unavoidable these should be noted and reasons explained for future guidance.

Evaluation. The evaluation of the project should be done both by the pupils and the teacher. The pupils should estimate the qualities of what they have done before the teacher gives his evaluation. The evaluation of the project has to be done in the light of plans, difficulties in the execution and achieved results. Let the students have self criticism and look through their own failings and findings. This step is very useful because as a result of the project, the pupils can know the values of the information, interest, skills and attitudes that have been modified by the project.

Record. A complete record of the project be kept by the students. The record should include everything about the project. It should include the proposal, plan and its discussion, duties allotted to different students and how far were they carried out by them. It should also include the details of places visited and surveyed, maps, etc. drawn, guidance for future and all other possible details.

(i) In project method of teaching the role of a teacher is that of a guide, friend and philosopher.

(ii) He helps the students in solving their problems just like an elder brother.

(iii) He encourages his students to work collectively, amicably in the group.

(iv) He also helps his students to avoid mistakes.

(v) He makes it a point that each member of the group contributes something to the completion of the project and in this process helps the shy and weaker students to work along with their class mates.

(vi) If the students face failure during execution of some steps of the project the teacher should not execute any portion of the project but should only explain to his students the reasons of their failure and should suggest them some better methods or techniques that may be used by them next time for the success of the project

(vii) During the execution step teacher also learns something.

(viii) Teacher should always remain alert and active during execution, step and see that the project goes to completion successfully.

(ix) During execution of the project teacher should maintain a democratic atmosphere.

(x) Teacher must be well-read and well-informed so that he can help the students to the successful completion of the project.

The merits of project method can be as under:

(i) It is a method of teaching based on psychological laws of learning. The education is related to child's life and he acquires it through meaningful activity.

(ii) It imbibes the spirit of cooperation as it is a cooperative venture. Teacher and students join in the project.

(iii) It stimulates interest in natural as also man-made situations. Moreover the interest is spontaneous and not under any compulsions.

(iv) The method provides opportunities for pupils of different tastes and aptitudes within the framework of the same scheme.

(v) It upholds the dignity of labour.

(vi) It introduces democracy in education.

(vii) It brings about a close correlation between a particular activity and various subjects.

(viii) It is a problem-solving method and places very less emphasis on cramming or memorising.

(ix) It helps to inculcate social discipline through joint activities of the teacher and the taught.

(x) A project can be used to arouse interest in a particular topic as it blends school life with outside world. It provides situations in which the students come in direct contact with their environment.

(xi) It develops self-confidence and sel-discipline.

(xii) A project tends to illustrate the real nature of the subject.

(xiii) A project affords opportunity to develop keenness and accuracy of observation and produces a spirit of enquiry.

(xiv) It puts a challenge to the student and thus stimulates constructive and creative thinking.

(xv) It provides the students an opportunity for mutual exchange of ideas.

(xvi) This method helps the children to organise their knowledge.

The drawbacks of project method can be as under:

(i) Projects require a lot of time.

(ii) Though the method provides the student superficial knowledge of so many things it provides insufficient knowledge of some fundamental principles.

(iii) In the project planning and execution of the project the teacher is required to put in much more work in comparison to other methods of teaching.

(iv) The teacher has been assumed as master of all subjects which is practically not possible.

(v) Good textbooks on these lines have not yet been produced.

(vi) It is an expensive method it involves tours, excursions, purchase of apparatus and equipment etc.

(vii) The method of organising instructions is unsystematised and thus the regular timetable of work will be upset.

(viii) The method may fit those who cannot listen but it is very questionable if it has the same value for those who can listen.

(ix) The method leaves a gap in pupils knowledge.

(x) It underestimates man's power of imagination which enables him to savour the full experience of another without the necessity of undergoing the experience himself.

(xi) Sometimes the projects may be too ambitious and beyond pupil's capacity to accomplish.

(xii) Larger projects in hands of an unexperienced teacher lead to boredom.

(xiii) The education given by projects is likely to emphasise relationships in breadth than in depth.

The project method provides a practical approach to learning of both theoretical and practical problems. If it is difficult to follow this method of teaching it would be better at least not to ignore the spirit of this method.

This method has been found to be more suitable for primary and middle classes and is of restricted use for high and higher secondary classes. This method may be tried alongwith formal class-room teaching without disturbing the school timetable. With this in view some projects may be undertaken by the students to be completed on certain fixed days of a week. Alternately first half of the day may be devoted to class-room teaching and the project work be carried out in the remaining half day. To help solve the problem of fund's shortage such projects be chosen which are self-supporting. As it is not suitable for drill and continuous and systematic teaching, it is not very desirable to use it freely.

Here are given some projects for a geography class.

Here are given some projects for a geography class.

Projects for Middle Class Students

(i) Running a shop (vegetable shop or cloth shop, grocer's shop, stationary shop)

(ii) Ploughing the field.

(iii) Running a post office.

(iv) Prepartion of models of houses, means of transport, etc.

(v) Studying the physical features of some area by making a 3-dimensional map, with the help of sand, paper, mache, etc.

Projects for Secondary

(i) Study of life in various parts of the world.

(ii) Preparing sand or clay models of different sections of the various river valleys. The Indus, The Ganges, etc.

(iii) Some mountaineous region scene showing railway line, bridge, cultivated fields, roads and other important features.

(iv) Preparation of economic and distributional maps of local area.

(v) Setting and running a geographical data museum.

(vi) Organisation of excursions and tours.

Inductive Method

In this method one is led from concrete to abstract, particular to general. In this method we prove a universal law by showing that if it is true in a particular case it is also true in other similar cases. Through these illustrations an attempt is made to elicit the new theory of knowledge from the students. This is a psychological and logical method. In this method the teacher should take the following precautions.

(i) He should not cite many examples otherwise the students feel bored.

(ii) The teacher should act patiently and make all possible efforts to elict the information,rules and theories from the students.

(iii) The teacher should encourage the students so as to develop their power of research and discovery.

This method is very useful for teaching of Geography. We have cause and effect relationship and this can be very easily clarified by use of this method.

Illustrations. Say our aim is to teach that in areas near equator, there is a good deal of heat and warmth. To achieve the aim the students be asked in a circle around the fire and an attempt be made to elicit the principle that on equator the sun rays are straight and therefore there is so much of heat. In the absence of any arrangement of fire in school we may draw a picture on blackboard and then elicit the principle with the help of questions.

Using this method an attempt should be made to elicit the principle that on the equator the sun rays are straight and so the place is hot. In the polar region the sun rays are slanting and so there is less of heat.

(i) It helps understanding.

(ii) It is a scientific method.

(iii) It develops scientific attitude.

(iv) It is a logical method and develops critical thinking and habit of keen observations.

(v) It is a physchological method and provides sample scope for students activities.

(vi) It is based on acutal observations, thinking and experimentation.

(vii) It keeps alive the students interest because they move from known to unknown.

(viii) It curbs the tendency to learn by rote and also reduces homework.

(ix) It develops self-confidence.

(x) It develops the habit of intelligent hardwork.

This method suffers from the following limitations

(i) It is limited in range and cannot be used in solving and understanding all the topics in geography.

(ii) The generalisation obtained from a few observations are not the complete study of the topic, to fix the topic in the mind of the learner a lot of supplementary in work and practice is needed.

(iii) Inductive reasoning is not absolutely conclusive. The generalisation has been done from the study of a few (three or four) cases. The process thus establishes certain degree of probability which can be increased by increasing the number of valid cases.

(iv) This method needs a lot of time and energy and thus it is time-consuming and laborious method.

(v) This method is not found to be suitable in higher classes because some of the unnecessary details and explanations may make teaching dull and boring.

(vi) The use of this method should be restricted and confined to understanding the rules in the early stages.

(vii) This method may be considered complete and prefect only if the generalisation arrived at by induction can be verified through deductive method.

Deductive Method

Deductive method is opposite of inductive method. In this

method the learner proceeds from general to particular, from abstract to concrete. Thus in this method facts are deduced or analysed by the application of established formula or experimentation. In this case the formula is accepted by the learner as an established fact.

In this method teacher announces the topics of the day and he also gives the relevant formula/rule/law/principle etc. The law/formula is also explained to the students with the help of certain examples which are solved on the blackboard. From these students get the idea of use or application of the concerned law/principle/formula. Then the problems are given to the students who solve the problems following the same method as explained to them earlier by the teacher. Students also memorise the results for future application

Following example illustrates the procedure.

Suppose the teacher has to explain to the students that in the Equitorial regions, it is very hot throughtout the year and in the polar regions it is very cold. The teacher will tell this thing at the very outset. Then contrary to the Inductive Method, he may put forward certain illustrations and then strengthen the knowledge of the students.

This method is not useful in lower classes but is a useful method for the students of higher classes.

1. It is short and time-saving and so this method is liked by authors and teachers.
2. It is a suitable method for lower classes.
3. It glorifies memory because students are required to memorise a large number of laws, formula, etc.
4. For revision of topic it is an adequate and advantageous method.
5. It supplements inductive method and thus completes the process of inductive-deductive method.
6. It enhances speed and efficiency in solving problem.

Limitations

1. It is not a scientific method.
2. It encourages rote memory because pure deductive work requires some law principle, formula for every type of problem and it demands blind memorisation of large number of such laws/formulas, etc.
3. Being an unscientific method it does not impart any training in scientific method.
4. It causes unnecessary and heavy burden on the brain which may sometimes results in brain fag.
5. In this method memory becomes more inportant than understanding and intelligence which is educationally not sound.
6. It is an unpsychological method because the facts and principles are not found by students themselves.
7. In this method student cannot become active learners.
8. It is not suitable for development of thinking, reasoning and discovery.

A careful consideration of merits and limitations of Inductive Method and Deductive Method leads to conclude that Inductive Method is the forerunner of Deductive Method. For effective teaching of Geography both methods are used because none is complete without the other. Inductive Method leaves the learner at a point where he cannot stop and after work has to be done and completed by deductive method. Deduction is a process that is suitable for final statement and Induction is most suitable for exploration fields. Induction gives the lead and deduction follows.

Socratic Method

In this method of teaching geography an effort is made by the teacher to systematize the previous knowledge of the students. For removal of any doubts in the minds of students they are brought on the proper track. Making use of Question-Answers an attempt is made to organise and systematise the previous knowledge of the students. For this the teacher should keep the following points in mind.

1. The curiosity of the students has to be awakened and the interest of the students has to be created in the subject matter of the lesson.
2. An all-out effort has to be made to associate the previous knowledge of the student with their present knowledge.
3. The mental status of student has to be kept in mind while teaching the new subject-matter. The teaching of subject-matter has to be modified in accordance with the requirements of mental status of students.
4. New knowledge has to be strengthened with the help of description, narration and discussion.

This method is quite useful for teaching of geography. This method is quite useful for big classes. While using this method teacher should take utmost care to put only such questions which help him in keeping up the interest of the students.

Textbook Method

In this method geography is taught with the help of textbooks. The relevant pages of the textbook are read by the teacher or he asks some student to read those pages of the textbook to the class. Teacher simultaneously explains the difficult terms, questions, etc.

This is not a psychological and scientific method because it is not possible to impart knowledge by reading the textbook or making the students to read it. It may create an atmosphere of boredom in the class-room and students lose interest in the subject.

Some of the limitations of this method are as under.

1. This method does not employ or use the maxims and principles of education.
2. This method narrows the out-look of students and they become inactive and lethargic. They do not participate actively in the acquisition of knowledge.

3. In this method the scope of revision is very limited and the knowledge acquired by the students is not permanent.

For teaching of geography, like other social sciences, this method is not useful. This method is not useful for imparting the real knowledge of geography. It develops a habit of cramming in the students which hampers the proper knowledge of geography. It is, therefore, advisable not to use this method.

Descriptive Method

In geography we have many such things whose pictures have to be drawn on the minds of students. It can be achieved by description. For this the description has to be vivid and lively. It is thus essential to make the description interesting and attractive. While making oral description an attempt be made to make use of models, charts, etc.

For presentation of geographical facts and for explaining their casual relationship the teacher has to give vivid description and present illustrations. Such a description is essential for awakening the power of imagination of students.

The description may be given in the form of a story, description of a travel, dialogue, etc. Finally an attempt be made to draw the substance so that the students have a thorough knowledge. While using this method teacher should not try to go very much in detail. Teacher should also encourage his students to actively participate in description and they be given enough opportunities to give vent to their feelings. Description should invariably be in simple language and lucid style. Teacher should never forget his basic aim of description is to draw a picture of the things in the mind of the students.

A list of topics that can be taught easily by descriptive method is given below

(i) Agriculture

(ii) Food habits, dresses, living conditions of people of different countries and geographical regions.

(iii) Water and rivers.

(iv) Living and working conditions of the workers of various industries.

(v) Markets and the description of various products manufactured in different places.

(vi) Geographical description of the discoveries of various regions.

(vii) The life of animals, mineral and natural wealth of different regions.

(viii) Description of mines, etc. and their working conditions.

(ix) Geographical environment.

An effort be made by the teacher to correlate the description with human life because it is only through such a correlation that the real purpose of geography teaching shall be served.

Story-telling Method

It is also known as *Narrative method* or descriptive method. In this method geographical facts are presented in the form of a story. In this method it is not possible to impart the element of character, plot, style, etc. which characterise any literary story. Moreover, it is not possible to present the entire perspective of human life in these stories. Because of these limitations this method is quite descriptive and narrative. Following types of stories may be narrated in teaching of geography.

(i) Stories depicting the life of people of various countries.

(ii) Stories connected with the animals and geographical environment of different countries.

(iii) Stories of different discoveries such as Columbus, Vasco de Gama, etc.

(iv) Stories of travels and excursions.

(v) Stories about conquest of man over nature.

(vi) Stories concerning human activities in the background of geographical factors.

Some educationists are quite apprehensive of the utility of this method for teaching of geography. In their opinion when the undeveloped minds are told the stories connected with the life of foreign countries they may not be able to grasp them entirely. Thus the stories and the knowledge contained them have little or no utility in such a case.

This method is quite useful for students of primary classes where we do not teach the geography of the world or of foreign countries. In lower classes we teach the geography of our country or the state.

Political Method

It is also known *as patriotic or Single country method of* teaching of geography. In this method the teaching of geography of any one particular country is undertaken. All the details of its lands, situations, natural conditions, climate, agricultural products, vegetation, etc. are discussed. The description of all these things is based on geographical factors of that particular country. When the description of one country is completed, we take up the description of another country. Thus, the geography of the whole world is taught in parts and countries.

Some educationists doubt the utility of this method. In their view the knowledge about one country given in isolation has little or no bearing on teaching of geography of the world. Moreover, in this method political condition of a particular country are not stressed. This method is not very psychological and scientific.

(i) This method is expensive.

(ii) This method is time-consuming.

Regional Method

Till the middle of twentieth century geography was taught on the basis of political divisions but now it has been replaced by regional method of teaching of geography. Now we take different countries with common physical features, climate, mineral wealth, economic progress, etc. at a time and study them together. In this method countries with common geographical features are studied together. It was Herbertson who gave impetus to this method by dividing the whole world into broad climatic regions. Now-a-days the natural regions method is more common and has become a universal method of teaching of regional geography of the world or of an individual country or a continent.

For his classification Herbertson used the criterion of climate and vegetation which means that all geographical factors have been taken into eonsideration but there is ample scope for modification of Herbertson's classification.

It is possible that natural regions may be different from political regions. In words of Prof. Macnee, "*The Regional Method of Teaching of geography is then, a method in which the area studied is divided into natural regions, each of which is studied separately*".

The most common procedure of this method is as under:

Location, structure, relief, drainage system and climate are considered first in the serial order and the students are told the biogeography of the region. Later on the distribution of minerals and their exploitation in the development of industries are studied. It is then followed by a study of population distribution, means of transport and communication, location of towns, etc. The region is then studied in comparison to other regions of the world.

Advantages of Regional Method of Teaching Geography. According to Prof. E.A. Macnee, "The chief advantage of Regional Method is that it is the quickest way of getting pupils to grasp the salient features of the geography of any area. No other method can give so quick a start or so sound a basis for furthur study."

Some merits of this method are:

(i) It is scientific, orderly and systematic method.

(ii) It provides a better understanding of geography and economics on time and energy.

(iii) It prepares the child to pursue independent study of geography which is very useful in individual method of teaching.

(iv) It correlates physical, natural, social, economic and other phases of man's life.

(v) It helps the child to understand the environment.

(vi) It helps to develop the power of observation, imagination and reasoning.

(vii) It broadens the vision of the child and helps him to understand the difference between man and man. Such an understanding is very useful for international understanding.

Limitation

(i) The boundaries of natural regions are not very clearly defined and one region therefore merges into another.

(ii) Sometimes we miss the smaller region while paying full attention to the broader regions. In this way a very vital point is neglected.

(iii) It is not possible to have a final division an regional basis.

If the world as a whole is to be studied then it be done through regions and if any part of world is to be studied it then it be studied under various heads such as structure, relief, climate, etc. already discussed.

After reading the regional geography of 2 or 3 countries the students be asked to take up an independent study of some other contries with the help of a good atlas. The regional method lends itself to independent study and it can be resorted to individual methods of teaching.

While studying by this method the following order of regions may be followed:

(i) Arctic regions and hot regions.

(ii) Tropical Forests and monsoon lands.

(iii) Mid-latitude grass lands.

(iv) Regions of Mediterranean climate.

(v) Mid-latitude forests.

Human Method

In this method man and human life occupies a very important place. In human geography we are concerned with the study of the progress made by man through his efforts and labour. This method is based on study of cause and effect relationship. Physical features and physical environments have a profound effect on man. In this method of teaching man is studied in relation to his geographical environment.

We have to allow for concession for freedom of human activities in study of human geography because human activities are not rigidly controlled by cause and effect relationship. The remarks of Prof. Macnee in this regard are quite correct. He remarked, "Geography is not a mere recital of unrelated facts. Most geographical facts are related to other geographical facts and it is the business of geography to elucidate these relations. In geography teaching, therefore cause and effect should be traced whenever possible and in particular the influence of physical and biological factors on human life."

Comparative Method

In this method students are encouraged to compare various geographical features. To start with, students are asked to know about the geographical features of their neighbourhood and then make a comparison with the features of city and village. They may then be asked to make a comparison of geographical features of a country with those of the other country. In this way the knowledge gained gets stabilised and it becomes permanent. In this method teacher is at liberty to proceed from known to unknown. The students, precious knowledge may be compared with the new knowledge acquired by him. This method is quite useful in assimilation of ideas.

The comparison may be carried out not only of the physical features of one region with those of another but for comparison purpose we can include the products and other things of one particular region and make a comparison of these things of the other region. In the words of Prof. Macnee, "Psychologists have emphasised the important part played in the assimilation of new ideas by the existing content of the mind. The mind tends to interpret the new in terms of the old. It is well, therefore, for the teacher, wherever possible to bring the new ideas which he wishes to present into relation with the previous experiences of the pupils; in other words, to track new knowledge on to old. This is the psychological basis for pedagogical maxim; 'proceed from known to unknown':"

While explaining the method he furthur remarked, "prompted by this ideas the framers of geography courses usually begin the primary courses with things that are familiar to the pupils, the school building and grounds, the village, the local river, the nearest railway line. From the pupils' home and from the things that he can see with his own eyes his geographical knowledge is extended outwards of the districts, state country and continent."

This method is not very useful in lower classes but is of great value for teaching geography in higher classes. Writing about the method Prof. B.C. Wallis has rightly remarked, "comparisons and contracts are the essence of geography teaching at senior stage."

This approach along with that of gaming approach have been added recently in the teaching methodology simulation or analogue is different from real world but it presents significant features of real world in order to make a worthwhile study. In this approach the processes or conditions or situations are re-enacted so as to indicate the basic structures and significant features. It motivates the students in the learning process and help him in making decisions. This approach can be usefully employed to teach mineral resources, location of industries, new towns, growth centres, etc.

This approach is quite similar to project method but differs from it in duration, planning and execution.

In view of the modern educationists, assignment is a well-planned learning situation created by the teacher. The objective of an assignment is to provide the pupil a direct, first hand and stimulating learning experience. The timing of assignment, duration and frequency will depend upon the purpose of assignment. An assignment should be specific and flexible. It is possible to classify the assignments under various heads. Some of these are as under:

(i) Assignments that aim at developing basic skills like using a textbook, a reference book, etc.

(ii) Problem-solving assignments. Such assignments aim at development of power of thinking and imagination.

(iii) Assignments on experiments and observations.

(iv) Assignments on making and handling tools.

(v) Assignments on map making, map reading and map interpretation.

(vi) Assignments for development of attitude leading to national integration and international understanding.

In the previous pages a number of methods of teaching geography have been discussed. Some of them have been recommended for use, some have been disapproved and some have been recommended for use with caution. Out of the methods available a choice is not entirely left to the whimes of the teacher but has to be made by the teacher in the light of the facilities available and nature of work to be done. It does not mean that a teacher may select any one method and then cling to it lavisihiy throughout his service or even an entire academic session. This is a great mistake because each method has its own merits. Our preference for any one method deprives us of the merits of other method. A good teacher should therefore try to imbibe the good qualities of all methods instead of depending on any one method. The teacher should keep himself on the right side of every method. The best method of a teacher is his own individualised and personalised method which is the result of his varied and long experience in teaching some of the points which a teacher must keep in mind are as follows:

(i) Heuristic approach be used to start a lesson. Thus the lesson be introduced in a problematic way so that the students feel that they are going to learn something really useful and worth learning.

(ii) He should choose a pupil dominated method in preference to a teacher dominated method.

(iii) He should have a bright manner of presentation and should illustrate his lesson with experiments, pictures, charts, diagrams etc. specimens and models are preferred for illustration.

(iv) Teaching should be made a cooperative enterprise. Teacher should give maximum opportunity of participation to the students so that they feel that their active participation is quite important for the solution of problem and successful growth of the subject.

(v) Teacher should make all possible efforts to properly correlate the topic in hand with other subjects.

(vi) Teacher should avoid the use of difficult phrases, expressions and lengthy definitions.

(vii) Though Heuristic approach dominates yet the historical method of teaching be utilized at places and the lives and achievements of famous geographers be told to the students. These are a source of inspiration to the students.

(viii) Instructional method and plans must be flexible. In a lesson if, in addition to planned illustrations and experiments students want some more experimental evidence then the teacher should make all possible efforts to satisfy the students.

(ix) After a constant use of some method, teacher can break the monotony by using project method and laboratory method.

Thus we conclude that no single method could be the best method and a good teacher will have to evolve his own individual method consisting ,of good points of all the methods. He will never become a slave to any method and will remain a true master of all of them.

With the development of the subject-matter and the knowledge of Geography, various methods have evolved and are being employed to impart its knowledge to the students. Teacher has to employ these methods, keeping in view the psychological requirements of the students. Students of different stages have different psychological requirements and so the method of teaching has to be modified accordingly.

1. Socratic Method or Question-Answer Method.
2. Inductive Method.
3. Deductive Method.
4. Lecture Method.
5. Text-Book Method.
6. Descriptive Method.
7. Observation Method.
8. Story-Telling Method.
9. Political Method of teaching of Geography.
10. Regional Method of teaching of Geography.
11. Human Method of teaching of Geography.
12. Comparative Method of teaching of Geography.
13. Project Method.
14. Dalton (plan) Method of teaching of Geography.
15. Laboratory Method of teaching of Geography.
16. Excursion Method of teaching of Geography.

• In this method of teaching of Geography, the teacher tries to systematize the previous knowledge of the students. The previous knowledge of the students is disorganised and scattered. By removing the doubts of the students, an attempt is made to bring them to the proper track. By questions and answers an attempt is made to organise and systematise knowledge of the students. In this regard, the teacher has to bear the following things in mind :

(a) The curiosity of the students as to be awakened and the interest of the student has to be created in the subject-matter of the lesson.

(b) A serious attempt has to be made to associate the previous knowledge of the student with their present knowledge. In other words, on the basis of the previous knowledge of the student, the new subject-matter has to be taught.

(c) The mental status of the student has to be borne in mind which teaching the new subject-matter. With the requirements of the mental status of the students, the teaching of the subject-matter has to be modified and organised.

(d) By description, narration and discussion, the new knowledge is strengthened.

This method may be useful in Geography, because here, an attempt is made to provide new knowledge to the students in the background of the previous knowledge. This is possible through question-answer method and it is the Socratic Method. In the classes this method can be more useful. While using this method, the teacher has to be very cautious. He has to put only those questions that shall be useful for keeping up the interest of the students.

• In this method, in order to find out a new theory of a new piece of knowledge, certain illustrations are given. Through these illustrations, an attempt is made to elicit-the new theory of knowledge from the students. Here an attempt is made to proceed from particular to general. From this point of view, this theory is quite Psychological and logical.

In order to use this theory successfully and scientifically, the teacher has to take the following precautions :

(a) The teacher should not give many examples. The example should be limited, so that the students may not get bored.

(b) The teacher should try to act patiently and try to elicit the rules and the theories from the students.

(c) The students should be encouraged so that their power of research and discovery may develop. With the help of the question, they may be encouraged to reach the desired goal.

This method is very useful for the teaching of Geography. We have cause and effect relationship. Through this method, this thing can be very easily carried out. An example will clarify it.

Suppose the student are to be taught that in the areas near equator, there is a good deal of heat and warmth. This may be taught with the help of the following examples :

The students should be asked to sit in a circle around the fire. Questions should be asked and attempt should be made to elicit the principle that on the equator the sun rays are straight and therefore there is so much of heat.

It is quite possible that there may not be arrangement of fire in the class room. In that case a picture may be drawn on the blackboard and, with the help of the questions, principle may be elicited. It is easy to draw a chart on the blackboard. This thing will facilitate the teaching.

While employing this method, the psychological requirements of ths students should always be borne in mind. An attempt should be made to elicit the principle that on the Equator the sun rays are straight and so the place is hot. On the other in the Polar regions the sun rays are slanting and so there is less of heat.

• In this method, first of all, the principle is enunciated. Then, on the basis of several illustrations, the principle is clarified. It is quite possible to enunciate various other acts on the basis of these principles. It may be done with the help of the following illustrations :—

Suppose the teacher has to explain to the students that in the Equatorial regions it is very hot throughout the year and in the Polar regions it is very cold. The teacher may tell this thing at the very outset. Then, contrary to the Inductive Method, he may put forward certain illustrations and then strengthen the knowledge of the students.

This method is not useful for the students of the lower classes. But for the students of the higher classes this method is very useful.

• This method is useful for the students of the higher classes. It may be employed in higher secondary, and university classes. In this method, the teacher, by lecture, tries to explain the facts to the students. He encourages the students to acquire knowledge and employ the acquired knowledge in life.

While delivering a lecture the teacher should determine the mental age and psychological requirements of the students. He should use such language which is intelligible to the students. But in practice it is not possible to do this.

This method is considered to be unpsychological. It is not considered scientific either. People have not favoured the use of this method in Junior High School classes and Secondary classes.

• In text book method, an attempt is made; to teach Geography with the help of the text books. The teacher takes to the reading of the text book or asks the students to read the text book. He goes on explaining the difficult and the complicated questions.

This method is also not considered psychological and scientific. It is not possible to impart knowledge by reading the text book or making the students to read it. This creates an atmosphere of boredom in the class room and the students lose interest in the subject-matter.

Text book method bristles with the following drawbacks :—

(a) The maxims and principles of education are not employed and used in this method.

(b) In this method the outlook of the students becomes narrow. They become inactive and lethargic. They do not take active part in the acquisition of knowledge.

(c) In this method there is very little scope for the revision of the subject-matter taught. The knowledge that is acquired by the students does not become permanent. In teaching Geography, like other social sciences, this method is not very useful.

Sometimes teachers try to give a substance of a lesson taught. By this substance, the students try to learn the subject-matter.

This method may be useful for the students in their case, but it is not useful for the real knowledge of Geography. The students develop the habit of cramming. The exercise of *Rote Memory* hampers the proper knowledge of Geography. It is, therefore, advisable not to use this method.

• In Geography, there are many such things whose picture has to be drawn on the minds of the students. This can be done only through description. The description has to be very vivid and lively. Only then the complete picture shall be imprinted. It is, therefore, very necessary, rather essential, to make the description interesting and attractive. While presenting oral illustration, models, charts, etc, may also be employed.

While presenting the geographical facts and trying to explain their causal relationship, the teacher has to present illustrations and give vivid description. With the help of this description, it is possible to awaken the power of imagination of the students.

This description may be in the form of story, description of a travel, dialogue, etc. In the end an attempt should be made to draw the substance so that the students may have a thorough knowledge. While employing descriptive method, the teacher should not try to go very much in detail. An attempt should be made to encourage the students to take part in this description. They should also be given an opportunity to give vent to their own ideas. Description should invariably be in simple language and lucid style. It should always be kept in mind that main aim of the description is to draw a picture of the things in the mind of the students.

The following subjects can be taught easily through descriptive method:—

(a) Agriculture.

(b) The food habits, dress and living conditions of the people-of different countries and geographical regions.

(c) Water and rivers.

(d) Living and working conditions of the workers of various industries.

(e) Market and the description of various things manufactured in different places.

(f) Geographical description of the discoveries of different regions.

(g) The life of the animals, minerals and the natural wealth.

(h) Description of the mines and such other things and their conditions.

(i) Geographical environment.

The teacher should try to connect the description with the human life. Then only the real purpose of the teaching of Geography shall be served.

• While going about to several places, the students get an opportunity to observe and see things for themselves. If the students are given an opportunity to acquire knowledge of Geography by observing things themselves, the knowledge shall be stable and shall have a practical value. The knowledge acquired through this method is complete, clear and perfect. Such a knowledge has practical value as well.

The students in the lower classes may be asked to observe geographical things in their environment, near their homes, villages and such other places. They may be asked to collect the geographical data after observation. This will give the students an opportunity to collect the geographical knowledge and data.

Observation method is useful for the teaching of the following branches of Geography :—

(a) Natural or Physical Geography, which includes mineral wealth, vegetation, production, trade, commerce, industry etc.

(b) Commercial Geography which includes crops, animals, methods of irrigation and such other things.

This method requires the following things :—

(a) The teacher should have properly observed and seen the things that he expects the students to observe. Unless the teacher has a thorough knowledge of it, it shall not be possible for him to impart scientific knowlege to his students.

(b) The observation should be accompanied by the collection of the necessary data.

This method has the following difficulties :—

(a) Sometimes when the teacher takes the students out, he has to tackle the problem of discipline as well. (b) It is not possible to observe things that are situated at a long distance (c) Sometimes it is difficult to get the permission of the guardians to take the students out for observation.

In spite of all these difficulties, the method of observation can be very successful in the teaching of Geography. As and when the circumstances permit, the subject must be taught properly through this method.

• This method is sometimes also called Narrative Method or Descriptive Method. It is based very much on the geographical background. Geographical facts are presented in the form of a story. It is not possible to impart the element of character, plot, style etc, in Story Telling Method of Geography. These elements are the special characteristics of literary stories. It is also not possible to present the entire perspective of human life in these stories, as it is possible in the case of historical stories. On account of these limitations the Story Telling Method of teaching of Geography is very much descriptive and narrative. Stories of Geograptey may be of the following type :—

(a) Stories connected with the life of the people of various countries.

(b) Stories connected with the animals and geographical environment of different countries.

(c) Stories of different discoveries such as Columbus, Vasco-de-Gama etc.

(d) Stories of travels and excursions.

(e) There may be stories about conquest of man over nature.

(f) There may also be stories concerning human activities in the background of geographical factor.

Some educationists have expressed grave doubts about the utility of this method in the teaching of Geography. They are of the view that when undeveloped minds are told the stories connected with the life of foreign countries, then it is not possible for them to grasp them entirely. In the absence of understanding, these stories and the knowledge contained therein is of very little utility.

In spite of all the criticism put forward against this method, it cannot be denied that Story Telling Method is useful for the teaching of Geography in lower classes. In lower classes we do and have to teach Geography of the world or foreign country. In these classes we teach Geography of our own country or the State. Under such circumstances the stories shall not go a waste.

• This is also called the patriotic or single country method of teaching of Geography. In this method we take up one particular country and give a detailed description of its lands, situation, natural condition, climate, agricultural products, vegetation, natural and mineral wealth, industry, means of communication, administration, economic progress, etc. The description of all things is based on geographical factors of that particular country. In this method we take each one by one. Once we have finished description of particular country, we take up another country. Thus the Geography of the whole world is taught in parts and countries.

Some educationists have expressed grave doubts about the utility of this method. They put forward the argument that knowledge of one country when given in isolation has very little bearing on the teaching of Geography of the whole world. It cannot be denied that Geographical features of different countries are sometimes same and similar. In this method of teaching of

Geography, very little stress is laid on the political conditions of that particular country. On account of this drawback, this method is not very psychological and scientific.

This method is expensive and time-consuming. While teaching Geography of different countries several things have to be repeated again and again. Things that a student has learned while learning the Geography of a particular country, are repeated again while reading Geography of the other country. This repetition sometimes leads to boredom and the students lose interst in reading.

• Sometimes the Geography was taught on the basis of political division. Now that method has been replaced,by the Regional method of teaching of Geography. Now we take different countries with common physical features, climate, mineral wealth, economic progress etc. at a time and study them together. In this method countries with common geographical features are studied together. Different regions have certain common features and certain contrasting features. It is possible that a natural region may be different from political region. In Regional Method countries with common Geographical features are treated as one unit. In the words of *Prof. Macnee,* "The Regional Method of Teaching of Geography is then, a method in which the area studied is divided into natural regions, each of which is studied separately."

This method of teaching of Geography has certain advantages. Prof. E. A. Macnee has written: –

"The chief advantage of the Regional Method is that it is the quickest way of getting pupils to grasp the salient features of the Geography of any area. No other method can give so quick a start or so sound a basis for further study."

The following are the chief merits of regional method –

1. This method is scientific, orderly and systematic.
2. It gives a better understanding of geography and economics on time and energy.
3. It deals the children to pursue independent study of geography and proves very useful in individual method of teaching.

4. This method correlates the physical, natural, social, economic and other phases of man's life. It helps the children to understand the drama of man being played upon the stage of nature.

5. It helps the child understand the environment, physical as well as natural and social. Therefore, it is uniformity with the modern conception of geography.

6. The method is based on casual relations therefore it develops the facilities of observation, imagination and reasoning. It is educative in itself.

7. It broadens the vision of children. They understand the differences in man and men. Various regions are scattered over the whole world in patches but the life over the whole region is similar inspite of political barriers. This understanding gives international understanding to the children.

This method has certain limitations as well. The boundaries of the natural regions are not very exactly defined and so one region merges into another. Secondly, it is possible that, while paying attention to broader regions, we may miss the smaller regions and neglect a very vital point. Thirdly, it is not possible to have a final division on the regional basis. There may be regions on the basis of different physical features such as climate, land etc.

In order to have a proper study of Geography, it was Herbertson who introduced this method. He divided the whole world into different regions. These regions were based on certain common natural features. Since that time, this method is being used and utilised.

For utilising the method of the teaching of Geography, the whole world is divided into different regions on the basis of the following features—

(a) The region of study.

(b) Its situation and its longitude and latitude.

(c) Area.

(d) Physical features.

(e) Climate.

(f) Vegetation.

(g) Mineral wealth and natural resources.

(h) Human and economic wealth.

• In this method of teaching Geography man and human life occupies a very important places. In Human Geography we study the progress made by man through his efforts and labour. In this method we always have an eye on the cause and effect relationship. Man is very much influenced by Physical features and Physical environment. In dealing with Geography through this method we study man in relation to his Geographical environment. In fact, the human being occupies the central figures in the study of Geography through this method.

While studying Human Geography, we study the contribution made by man in the development of cities, various industries, means of transport and communication, business and other economic activities.

In Human Geography we have to give concession for freedom of human activities. Human activities are not rigidly governed by cause and effect relationship. They have some element of freedom in them. It is quite possible that one group of human beings may act differently in comparison to the other group of human beings. This fact has to be kept in mind while studying causal relationship in Geography. Prof. Macee has, in this regard, very correctly remarked :

"Geography is not a mere recital of unrelated facts. Most geographical facts are related to other geographical facts and it is the business of Geography to elucidate these relations. In Geography teaching, therefore, cause and effect should be traced wherever possible and in particular the influence of physical and biological factors on human life."

• In this method of teaching of Geography, the students are encouraged to compare various Geographical features. In the beginning they are asked to know about the Geographical features of their neighbourhood and then compare these features with the features of city and village. The teacher of Geography may also compare the Geographical features of a particular country with the geographical features of other countries. This Comparative Method is helpful in making the knowledge stable and permanent. In this method the teacher may proceed from known to unknown. The student must be having some knowledge. This knowledge may be compared with the new knowledge and it would provide them with an opportunity to strengthen their experiences. In the words of Prof. Macnee, this method is useful for assimilation of new ideas.

In this method it is possible to compare not only the physical features of one region with the other but also the products and other things of one particular region with that of the other. In the words of Prof. Macnee, "Psychologists have emphasised the important part played in the assimilation of new ideas by the existing content of the mind. The mind tend to interpret the new in terms of the old. It is well, therefore, for the teacher, wherever possible to bring the new ideas which he wishes to present into relation with the previous experiences of the pupils ; in other words, to track new knowledge on to old. This is the psychological basis for the pedagogical maxim ; 'proceed from the known to unknown'."

Explaining the method employed here, he has remarked, "Prompted by this idea the framers of Geography courses usually begin the primary course with things that are familiar to the pupils, the school building and grounds, the village, the local river, the nearest railway line. From the pupil's home and from the things that he can see with his own eyes his geographical knowledge is extended outwards of the districts. State, country and continent."

This Method is not very useful in lower classes but it can be of great use and value for teaching Geography in higher classes. Prof. B. C. Wallis has rightly remarked :

"Comparisons and Contracts are the essence of Geography-teaching at senior stage."

• We all know that in Project Method, the students are given certain projects and problems. They carry out these projects and solve the problems and learn Geography. Students are encouraged to fulfil their projects in the background of natural settings. The teacher has very little to do. He formulates the directions and directs the students to go on that path. He encourages the students to take independent activities. Students have a good deal of freedom to complete this pioject.

The project may be of an individual or collective type. In individual projects the students have to do the work independently but in collective projects it is the group of the students that has to fulfil the task.

In Project Method the teacher has to draw up the project well in advance. He has to be an imaginative and competent sort of person. These projects, have to differ in accordance with the mental status of the students. For the students of the lower classes the projects shall be of a simple nature and for the students of the higher classes the projects shall be difficult ones.

The Project Method has the following advantages—

1. The students have a clear picture of the project and the aims and they continue to work accordingly.
2. In this method, there is a good deal of activity and so the knowledge is founded on solid base.
3. Since the students have to work in realistic circumstances, they develop an attitude of realism.
4. In projects, the students get a pragmatic education. They learn various things with reference to their utility in life and so they acquire a pragmatic attitude towards life.
5. Since the projects have a bearing on life, the students also develop an attitude of interest for life.
6. Students have a good deal of freedom in this method. They continue to work independently and so the originality of the students develops.

Every Project has the following steps to be followed :

1. Dialogue to talking,
2. Manual work or handicraft,
3. Project and study,
4. Drawing of the outline of the project.

A project may deal with any of the aspects of life.

The students may he asked to draw a chart for record of the weather, they may be asked to draw a model of the map of the district or the State, they may also be asked to run the farm of the school successfully and they may also be asked to draw a model of the railway station.

• This is plan of the teaching of Geography which tries to encourage the students to take to self study or independent study. In fact, this method was first introduced by Miss Helen, a teacher ot America. She had the idea of training the students in discipline and co-operation.

In this method the whole lessen is divided into certain parts. The students are supposed to complete certain parts in a specified period. The students are free to divide their time for the study. The teacher is there to direct and guide. He encourages the consultation as and when required.

In this method there are no class-rooms. Class-rooms are like Laboratories and they are also termed so. In these laboratories, the students carry out their work. They are free to carry out the work independently.

Prof. J.E. Parkinson has laid down certain directions and plans in this regard.

(i) In one plan, he expects the students to draw two maps, depicting the climate of India. He expects the students to plot the lines of temperature showing 80°, 75°, 60° and 55° in the month of January and 90°, 85° and 80° in July. These two lines are to be ploted separately.

(ii) Which parts of India are extremely cold and extremely hot ? Explain with causes.

(iii) What is the temperature of Delhi, Madras, Shikarpur and Lahore in the months of January and July ?

Similarly, other plans may also be drawn and the students may be asked to learn Geography through this method.

• In this method of teaching of Geography, the subject is taught like a science subject. Certain experiments are carried out in a laboratory like Geography room. The teacher may demonstrate any experiment and the students shall try to follow it. The rainfall may be called and measured. The teacher may do so with the help of an apparatus. The students may be asked to observe it and try to repeat the performance. The students may also be encouraged to do the work independently.

The knowledge that is acquired by draw out conclusions and finding out results is really stable and useful in future life. Students may also be asked to draw charts, models, maps etc. They may also be encouraged to find out the direction with the help of the compass. The revolution and the rotation of the earth may also be explained with the help of demonstration.

• In teaching of Geography excursions occupy an important place. In excursions and travels, the students get an opportunity to observe and see things by themselves. In fact, excursions are a part and parcel of observation method. It shall not be improper to call the excursion method a projection of observation method. In excurisions the students acquire the practical knowledge. Educationists have laid down that excursions should be formed a part of the teaching of Geography since the early stages. In lower classes students have a good deal of time and so it is possible to plan excursions. The excursions should begin from the observation of the hills and valleys that are situated in the neighbourhood of the school. This may go on the observation of the things of higher importance.

Excursions have the greatest advantage of breaking the monotony of the class-room. In class-room the students have to read the subject in a monotonous atmosphere for a number of days. Once they come out of the class-room, they find a change and this change is helpful in strengthening the interest of the students in the subject-matter of Geography.

In higher secondary classes when the students have developed mentally and physically and are competent enough to know about the responsibilities, they may be taken out on long excursions. James Fairgrieve has very rightly summed up the importance of this method in the following words—

"More Geography is learned by feet rather than head."

While the students are on excursions, the teacher should provide them with an opportunity to express their views about the things observed. This would also develop their power of expression. Before expressing a thing, a person has to organise his thoughts. Excursions would also help in this direction.

The excursions should not be very long. Excursions should invariably be limited and properly planned. Maximum attempts should be made to make proper use of the time. Utility of the time should not spoil the interest of the students in the subject-matter.

While the students are on excursion, they should be encouraged to take down the notes of the things that they have observed. This is possible in higher classes and higher secondary classes. Students should be encouraged to carry note books and pencils with them.

It may not be possible for the students of lower classes to take down notes but for the students of higher classes it shall not be difficult.

It is advisable to divide the whole class of students into groups. Each group may be asked to observe a particular aspect of nature of geographical environment. Then these groups may be asked to exchange notes. This exchange of notes would encourage the students to acquire knowledge independently and in a more scientific manner.

After having completed the training or excursion, the students should be encouraged of study all those things in the maps. This would strengthen their knowledge and encourage them to proceed from concrete to abstract. Students should also be encouraged to write out in detail what they have seen in excursion.

The students should also be encouraged to make certain collections while on excursion. Those pieces collected by the students should be lodged in the Geography museum. The lot would also enrich the. Geography museum Prof, E. A. Macnee have described the importance of this method of teaching of Geography the following words : –

"It is essential that the foundation of Geographical knowledge shall be laid in the field. No amount of reading from books can' make up for a practical knowledge gained by looking at the earth which the child is studying. It follows that from the very early stages expeditions should form part of Grography."

This method can be successful only when the teacher himself is fond of excursions and is prepared to take out the students on expeditions and excursions in a scientifically planned manner.

The teacher should also be well aware of the requirements and' difficulties of an excursion. He should be prepared to face them. Only them it is possible for him to work out this method sucessfully.

1. Teaching of Geography is carried out through several methods. Following are the important methods that are employed for the successful teaching of Geography.
2. Socratic method, in other words the question-answer method. Here attempt is made to impart new knowledge on the basis of previous knowledge.
3. In Inductive Method certain illustrations are given and then an attempt is made to elicit the new theory or principle out of the students.
4. Descriptive Method of teaching of Geography attempts at presenting a de-scription of the thing before the students. Certain subject-matters of Geography, such as agriculture, market etc., can easily be taught through this method.

5. In Observation Method the students are encouraged to observe things by themselves. This method involves certain difficulties.

6. Lecture Method of teaching of the Geography is useful for the teaching of Geography to higher classes. Here the teacther tells the lectures and the students try to grasp them. This method makes the students inactive.

7. Text Book Method implies that the teacher students shall read the text book and impart to the students the knowledge of Geography. This method is also not very scientific.

8. In Story-telling Method the subject-matter of Geography is presented before the students in form of stories. The stories deal with various aspects of geographical environment.

9. Political Method of teaching of Geography various political divisions or countries of the world are taken up one by one and their Geography is studied. Till very recently this method was very popular.

10. Regional Method of teaching of Geography implies that the countries having common Physical and Geographical features and shall be studied together. The whole of the world has been divided into certain physical regions.

11. Human Method of teaching of Geography keeps human being as the centre of study. This method is more concerned with the human activities than other things.

12. Comparative Method of teaching of Geography provides opportunity to the students to compare things of one particular region or place with the things of other regions or place. This gives a solid foundation to the knowledge of Geography.

13. Project Method of teaching of Geography gives the students certain projects and the students have to fulfil them.

14. In Dalton Plan the Geography is taught like other subjects.

The lesson is divided into certain parts and the students are left free to carry out the plan.

15. Laboratory Method of teaching of Geography or Scientific Method of teaching of Geography implies that the Geography shall be taught like a science subject. In this method the Geography room is treated as a laboratory or a science room where practical experiments are carried out and students learn Geography.
16. Excursions form an integral part of the teaching of Geography. Excursion Method not only provides the students with an opportunity to observe things by themselves but it also provides them with an opportunity to organise their knowledge.

Man is constantly acquiring new experiences. With his development in the world, he tries to gain new experiences. In this method of education, the natural experiences of child form the basis of education. Here the teacher has to proceed on the basis of the experiences acquired by the young men in the modern would of education this method occupies an important place. It is supposed to be more scientific and psychological as compared to other methods of education.

In India basic education has acquired the status of national pattern of education, specially at the primary stage. As we all know, it is craft centred method of education. Here the students are encouraged to do things by their own hands and thus acquire knowledge. This method of education is very much akin to basic education. The two can go together to a great extent.

Combination of theoretical knowledge and practical life. In life we acquire theoretical knowledge. This theoretical knowledge shall be of no use if it cannot be put into practical use. In fact, theory and practice have to go together. Learning by doing is the basis of the logical method of teaching. The students are made to learn by practical experiences. They have to work according to a set pattern. A project is drawn and the whole project is divided into smaller projects. The teacher of Geography provides the knowledge of the subject to the students with the help of these projects. These projects are of a varied nature and so the student is able to know about the various aspects of the subject through this method. The project and the working of this method is so evolved that the student does not feel that the work is going on. The student feels at home in the whole set-up. Through his questions and answers he *is* able to organise the whole of his knowledge and ideas.

Environment and experiences. The child lives in the society or the social environment. This social environment is brought with activities. Various types of activities are going on in the society. This society has diverse activities. These activities continue to take place. These activities add to the experience of the child and so he acquires knowledge which is useful in life. This method is based on the following three types of environment :

1. Physical or natural environment;
2. Social environment;
3. Practical work or trade.

Natural or physical environment. Man is born in the free atmosphere of nature. He sees various natural objects all around him. By coming in contact with these natural things, he acquires new knowledge. Every day in the morning he sees the sun rise and in the evening sees its set in. The process of the day and night goes on. He also acquires the knowledge of the fact that sunrise causes warm and heat and in the night there is cold. When at night the child sees the moon and the stars, he feels happy. In the summer the sun shines in such a manner that the sun rays straight and they cause heat and temperature. In the winter season it is not so. During rainy season there is rainfall and in the winter reason the day is short and the night is long. On the other hand, in the summer season the day is long and the night is short. When the rain falls during the rainy season, we see the water flowing. This also gives an idea that the water flows from an elevated place to a lower place. All these natural activities of the environment add to the experience of the child. He also sees the agricultural products of his atmosphere. These agricultural products provide him with some knowledge and new experiences. It is the duty of the teacher to direct all these experiences in the proper manner. These experiences have to be properly organised. In this process, it is possible for the teacher to provide certain new experiences to the students. New things are also known to the young boys and girls. Here in this method, on the basis of the unknown experiences, certain known facts are taught.

Geography is very much related to nature. Therefore, through this method it is possible to teach Geography more successfully. The students may be taught about the things that they do not know, with the help of their known experiences. Thus the students may be encouraged, in a natural manner, to proceed from known to unknown.

Social environment. Man's sociality is a well known fact. It is not possible to separate man from society. He starts with the assumption that the world is confined within society. It is as a member of the society that the performs various activities and takes to new processes. It is in the society that he learns activity. He takes part in various social activities, religious ceremonies, social customs, pilgrimages, etc. He is not only a passive looker of all these social activities and customs but also plays an active part in it. It is through the social environment it is possible to have an idea of the importance of various activities of contemporary value and social importance. In our day-to-day life we use various things that are imported ones. With the help of this practical experience it is possible to have an idea of import. Sometimes we see that people who are agriculturists see that there is surplus of foodgrain. The student sees that his father has sold a surplus grain to some trader. The trader carries this grain away and sells it in ths market. Thus, there is training of import. While learning about export and import, the student also learns about trade and business. He sees several things arranged for several occasions. He also sees that on certain occasions certain things are utilised for decoration. These pieces of decoration are the result of industry of handicraft. This gives him a knowledge about that.

The teacher can utilise various social functions, customs and festivals for teaching of Geography to the students. He may draw a plan and list of all these things and teach the students about all these things. By this method it shall be possible to place many things in the minds of the students in a natural and spontaneous manner.

Industry or practical work or trade. Through this method or Project Method it is possible to teach the students about trade. A detailed plan may be drawn about collecting the raw material and doing many things in this regard. The students may be asked to perform jobs in regard to this. It would provide them with an opportunity to learn about all these things. They shall also have a detailed knowledge of the various aspects of a particular trade or industry.

In this process it shall be possible to have a study of the local conditions and local environment. Students may be asked to take up some work of some small scale industry and acquire a solid knowledge about trade and its working. For example, the students may be shown the process of jaagary making and this may give an idea to the students about the process of preparation of sugar. The students may also be told about the process of carrying the sugarcane to the mills and preparing sugar. They may also be given an idea of export and import of sugar. This would provide them with an opportunity to study about various means of communication and transport and their Georaphical method.

From this thing it is well evident that this method can be very helpful in the study of Geography, Such a knowledge is practical and useful. In future, the student is capable of giving a practical shape to his knowledge. He can have proper ideas of social and natural environment and utilise the knowledge of these things for establishing or running a particular industry or trade. This would be helpful for the future life.

1. Teaching by the method of learning by doing or Project Method can be very useful for the teaching of Geography.
2. In this method there is combination of the theoretical knowledge as well as practical knowledge.
3. This method implifies study of the following types of environment.

(a) Physical or natural environment.

(b) Social environment.

(c) Practical knowledge of trade or some industry,

4. Teaching by this method, which is also called the Project Method, implifies that the student shall learn about natural environment and social environment and try to put the whole knowledge into practical form.

5

Role in Teaching

Recent years have seen both a decline in the price and a rise in the power of personal computers. You can get a fairly basic word-processing kit, including a monochrome monitor, dot matrix printer and word-processing software, for around £400; Whereas £1,500 would buy you a powerful and sophisticated IBM-compatible personal computer (PC) with a built-in integrated suite of software (word processing, database, spreadsheet, graphics, communications, etc.), DOS and Windows operating systems, colour monitor and a bubblejet printer.

There may be a temptation for a community information service to assume that a computer is now a necessity for its work, before asking the obvious question: 'What do we need one for?' Consideration also needs to be given to the question of who is expected to use the computer. If your service relies on volunteers, they may have an aversion to new technology or simply not work long enough to become familiar with and confident in using a computer. Before plunging into the murky waters of information technology (IT), you should first of all ask the kind of basic questions that needed to be addressed when setting up your service, such as 'Why do we need IT', 'What functions do we want it to perform?', 'What system is going to meet our needs?' 'Who is going to use the system?', 'Where can I get advice?', 'What training will be required?', and so on. There are many reasons why an information service might want a computer but they may not necessarily all be the right reasons. Some wrong reasons are:

- everybody else has got one;

– to improve the image of the service;

– to sort out our database /statistics/ financial accounts, which are in a mess.

This latter brings to mind the computer cliche 'garbage in, garbage out', namely that if you put rubbish into a computer, you can expect to get rubbish out. Before inputting any information into a computer, you must first have a logical and organized manual system. The computer won't do it for you.

Some right reasons, might be:

– to provide faster and more timely access to information;

– to facilitate access to a wider range of information;

– to provide more sophisticated access to information;

– to enable more people to have direct access to information.

Before making a decision on what equipment to purchase, consider what functions you want the computer to perform. These might be one or several of the following:

– database management;

– recording statistics and, possibly, producing these in graphic form, i.e. as bar or pie charts, graphs, etc.;

– running welfare benefits and other programs;

– running a local view data system;

– online access to other external databases;

– word processing;

– financial accounting;

– desktop publishing.

If you require most of these functions, a fairly powerful machine would be necessary but you might be better advised to consider more than one computer or even linking them in a local area network (LAN). A LAN enables personal computers to commu-nicate with each other and share resources such as software and printers. Usually, a LAN is driven by a computer with a large hard disk which contains the software programs and the data input by the rest of the PCs or terminals on the system. It also provides access to shared printers on the network and to central back-up facilities.

Scope and Sphere

There are several ways in which you might set about choosing a computer, depending on the level of knowledge of staff in your organisation. Let us assume elementary or no knowledge of computers, in which case the options might be the following:

Dealers-may be OK if you know one who can be trusted or is recommended, but computer salesmen, like car salesmen, frequently try to get you to buy a machine of a higher specification than you need and blind you with technical jargon. Also limits your ability to shop around.

Consultants-usually expensive unless you can beg or borrow their services. Have a tendency to recommend separate software packages for each function or even writing a program to match needs exactly, rather than considering integrated packages which may require some compromise. OK if all the separate parts can work or are not required to work together.

Other organisations in the same sector who use computers in their work may be able to recommend equipment and software from their own experience. However, they may be reluctant to admit shortcomings and the equipment/ software they use may be out of date, given the speed of developments in this area.

Networks who support advice services or community and voluntary organisations, such as Community Computing Network (65 Litchfield Road, Cambridge. CBI 3SP) or the Computer Develop-ment Unit of LASA (2nd Floor, Universal House, Wentworth Street, London El 7SA Tel. 071-377 2798). Apart from giving direct advice themselves, they may be able to put you in touch with others who can help.

Within the space of this book, it is not possible to consider all the potential uses to which a community information service may wish to put a computer. I have therefore concentrated on those aspects which, though not peculiar to information services, are a major feature of their work, namely database management (including view data and access to external databases), welfare benefits programs and enquiry statistics.

Technical Management

There are a number of reasons why a community information service would want to keep its information file on computer:

- beyond a certain point, a manual information file becomes unwieldy to use and update, whereas a computer database offers speed of access and ease of updating;
- complex searches involving, for example, subject, place and clientele, are extremely difficult and well nigh impossible to carry out with a manual system. A good computer database management system allows searching of the database by a combination of terms;
- individual records or subsets of the database can be printed out on demand in a variety of formats, e.g. as mailing labels, lists, standard letters;
- through networking, online or exchange of disks a computer database can be shared with other workers or organisations;
- customers can be given direct access to the database through public access terminals in your centre(s) or through a viewdata system;
- entries can be fed into a word-processing or desktop publishing package and printed out as leaflets, directories, handbooks, etc., either directly or, more usually, by preparing a master copy which is then printed by offset litho.

A computer database is made up of two parts—the software, sometimes referred to as DBMS (database management system) and the database file, which is very much like a manual card index system in that it contains individual records made-up of a number of fields (e.g. name, address, telephone number, hours of opening, etc.), into which bits of information (data) are entered (input). Most database systems store data in a highly structured form but there are some exceptions, known as free-form' or text-retrieval databases, which automatically index all significant words in a document.

Some database systems allow information to be viewed or edited either in tabular form, with each record represented by a row and fields as columns, or a record at a time. The tabular approach is fine if the fields in each record are short but is less convenient where you have lengthy fields. This can usually be circumvented by limiting the number of characters in each field, but then you cannot see the record as a whole. There are basically two types of database management systems: a simple DBMS produces a single file (sometimes called flat file) of records that have a predetermined number of fields and field lengths. This does not mean that field lengths cannot be varied or fields added or deleted, but any changes affect all the records in the file. A flat file may be adequate, say, for a database of community organisations, provided you have reasonably anticipated all the fields and field lengths that you are likely to require.

However, it will not be suitable for a situation where you want to create several different files and have the ability to link them. For example, in addition to the database of community organisations, you may want databases of leaflets, booklets and pamphlets; 'hard' information; individuals who can provide help; and enquiries plus the ability to search on all of them simultaneously. In those circumstances, you are more likely to need a relational DBMS, which would enable you to form links between the different files through the use of common denominators, such as subject or classification fields, client reference number, etc.

Examples of flat file systems are Cardbox Plus (used by Help for Health for its database), Q&A, and FileMaker Pro. Most database functions that come as part of a suite of integrated software, such as LotusWorks, will be flat file systems and may not be sophisticated enough to cope with anything but a simple database. Some of the leading relational systems are DataEase, Paradox, and dBase systems (dBase IV, FoxPro, Clipper). I have used for a number of years a system called Superfile which, at the time, had the advantage of not requiring any programming knowledge from the user. However, most of the database systems have become more user-friendly over the years.

The price you can expect to pay for a DBMS can range from £ 250 to £ 750 but some suppliers offer substantial discounts to voluntary organisations and charities.

Further Options

Before choosing a database management system, you should first of all draw up a shopping list of requirements and questions that you need to ask, such as the following:

- Is there a maximum size of file that the system can handle? In most cases this will depend on the size of your computer's memory but some systems may operate more slowly as the database grows beyond a certain size.
- Is there any limit on the size of records, the number of fields in a record, or the size of a field? If so, is this likely to be a problem?
- Is it possible to add, expand or delete fields from a record without difficulty?
- Is it possible to print out all or a selection of records and fields within records in a structured format?
- Can the data be fed into other software packages to produce lists, standard letters, mailing labels, etc.?
- What features does the system provide for searching records? For example, wildcards (* ? =) are a means of truncating search terms to take account of varying forms or spelling, e.g. ORGAN will find any first word in a field beginning with the letters O R G A N, such as 'organize', 'organisation' etc.; 'sounds like' will find records with similar sounding words to the search term, e.g. FAIR and FARE; or Boolean logic will logically link or exclude terms

to narrow the field of search, e.g. A and B, A or B, A-G but not C, etc.

- Is there a facility to check on the validity of entered data?
- Is there provision for constructing user-friendly menus?
- How much knowledge is required to set up a database? How long does it take to acquire that knowledge? Can it be self-taught?
- How good is the documentation that accompanies the system?
- Is there a multi-user version of the software?
- What support is offered by the supplier? Is there a user group?

Having bought your software and installed it on the computer, the next step is to create the database(s). Each database management system will have its own methods for setting up the database and this section can give only a few tips from experience that should apply to whatever system you have chosen. First determine a structure for your database. If you are moving from a manual database, that structure may already exist.

The method of determining a structure for a database is similar to that for a manual system, as set down in Chapter Four. However, in addition to identifying what fields you require, you will also need to determine field lengths. Be generous, if your system will allow, so that you are not continually changing field lengths. Separate fields will need to be given field names or tags to which the computer attributes information that is being input.

For example, you might decide to call the 'organisation' field ORG and the 'address' field AD. Where a field consists of several lines, such as an address, it is advisable to split these into separate fields, particularly if you want to search on individual elements of an address field or to print them out as separate lines. An address field might thus be divided into two or three separate fields for building/house name, street, community/ neighbourhood /village and fields for town county and postcode. So your tags might look like AD1, AD2, COM, TOWN, COUNTY, PCODE. In some cases, a record might contain several repetitions of the same field types, e.g. names and addresses. Every time these occur you could give them the same tags, but this may cause problems when conducting searches or printing out information.

For example, if you wanted to see or print out a list of organisations in, for example, the 'Parkside' neighbourhood, the computer would also throw up records for, say, the secretary or second contact who lives in the 'Parkside' neighbourhood, if they all have the tag COM. The simplest way to get round this is to add to the root name for tags a separate number for each occurrence within your record structure, e.g. COM1, COM2, COM3, etc.

There are occasions when it is advantageous to use the same tag for several fields:

1. You might, for instance, want to have several fields for subject headings. By giving them the same tag name, this will ensure that, in whatever subject field a particular term is entered, the computer will throw up the record when a search is made under that term. It will also ensure that when records are printed out, the record will appear under each subject heading.

2. When you want to link files in a relational database system, this can be achieved by having a field with the same tag name appearing in each file, e.g. subject, name of organisation, client, etc. A search on that particular field will throw up records in all the files bearing the term entered.

It is advisable to have the database form in the same order as the form that you send out to organisations for their information, as this makes it easier for the person inputting the information. One of the advantages of having a computerized database is that it enables you to automate administrative processes.

For example, update letters can be customized and printed out as you determine. If you want to update continually throughout the year rather than in one session, then you will need to build into your record structure, field that enables you to do this, e.g. date record last updated, or added, AGM date. Dates must be entered in a consistent form. Alternatively, you could update a section of the file each month by the initial letter of each organisation, e.g. Month 1: A-B, Month 2: C-D, and so on. When sending out update letters or forms for information about new organisations, if people's names and addresses are going to be recorded, make sure that you conform to the requirements of the Data Protection legislation by including a statement to the effect that: 'This information is being stored on a computer. Please indicate any items of information that you do not wish to be recorded.' Details of the Data Protection legislation are available in a series of free booklets from the Office of the Data Protection Registrar, Springfield House, Water Lane, Wilmslow, Cheshire SK9 5AX.

When sending out an update letter, it is also helpful to send a printout of the organisation's current entry as a prompt for any changes that may have occurred and to save the secretary time in filling out information that has not changed.

All database systems will have some facility for sorting records according to predetermined parameters, e.g., alphabetical by subject, then alphabetical by name of organisation or by date, record number, place, etc. You can usually set up several sort codes for different purposes. The sorting facility is used mainly as a prerequisite when printing out records as a list. For this, you will use another element of a database management system, the report function. (name may vary according to DBMS used). This enables you to print out information in a predetermined format, using all or a selection of fields in a record. Again, more than one report can be set up to take account of different uses. In some integrated packages, the database records have to be fed into the word-processing package for printing out.

Information Treasure

You will need to consider potential uses of the database. Is it a tool for the staff alone to use in answering enquiries? Are you going to allow public access to records either as printouts or through an online terminal? Are you going to make the database available to other organisations through exchange of disks or even sell it to interested parties? The answers to some of these questions will have implications for the kind of hardware and software you choose, and therefore need to be decided at an early stage.

For example, if you decide to allow public access via an online terminal, apart from the additional terminal and keyboard you will also need a multi-user version of the software which must be capable of building in safeguards to prevent the public either accidentally or deliberately erasing or changing records. Some database systems offer run-time versions of the software at a substantially lower price. These allow the system to be run but cannot be used to make changes to it or to develop something new. A good example of this is Help for Health's Cardbox database, where subscribers receive a run-time version of Cardbox and regular updated disks of the database. Obviously, a run-time database will not be as up to date as a true online system but could be a cheaper and safer alternative. You can also get video-text packages which run on PCs and enable you to marry attractive graphics with a database. A good example is the TAP (Training Access Point) terminals located in various public buildings to dispense information on training opportunities, both local and national. The national information was obtained through online links with remote databases. The local information database is maintained on a master PC and then transferred by disk at regular intervals to the PCs driving the TAP terminals. The advantages of this kind of system are:

- eye-catching graphics can be used to overcome the public's reluctance to use computers;
- protects your main database;
- less staff-intensive.

The disadvantages are:

- the information is not as up to date as a true online system;
- a PC is occupied just in running that function;

– it can become monopolized by young people who think it's the latest arcade game;

– if a printout facility is offered, this can easily be abused, requiring frequent staff attention;

– there is a need to make the equipment inaccessible or tamper-proof

PC-based video-text terminals have been used to good effect by some commercial organisations to provide local information and advertising. You find these most often in the windows of tourist information centres, the Computer display being operated by a touch-sensitive keypad attached to the window. Another variation is to get a graphics package, such as Animator, which has the facility of enabling the computer to rotate a series of frames of information at set intervals. Several years ago COIC (Careers & Occupational Information Centre) offered a video-text package called Rotaview which enabled users to create colourful graphics and link these with a database.

The system was used to prepare an off-line database, to access or download frames of information from Prestel, or to operate as a mini-viewdata service with users dialing into the database for information. Another attraction of Rotaview was its carousel feature that enabled up to 80 frames of information to be scrolled at intervals. A particular use for this type of feature in an information centre would be to display essential information to the public out of hours. Rotaview was marketed at schools, colleges and public libraries but, alas, was developed only for the BBC micro and is no longer available. However, with infinitely more powerful PCs around today, there must be similar software on the market, if you are interested in this way of displaying information.

Store of Knowledge

Using a PC is not the only way of setting up a community information database. There are other options which may be open to services which are part of a much larger organisation, like public libraries, and are designed to cope with extremely large databases and/or allow wider access. In the early 1970s British

Telecom (or The Post Office as it then was) developed a viewdata system called Prestel which enabled users to access thousands of pages of information on all sorts of topics via the medium of the telephone and specially adapted television sets (and later also PCs). The system has never quite lived up to its early promises but is still going strong. A number of public libraries were involved in the early trial of Prestel and recognized the potential of the system, if not of Prestel itself. Eventually, local authorities began to set up their own viewdata systems of information about council services and other local information. The public could access the system either directly from home or through terminals located in libraries and other public buildings. In some instances, the library service is responsible for maintaining the database, in others another department of the local authority. Viewdata systems offer the following:

- access to large amounts of continually updated information;
- use of graphics;
- public online access from home, workplace or publicly located terminals;
- centralized updating of information.

Some disadvantages are:

- they need dedicated teams to maintain the database;
- many clientele of community information services would not be able to afford equipment to access the database or would be afraid of using a computer;
- limitations on the amount of information that can reasonably be presented by the system.

Some public libraries, like Berkshire, are beginning to recognise the income-generating potential of viewdata, with electronic Yellow pages, teleshopping, rental pages, and closed user group facilities. Apart from running viewdata systems, mini or mainframe computers can also be the hosts for community information databases using such software as IBM's STAIRS (Storage and Information Retrieval System). Some libraries set up their databases on a mainframe computer from the start; others, like my own, have transferred from a PC-based system. Some advantages of using a mainframe computer are:

- almost limitless power;
- speed of operation;
- updating from multi-access points;
- online access from other council departments, the public, etc.;
- possible links into computer issue systems;
- feedback from other departments/ organisations using the system.

Disadvantages are:

- they are not particularly user-friendly - no use of graphics;
- it can be difficult to maintain consistency of input and updating with multi-access;
- they take second place to other council programmes, such as payroll.
- you need to 'log on' each time the system is used.

Reference was made above to possible links between mainframe-based community information files and library computerized issue systems. In fact, a number of these systems now offer add-on features for storing community information themselves. The advantages of these are:

- access to database through every library in the system;
- public access through OPACs (Online Public Access Terminals) or, in some cases, dial-in facilities;
- multi-access to inputting and updating database.

Disadvantages are:

- they can slow down issue system;

- they are not usually accessible by other council departments;
- with multi-access, it can be difficult to maintain consistency of inputting and updating;
- as with viewdata systems, information is usually limited.

Inevitably, with a technology that is developing so fast, there will be new systems for presenting information coming along. Glasgow has been experimenting with HyperCard, which allows the user to search through text, pictures, numbers and instructions to gain information about the city. Before long someone is bound to be using CD-ROM or interactive video.

Various Systems

Another use for your PC might be to link into other remote databases such, as a local authority's viewdata system. To do this you will need' a modem, to link the PC to the telephone network, and communications software, which could be a separate package or part of a suite of software such as LotusWorks or Windows 3.

Most online databases, except for local viewdata, are not appropriate for community information services, but there is one that is: Volnet UK, operated jointly by The Volunteer Centre UK and the Community Development Foundation. Volnet UK is an online information service containing thousands of references to press items, journal articles, reports, books and current research projects on community development, voluntary action, youth affairs, child care and social policy issues, stored on an easy-to-use computer database. For a modest annual fee (00 local community/ voluntary agency, £90 national/ regional voluntary agency, £150 central/local government department) you get unlimited access to the database (no charge per second or minute), a telephone help-line, plus a photocopy service for articles, for which a small charge is made. Details from Volnet UK, Community Development Foundation, 60 Highbury Grove, London N5 2AG.

Various Programmes

Providing welfare benefits information and advice can be

notoriously difficult because of the complex legislation, which is why some advice centres and public library community information services are harnessing the power of PCs to help them. These are usually designed for use by advisers although, over the years, some attempt has been made to develop client-operated systems, largely without success.

Welfare benefits programs contain the rules of the benefits system and present on the computer screen a series of questions. The adviser, in consultation with the client, types in the details and the computer works out whether the client is entitled to benefit and, if so, how much. The results can usually be printed out and given to the client to take away. The main benefits covered include Income Support, Housing Benefit, Family Credit and Community Charge Benefit. The advantages of these programs are:

- consistency;
- they do not let you forget little-used regulations or passport benefits, where claiming one benefit, automatically entitles the client to others;
- a novice worker can tackle more complex cases;
- 'what-if' calculations can be done speedily;
- printouts of results can be obtained;
- some clients like the computerized approach and are reassured by it.

Some disadvantages are:

- they are only as accurate as the information input;
- the benefits, system is so complex, programs are bound to have quirks;
- an experienced adviser can usually work faster than the program;
- they ran lead to over-confidence;
- some clients can be intimidated by a computer and find it intrusive;
- they are no substitute for experience.

For more details, on the main welfare benefits programs available and their features, addresses etc., see the *Computanews* factsheet Welfare benefits programes.

Many a Programme

There are other PC-based programs and databases available on such areas as debt advice calculations and sources of funding from charitable trusts. Resource Information Services, in conjunction with LASA's Computer Development Unit, has developed a database of advice agencies in London which became functional in autumn 1992. A good way of keeping up with the latest developments in programs for advice work is to take out a subscription to the excellent bimonthly periodical *Computanews*.

Data and Figures

Collating and manipulating statistics is one area where computers have a distinct advantage. They can do in seconds or minutes what would take hours of work manually. However, if all you want the computer to do is add up and produce totals in broad categories, then you might as well stick to pencil and calculator. But, for detailed analysis of enquiries and graphic representation of information by means of pie or bar charts, graphs, etc., you will need a computer program. There are two options: either devise your own system using a spreadsheet package or a relational database system linked with a spreadsheet package, or buy a specially designed program. A lot of the pioneer work in this field has been carried out by LASA's Computer Development Unit which, some years ago, developed CRESS (Client Records and Enquiry Statistics Service) and is currently engaged on developing a model recording system called STATS. Finally, there are many more uses to which a community information service might wish to put its computer, e.g. word processing, accounts, graphics, desktop publishing, but these aspects apply to many other organisations and it is beyond the scope of this book to cover them.

6

Role of Teacher

Teacher occupies a very important place in the scheme of education. Without a well equipped teacher, teaching of a subject cannot go on. It may be possible to continue the teaching of purely literary subject having a scientific bias, it is not possible to go on without a properly equipped teacher. In subjects involving observation and collection of data, direction of a teacher is very necessary. Without his co-operation and direction teaching work cannot go on successfully.

Geography is such a subject which has the qualities of art as well as science. If on the one hand it has the qualities of a literary subject, on the other it has the qualities of a scientific subject. The practical knowledge is required at every step. Students have to be acquainted about the countries about which they do not know anything. Their imagination has to be excited so that they may know things properly.

In teaching of Geography maps, charts, diagrams etc. form an integral part of the scheme of teaching. These things cannot be used without the proper guidance of the teacher.

For the teaching of Geography it is necessary to have direct observation of the environment and the physical conditions. Students have to be encouraged to observe things by themselves and have-proper assessment and knowledge of the subject-matter, this work has to go on in a well-graded and proper manner. Only a successful teacher of Geography can encourage the students to resort to this method. In rural areas various types of crops, such as wheat, maize, jute, etc. are grown. In market we find things made of textile, steel, etc. All these things are produced and grown under certain geographical factors whose knowledge is very necessary and useful for the students. Only the teacher of Geography can help the students to know about all these things.

A teacher of Geography can play his part successfully when he is able to guide the students to acquire knowledge of the subject in a scientific and thorough manner. In order to be able to do this he should have the following qualities in him :

Different Angles

A teacher of Geography should have a thorough knowledge of the subject. It does not mean that he should have read taxt-books only. It requires that he should have grasped the spirit of the subject and studied it in the proper perspective. On the other hand the teacher of Geography should also be a student sort of person. His reading should not cease after he has completed his education for a particular degree. He should continue to be a student throughout his life.

A teacher of Geography should not have only read the subject he should have grasped it properly. Once the teacher has grasped the subject properly, he can present it before his students in the proper manner. The teacher of Geography should also be upto date-in the knowledge of the subject-matter. This does not mean that he should be a specialist. A specialist is useful person for higher education. For secondary classes he should be able to present the fact of Geography in a Psychological manner. This he can do when he is aware of the fact that social sciences are a developing subject.

No teacher can be successful in his task if he does not possess a thorough knowledge of the child psychology. Children of different stages have their own psychological requirements. Teaching of a subject is based on these psychological requirements. Unless the teacher has thorough knowledge of educational psychology and knows the psychological reqirements of the children, he cannot impart the knowledge of the subject in the proper manner.

The knowledge of child of psychology enables the teacher to know what method should be employed for the children of particular age. This knowledge can bring a good deal of success to the teacher.

Along with the knowledge of the psychology, the teacher should also know about the various methods of the teaching of Geography. For different stages, different methods are useful. These methods are employed according to the psychological requirements of the student. When the teacher is aware of the various methods of teaching he can employ them very successfully.

A student at the age of fourteen is fond of excursions and going about. For a student of this age excursions and travels can have a good deal of educational requirement of the child and knows about the importance of travels and excursions in the teaching of Geography, he can very safely co-ordinate the two and make the teaching successfully.

The teacher of Geography should be a keen observer. We have seen it more than once that, excursions and travel form an integral part for the teaching of Geography. While going about the teacher and the students have to observe things and collect suitable material. If the teacher is keen to observe, he can have the students collect things and make proper use of the subject-matter.

Along with keen power of observation the teacher of Geography should also have good power of imagination. Observations coupled with imagination can lead along way to the success of the teaching of the matter.

Natural environment have a good deal of influence on the life of man. This influence can be properly studied through observation and imagination. We observe this influence at one place and on the basis of imagination which visualize its effect in other places. The teacher of Geography has to acquaint his students about all these things. Unless he has power of observation and strong imagination, he cannot present the Geography of foreign countries before his students in a vivid and attractive manner. These two qualities help the teacher to present the subject-matter of Geography in a lively and interesting manner. It is not necessary that all students should have seen desert or a hilly place. With the help of imagination and observation the teacher can make the student visualize and understand the life in desert and hilly place. He can also make them understand about the way of life of all these places. In fact these two qualities help him in making the teaching of the subject-matter interesting.

The teacher of Geography must have the knowledge of the curriculum and syllabus of other subjects. He should know about their developments and requirements of teaching. This is necessary because Geography is a subject which has the element of science as well as the humanities. It has to be taught in both the ways. A teacher who has no knowledge of the subjects of science shall not be able to do justice to the subject. Similary a teacher who has no knowledge of the curriculum and syllabus of humanities shall also not be able to teach the subject successfully. For teaching the physical Geography in a successful manner the teacher must have the knowledge of the principles of science. In higher classes Geography science is an essential part. A teacher who has knowledge of the principles of science can handle various geographical apparatuses such as Thermmometer, Rain Gauge. Barometer, etc. successfully and confidently.

With the help of knowledge of other subjects, it is possible to establish co-relationship of Geography with other subjects. We have already seen that Geography is related to Language, History, Mathematics, Art, Gardening. With the help of the knowledge of these subjects, thes teaching of Geography can be made interesting and lively. Teaching of a particular topic of Geography can be strengthened with the help of the examples from other subjects.

Knowledge by Practice

Geography is a subject which is based on cause and effect relationship. In teaching of this subject everything has to be explained on the basis of the cause and effect. In order to explain the cause of various events, the teacher of Geography should be read with the material that may explain the cause. It is with the help of the maps, charts, diagrams etc. that the cause and effect relationship can be properly explained.

On account of the cause and effect relationship, in the teaching of Geography, models, charts, sketches, etc. occupy an important place in the teaching of Geography. In primary classess models are very important. In secondary classes it is charts and the maps that pay a vital role. The teacher of Geography, while explaining a thing or the point has to take help from maps and charts to explain his points fully well to his students. These teaching aids make the teaching of the subject interesting and lively. The teacher of Geography must be skilled in handling these aids. He should also be good at drawing of the charts and maps. Unless he is good at drawing maps and charts, he shall not be able to draw them on the black-board. If a chart is drawn on the black-board it will be possible for the student to understand the subject-matter successfully with the help of those charts and maps. In short, it means that the teacher of Geography should be able to handle and make the charts, maps, models etc. successfully and properly.

If it is possible to arrange the curriculum on the basis ol season and weather, the teaching can be made realistic and interesting. If the teacher wants to teach about rainfall and he can do it during rainy season, the knowledge shall be stable and permanent. Similarly, lesson about crops may be taught in the season when the crops are grown. During winter season the frost, log, etc. may be taught. The teacher must have the capacity to organise and arrange the subject-matter according to season. He should be all along alive to this requirement of the students and try to teach successfully. This thing has a good deal of utility in the teaching of the subject.

The teacher of geography should have a scientific way of thinking. He should be able to impress upon the minds of his pupils the cause and effect relation in the world of geography. He should suggest the children not to take things for granted without scientific verification. Heuristic attitude in Geography will be the most educative for the childern.

Various Potentials

In fact geography is a subject of maps. The teacher of geography must be able to draw maps, sketch maps and diagrams on the black-board. Geographical facts can best be brought home to the children with the help of such aids. But ready-made aids of this kind are not available and controllable at every step. Therefore, the teacher should be able to draw maps and sketches freely.

The teacher of Geography should be a good story-teller. He should have the capacity to draw and frame stories connected with various geographical aspects and present them before the students in a successful and interesting manner. The quality of the teacher can be of great use in lower classes. The teacher should be interested in story-telling and writing out stories. A teacher of Geography with this quality can be really successful.

It is necessary to have a good collection and museum of the things of geographical importance. Such a collection makes the teaching interesting and lively. The teacher of Geography should have interest in collecting things of geographical importance. He should also have interest in organising and arranging a museum. If things of geographical importance are presented in their real form before the students, the teaching becomes interesting and lively. Then it becomes possible for the student to know about soil, rocks, stones, etc. These things can be presented before the students if they are lodged in a museum. This museum can be arranged by the teacher only and unless he has interest, he shall not be able to do it. Same is true of maps, charts, coins, etc. Unless the teacher is fond of collecting things of geographical importance he shall not collect the chart showing the inhabitants of different countries and the routes of sea, land, etc.

It is necessary for every teacher to have qualities of leadership and direction. Unless the teacher has these qualities he shall not be able to handle his students successfully. In a subject like, Geography, these things are all the more important. The teacher of Geography has to take his students out for travels and excursions. In these travels and excursions only a successful leader can guide his students properly. He can maintain discipline effectively only if he has these qualities in him. It is, therefore, necessary for the teacher of Geography to have qualities of leadership and direction in him.

Travels and excursions form an integral part of the teaching of Geography. Unless the teacher himself is interested in excursions and travels he shall not be able to take his students out for such jobs. In these travels and excursions the students acquire knowledge directly. They are able to see various things with their own eyes and also observe geographical phenomena. By direct observation the students acquire knowledge successfully, easily and effectively. Direct knowledge is always better than indirect knowledge. Knowledge acquired with the help of the books is not so lasting as the knowledge acquired with the help of the eyes and ears.

Excursions imply keen observation. If the teacher is fond of excursions he shall also be able to guide his students in the observation of geographical things. In this manner he shall be able to do justice to his job.

We have already stated that in Geography cause and effect relationship plays a vital role. The teacher of geography must have the capacity to explain the geographical causes in a clear and food manner. There are also factors that are responsible for the control of geographical events. We have already talked about them. They include geographical conditions, climate, ways of living etc. All these things are influenced by the controlling factors of Geography. The teacher of Geography must know about them and must be able to explain these things to his students successfully and effectively.

Every subject is taught on the basis of certain aims and objects. The teacher has to remain alive to these aims and objects. Unless, he has the aims and objects he shall not be able to teach the subject effectively and in an interesting manner. If the teacher of Geography continues to assess the extent to which he has been able to teach the subjects on the basis of the aims and objects, he shall be able to teach successfully.

The teacher of Geography should be able to infuse regard for the subject and interest in it. This can be done by handling the subject in psychological manner. The teacher may by his personality and method, incite the students to study Geography and take interest in it.

Intelligence and Wisdom

In the words of an eminent writer "One of the aims of teaching geography is to produce international understanding in the children. They are to learn how every individual, every country and every community is dependent upon other individuals, countries and communities. They must understand how physical, natural and social environments are invisible effective in binding us all together. But these secrets can be taught effectively only by such a teacher who himself has faith in international ideas and who appreciates world citizenship. The teacher of geography must be able to rise above political boundaries. A natural region is the natural geographical region and not a politically democrated country."

Every teacher has to be idealist. It is equally necessary for the teacher of Geography to be idealistic. His attitude of teaching as a subject should be based on philosophical foundations. Through these bases he can help the students to develop in them the feeling of world brotherhood and world fraternity.

1. The teacher of every subject has to possess certain qualities in order to teach his subject successfully.
2. This is true about the teacher of Geography as well. Since Geography is Art as well as Science. The teacher of Geography must have the qualities to do justice to subjects of both these types.
3. The teacher of Geography must have the following qualities in him :
   (a) He should have a thorough knowledge of the subject.
   (b) He should also have knowledge of child psychology.
   (c) He should have knowledge about various methods of teaching. In this respect the knowledge should be upto date.
   (d) The teacher of Geography must also be a keen observer. He should have the capacity to observe things keenly.
   (e) The teacher of Geography must have the knowledge of curriculum and syllabus of other subjects as well.

This 'knowledge would help him to do justice to his subject.

(f) The teacher should have the knowledge and practice of handling various teaching aids such as models, charts, sketches, diagrams, etc.

(g) The teacher of Geography should be capable of arranging his curriculum and syllabus with an eye on the season. If a particular thing is taught in the season in which it can be practically seen, the teaching shall be effective and interesting.

(h) The teacher of Geography should be a good story-teller.

(i) The teacher of Geography should have interest in the collection of the things of Geographical importance.

(j) In order to be able to guide the students properly and keep discipline, the teacher of Geography should have the qualities of leadership and direction in him.

(k) Since travels and excursions form an integral part of the teaching of Geography, the teacher of the subject should have love for travels and excursions.

(l) The teacher of Geography should be capable of explaining to the students the geographical causes and the factors control various geographical events.

(m) The teacher of Geography should be alive to the aims and objects of the teaching of the subject and he should also continue to assess the extent to which he has succeeded in achieving these aims and objects.

(n) The teacher of Geography should also have the capacity to inculcate interest and respect for the subject.

(o) Finally, the teacher of Geography should be an idealist and his attitude of teaching the subject should be based on philosophical bases.

Ours is a country of villages and whole of the India live in villages. So, after completing my studies, I would like to be appointed as a geography teacher in a village school. When I would join the school I shall first of all acquaint myself with physical, natural and social environment of that village. I shall visit the surrounding fields and study life of the people inhabiting in the village. I shall also acquaint myself with the trade of village and know what commodities are exported and what are imported.

The students of the college would be mostly from the agricultural class and be studying agriculture as compulsory subject. So, I shall make my teaching of geography on the actual experience of the agriculture. I shall follow the following devices to make my teaching effective :

Rambles in the countryside—I shall take my students to the countryside—Fields, forest and hills. They have already visited these places but their visits were not systematic and well-planned. I shall narrate to the student about the important things and pass over the unimportant ones.

Visits to the centres of trade and industry—I shall also take my students to the centres of trade and industry. I shall tell them that society has exploited geographical resources to the benefit of man. In the industrial centres, the process of exploitation is going on. By visiting the centres of trade and commerce, students shall have actual understanding of the fact that how our daily needs are met.

Exploitation of the experience of children—I shall also make the actual experience of the children the basis of teaching. My whole teaching would be based upon the knowledge of the students that they have gained earlier.

Home-geography the starting point—Home geography shall be the starting point of my teaching. While teaching about the agricultural products of America, I shall base the new knowledge on their already attained knowledge of Home-geography. In this way I shall be able to base their new knowledge on sound footing. My teaching based on the Home-geography shall be interesting for the students and so they would grasp, the subject without difficulty.

Use of project method—Occasionally I shall follow project and problem methods. Such devices will be occasional but well-planned.

Play-way method—I shall dramatise suitable geographical lessons and will use other play-way methods also.

The use of pictures and maps etc.—I shall use illustrative aids of various kind. I shall show them beautiful pictures on various topics such as children and busy people of distant lands, snow-capped mountains, mighty rivers, magnificent buildings, lofty trees and strange animals. These pictures will not be shown at random but will be exhibited in connection with lessons which they are learning.

Geography room—I must have a fully equipped geography room to produce good atmosphere for the subject. The pupils will be encouraged to help in the equipment and upkeep of the geography room.

Library books—I shall provide interesting and well-illustrated library books to the pupils to create interest in the subject. The books will be selected very carefully.

The use of epidiascope, magic-lantern and film strips—I shall provide a projection for the effective teaching of geography. I shall use epidiascope, magic-lantern and film strips regularly to make my teaching interesting and effective.

Other audio-visual aids—I shall exploit radio also for this purpose. There are often broadcasts of useful lessons connected with geography. I shall have a radio-set for the school. Other available audio-visual aids will also be exploited.

Construction of models and maps etc.—I shall encourage the pupils to prepare geographical models, map and illustrative aids themselves. I will satisfy their urge for construction and develop their interest in the subject.

In order to create interest in geography, as a new teacher I shall do the following—

1. I shall take my students to the countryside and teach them systematically.

2. I shall arrange visits to the centres of trade and industry so that student may understand how their daily needs are met.

3. I shall exploit the experience of the children and base my teaching on Home-geography.

4. I shall use Project-Method and Play way-Method for teaching Geography. I shall make proper use of pictures and maps, Geography room, Library books, epidiascope, magic-lantern and nun-strips, audio-visual aids etc. I shall also say the students to make models and sketch maps by themselves.

7

Current Setup

Information is the life-blood of a community information service and the information file is at its heart. Unless the heart is sound and continually pumping a supply of regularly renewed and fresh information into the system, it will not function at its best. Therefore, it is important to give extra care and attention to planning the resources needed to set up a sound information base and a workable system for keeping it up to date.

Some basic things you will need to consider are as follows:

- How is the information to be collected?
- What method is to be used for processing and storing information?
- How is the information to be retrieved?
- What size is the file likely to be?
- What areas, geographical and subject, is the file to cover?

In addition, you will need to consider how the information is going to be disseminated, if it is not just for internal use; but that is the subject of the next chapter. The kind of system you choose and the degree of its sophistication will depend on the nature of your information service, the size and complexity of the information you need to store, the staff, and the financial resources available. When designing a system, make sure it is readily understandable to all those using it-volunteers and public included-and not just to professionals.

Area of Operation

In identifying the need for your community information service, you should have reached a decision already on the community to be served. This may be either a geographical community or a community of interest or both. Either way, you will still need to make a decision about the extent of your information base. For example, a neighbourhood information service must decide what information to collect on the wider area-town, county, region, nation-outside its local community. An information service aimed at a fairly wide area may need to limit its interests to a particular sector of the community or to a particular range of subjects, e.g. the low paid, those receiving income support, or those with debt problems. Even an information service in support of a local campaign may benefit from collecting information on similar campaigns or problems country-wide.

Different Kinds

The information base of your service is most likely to include the following types of information:

Soft information– details of clubs, societies, Organisations and services; individuals; events, etc. Usually this information will not be available in a published form, or at least not in sufficient detail, and it will be necessary to make a conscious effort to collect it. This information may comprise the major part of the resources file.

Hard information– factual information on a specific subject e.g. benefit rates for single-parent families, how to get legal aid, how to change your name. This information will be available in a variety of Banns, some ephemeral such as leaflets, pamphlets, booklets, broadsheets, posters, periodical articles, etc. Such items are usually kept in a vertical file, in storage boxes or similar receptacles and accessed via some form of index or classification scheme. Other hard information may be in the form of books, multi-volumed reference works, law books, or even audiovisual forms. If there are many items of this type, they will need to be classified and shelved.

Supplementary information – information already produced in a particular format-directories, handbooks, diaries, annual reports, constitutions, newsletters-of Organisations appearing in your information file.

The Software

It is highly unlikely and undesirable that an information service should need to 'go it alone' in the collection of information. Such is the volume, complexity and variety of sources of information in present-day society that, unless your service has very narrow terms of reference, it will be virtually impossible for it to collect and keep up to date all the information that is required.

Therefore, it is important that you first of all identify the information providers, support services and 'gatekeepers' in your community and establish effective contacts with them. These links may already have been forged in the process of conducting a community profile. They now need to be fostered and strengthened, so that there can be a mutual exchange of information. These contacts will also be able to provide you with useful feedback from the community as to the success or otherwise of your service. The network of contacts can be maintained on a fairly casual basis as the need arises, or you might want to formalize the arrangement. Some ways of doing this include irregular 'get togethers', informal luncheon clubs, regular meetings with agendas and minutes, or the circulation of a newsletter or bulletin. Other activities that could develop out of such meetings are joint collection of information, shared publicity, compilation and publication of directories, information handbooks and leaflets, training, and general discussion of common problems. Collecting information is a time-consuming process and there is no one method of going about it. You will probably have to use a combination of several techni-ques to build up a satisfactory information base. One thing definitely to be avoided is duplicating work that has already been done. So first of all identify the following:

Existing information files. Contact all the other community information services, council departments and Organisations who are likely to maintain information files and ask if they would be willing to share this information. Try to offer something in return, either an exchange of information or some other help you can provide.

Local directories. There are several types of directories that may be available in your area and which are useful sources of soft information: (a) local government authorities often produce directories or town guides of their area which contain a certain amount of local information or they may produce a guide to council services; (b) telephone directories, especially Yellow pages which have an alphabetical subject arrangement; (c) area directories, such as those produced by Thompson's Newspapers, which are similar to Yellow pages but also contain a section of community information-your local newspaper may produce a directory of local services, sometimes in conjunction with local information groups; (d) citizen's guides may also be produced by the local newspaper as a supplement to an existing newspaper; (e) CVSs or RCCs sometimes produce directories of voluntary Organisations in their area or you may find these listed in your local CVS/RCC annual report; (f) directories covering a special subject, such as accommodation, halls for hire, etc.; (g) directories aimed at a particular interest group or groups e.g. people with disabilities or senior citizens.

National directories are useful not only for the wider network of services but also for identifying local offices of a national Organisation.

Other methods to use in building up your information base and maintaining its currency include:

Looking and listening. A lot of information can be gathered by simply walking around your community, looking at notice-boards, picking up leaflets, or attending open meetings, fairs, fetes and other community events. This method of collecting information is unpredictable and requires more than a 9-to-5, five-day week.

Contact with individuals. People are a major source of information in any community and there are always those to whom others naturally go for information. Try to identify such people and enlist their help, possibly by offering something in return-bartering is a time-honoured system! Direct contact with individuals in other information services and Organisations is often a better way of eliciting information than impersonal methods and also paves the way for further cooperation. Pay regular visits to such centres.

Scanning newspapers, magazines, newsletters, etc., can turn up details of new Organisations; changes of personnel, premises or hours of opening; new services introduced; and may highlight problem areas where information may be needed.

Other documents, including council minutes and agendas, planning regulations, annual reports (ask to be put on mailing lists for these), leaflets and manifestos.

Media publicity Local press, radio and cable television stations may be prepared without charge to put out a call for Organisations to contact your service. If not, then consider inserting an advert or, where there is, a local directory produced, have a tear-out slip included for Organisations to fill in and return to you. As a result of these various methods, an amount of raw material will have been obtained which may be of use to your information service. How accurate, up to date and complete the data is will depend very much on the reliability of the source. In most cases, unless you have every confidence in the source, the information will have to be checked before it is entered in a more permanent form in your resource file. So, at this stage, simply record it onto say a scrap 5in x 3in card and put it into a temporary file.

The information you have obtained will be of several different kinds but the most common will probably be that relating to Organisations, clubs and societies. This is the most difficult type of information to collect since it is ever changing and therefore unrelenting effort will be required to achieve even reasonable completeness or accuracy-100% will be impossible. However, with a good system for collecting and updating the information, you should be able to build up and maintain an acceptable file.

A lot of staff time will be needed to carry out this work, so first of all investigate whether there are other local information services that need this type of information and would be willing to help in its collection. It may be possible to collect the information through an umbrella group, where the work can be framed out so that it is not too great a burden on any one Organisation. Alternatively, a joint approach can be made on behalf of a number of Organisations.

Ideally, the most effective way to collect information of this kind is to pay a personal visit to each Organisation or service, but rarely will that be possible without extensive staff resources or a very small community. The cheapest and quickest way to collect this information is by telephoning. Prepare a standard list of questions to ask so that entries in your information file follow the same format.

Telephoning is only practicable if you have a reasonably small number of Organisations to contact, say up to one hundred. If visits and telephoning are ruled out, then the information can be collected initially by postal questionnaire, with a request for up-to-date information sent at least once a year and also when it is known from other sources that changes have taken place. A covering letter should be sent with the questionnaire or update request, explaining "Why the information is needed and asking for cooperation. If the information is to be passed on to other Organisations or commercial bodies, either free or for payment, this should be drawn to the attention of the recipient of the questionnaire, so that they have an opportunity to decline to give the information or insist that it is not so disseminated. If the information is to be stored in a computer, then you will need to meet the requirements of the Data Protection Act.

If it can be afforded, include with your questionnaire some means of returning it free of charge, as this will significantly improve the response rate. Separate forms may be required to collect different kinds of information. The following is a suggested list of headings which you might need to include on forms for collecting information from two of the most common types of Organisations.

Clubs and Societies

- Name: the name by which the club is best known, plus the full name if different. Indicate relationship to larger body, i.e. branch, regiment, lodge, etc.

- Secretary's name, address and telephone number or those of a similar person if the Organisation has no secretary.
- Place, day and time of meetings.
- Purpose of Organisation if not self-evident from the name.
- Eligibility: any restrictions by age, sex, ethnic group, occupation, status (single, divorced, widowed) etc.
- Subscription: any charge to become a member or to attend meetings.
- Annual general meeting: the date of an Organisation's AGM can be a useful indication of when to send out update forms as this is when officers or policies are likely to change.
- Other officers: names, addresses, telephone numbers of treasurer, president, chairman, publicity officer, membership secretary, etc.
- History of the Organisation including special events or persons associated with it.
- Publications: newsletter, diary, commemorative brochures, annual report, etc.
- Date the information was obtained and/or last updated or checked.

Agencies and Organisations providing a service

- Name: popular name and full name, e.g. CHAT (Come Here and Talk), SHAC (Shelter Housing Action Centre), plus relationship to parent body where necessary.
- Address: street address and postal address, Post Office, box number if used.
- Telephone and fax number, including-service number, administration number, after-hours or hotline numbers.
- Contact person: personal name, title and address, if different from above.

– Hours of opening: days and times; note if seasonal, e.g. holiday period, term time.

– Services provided: advice, counselling, practical help, etc.; types of enquiry the service would like to have referred to them.

– Eligibility: age, income, sex, residency, status.

– Application procedures: walk-in, appointment or waiting list; what papers or documents need to be brought.

– Cost: free, fees, means-tested, donations; any facilities for payments to be spread over a period; help available from local or central government, charities, etc.

– Geographical area served: neighbourhood, city, county, region, adhoc area; no geographical restrictions.

– Branch offices: extension bureaux, mobiles, surgeries, etc.; include hours of opening, routes and times of stops.

– Director, administrator or executive director of the service; name and telephone or extension.

– Volunteers: does the service use volunteers and for what purposes? Method of recruitment.

– Publications: directories, handbooks, leaflets, annual report, etc.

– Funding: local government grant-aided, donations, etc.

– Special facilities: foreign languages spoken, access and facilities for people with disabilities, photocopying or fax service, escort, advocacy, etc.

– Transportation: how to get to the service, e.g. bus route numbers, underground line and station, etc.

– Date information was obtained and/or last updated or checked.

These two lists represent most of the facts that a community information service might need to know about an Organisation or service. In practice, depending on the scope of your service, it may not be necessary to include all the fields in the questionnaire. It is a good idea to get the person filling in the questionnaire-to-sign it, thereby giving the information service some-protection against claims of giving out wrong information—a not uncommon occurrence, especially when the information is committed to print.

There are other types of 'soft' information that your service might need to collect, for example halls for hire, places of local worship, accommodation, 'What's-on' events, local industry. The procedure is much the same:

- Decide what information you need to know.
- Devise a standard format or list of questions to ask.
- Identify possible sources of information.
- Decide which method or methods to use to collect the information: telephone, personal visit, postal questionnaire, press advert, etc.

How to Store 'soft' Information?

There are various methods that can be used for storing information:

A list is easy and quick to consult, can be photocopied for clients to take away and can be faxed, but has very little flexibility for inserting and updating information.

A strip index provides flexibility, can easily be photocopied, and is available in various forms: large binders holding many pages, smaller folders containing just a few pages, address books, wall-hung panels, rotunda units, etc. Strips are available in several colours, which allows for a simple categorization, and various widths. Even so, they are limited as to the amount of information that can be contained on them. It is also not quite as easy to insert new strips as the manufacturers claim.

Cards are still one of the most commonly used systems for storing information. They are infinitely flexible, easy to insert and update, can be sorted into any preferred order, and require very little technical know-how. The most popular sizes are 5in x 3in, used mainly for indexes or temporary information waiting to be checked, 6in x 4in, and 8in x 5in, which are large enough to contain sufficient information about most Organisations or services and to be preprinted with a standard grid for recording the information. There are more superior types of card files available, such as the Rondofile or Rotadex systems which use custom-designed stationery and therefore tend to be more expensive. With systems that use standard cards, you can-if you are hard-up or want to save trees-use the reverse of scrap cards. Card files have a number of disadvantages: they are not so easy to carry around, they arc not easily reproducible if someone wants a copy of a particular section, multiple access (e.g. by name, subject, area, service, etc.) requires duplication of cards, and the updating process can be tedious.

You may still find around edge-punched cards which offer a primitive type of multi-access to the information on the card-through the strategic use of knitting needles or rods. Personally speaking, I would save up and get a computer.

Loose-leaf binders with one sheet for each entry, sometimes called 'sheaf' binders, have a similar flexibility to cards. They are slightly slower to add to and amend but are more portable. They are suited best for alphabetical arrangements as they are difficult to guide.

Microcomputers now have the capacity to handle immense information files that can be accessed by any number of predetermined variables or even free-text searching by keyword, depending on the software used. With a printer attached, all the information or sections of it can be printed out on demand or to provide a master for printing by conventional methods. Personal computers now begin at prices that bring them within the range of most community information services. However, there is danger in automatically seeing the computer as the best solution for maintaining your information file, as this may not always be the case. A lot depends on the size of your file and its complexity, what you want to do with the file, and to what other uses you want to put the computer. The importance of the computer in, information and advice work is such that it merits a chapter to itself, and you will find these and other aspects.

Filing System. Whichever method is chosen for physically storing the information, except for that by microcomputer, it will be necessary to decide the best way of arranging entries so that the information can be retrieved swiftly and accurately. In order to ensure that the total resources of your information service are used to the full when answering an enquiry, it will help if the system used to organize the information file can be integrated with that for the vertical file and the book-stock. This point needs to be borne in mind now, although it will be dealt with more fully later.

The bulk of the information file is likely to comprise 'soft' information -which you have collected about Organisations, clubs, societies and services and, to a lesser extent, about individuals who are a valuable source of information or advice, plus items of 'hard' information not available or conveniently available in printed form. There are several ways in which you might want to retrieve this information-by the names of the Organisations, by subject (i.e. area of interest), by clientele, by the type of service (e.g. counselling), or by place. In practice, the 'clientele' and 'type of service' approaches are usually catered for through the subject file rather than, as separate files.

Organisations file: The master file for the whole system will usually be an alphabetically arranged sequence of entries by name of Organisation. It is generally recommended that the full, official name of the Organisation is used, with references from other forms of the name. In practice, it does not really matter as long as there are references from the alternatives to whichever form is chosen. There is a good argument for putting the main entry for an Organisation under the form of name by which most people refer to it, even if this differs from or is an abbreviation of the official name. This is especially so where the file is to be used by the public.

In addition to details of Organisations, each entry in the master file may also contain certain 'housekeeping' details relating to the maintenance of all the information files, plus references to appropriate headings in the subject file, where relevant information can be found, and a classification number.

Subject file: Most enquiries received by a community information service are likely to be about the need for a service or activity or for help with solving a problem, rather than for information on a specific named Organisation. So the information you have collected about Organisations, services and individuals will also need to be accessible by the services and activities they provide. There are two ways this can be achieved, by either using a subject index or having a subject file of Organisations. In both, you will need to choose or adopt a set of subject headings which will adequately describe the information on file or elsewhere in the system and the interests of your clientele.

If you are compiling your own list of subject headings, choose terms that are in common use by your clientele, especially if they will be consulting the files directly, rather than the 'official' term, e.g. OUT OF WORK or ON THE DOLE instead of REDUNDANT. Always refer from alternatives not used to the chosen term.

A subject index is rather like the index to a book. It is an alphabetically arranged file of subject heading cards on which reference is made to where information on that subject can be found. The cards themselves do not contain information. The subject index can contain references to Organisations, individuals and other supplementary material such as pamphlets, periodical articles, audiovisual material, books, etc.

A subject file consists of an alphabetically arranged set of subject heading cards behind which are filed copies of the Organisation cards appropriate to that heading and possibly cards containing items of 'hard' information. An alternative is to arrange cards according to a classification system either devised by yourself or adopted from another service, such as the NACAB classification scheme.

Place file: Where an information service covers a number of distinct towns, villages or neighbourhoods, each having a similar range of Organisations, it may be helpful to have a file that can be accessed by place. There are a number of options. You could sort the Organisations file initially by place, especially if it contains few Organisations whose responsibilities extend to the whole area covered by your service. Alternatively, if most of the Organisations are prefixed with the name of the place (e.g. EXVILLE ATHLETIC CLUB, EXVILLE COUNCIL FOR THE DISABLED), the alphabetically arranged master file will automatically bring together those from the same location, provided inverted headings have not been used.

Some arrangements will have to be made for Organisations which do not conform to the pattern, either because the place-name does not feature at the beginning or because it is not contained in the name of the Organisation at all. In these cases, an additional card can be made out with either an inverted heading (e.g. EXVILLE, ROTARY CLUB OF) or the place-name can be prefixed.

The third option is to have a separate file of Organisation cards arranged initially by place and then alphabetically by name of Organisation or by subject.

Filing alphabetically. Filing alphabetically is not quite as simple as ABC, as any librarian will tell you. There are two recognized methods, known as 'word by word' and 'letter by letter'. In word by word, entries are initially sorted by the first word in the heading, then headings that begin with the same word are sorted by the second word, and so on. Another way to describe this method, which may be more helpful, is to treat spaces between words in a heading as an imaginary letter coming before 'a' in the alphabet, then sort letter by letter.

In letter by letter, you simply ignore any spaces in the heading and sort one letter at a time from left to right. Here is how a small group of headings would look sorted by the two methods:

Word by word	Letter by letter
Do Something! Boys Club	'Dog And Bone' Darts Team
'Dog And Bone' Darts Team	Dogsbury Residents'
Dog Sniffers Anonymous	Association
Dogs Homes	Dogs Homes
Dogsbury Residents'	Dog Sniffers Anonymous
Association	Do Something! Boys Club

There are several other niceties to do with filing alphabetically but we only need mention here that hyphens are treated as spaces in word-by-word sorting and numerals are spelt out as said, so that 1900 (the year) is considered for sorting as Nineteen Hundred and 1,900 as One Thousand, Nine Hundred.

File 'housekeeping'. In addition to the information needed to answer enquiries, there are other items of information to do with the maintenance of the file which may usefully be included on each entry, such as the following:

- the date the information was obtained, last updated or last checked, which will indicate not only the degree of reliability to be placed on it but also when to update;
- the date a questionnaire or update letter was sent - a check for chasing up non-returned forms;
- additional contacts or other information which does not fit into the main part of the entry;
- subject headings used in the subject file;
- place headings used in the place file, if not obvious from the name of the Organisation;
- feedback-comments from users of the service;
- 'tracings', i.e. a list of other cards that refer to they can be traced and amended or withdrawn when necessary.

The amount of this 'housekeeping' information you need to include will depend on how sophisticated you need your file to be. The bigger the information service and the larger the file, then the more likely it is that you will need to introduce a systematic procedure for processing information. In such a case it is usual for the housekeeping information to go on the reverse of each entry, using a standard grid like the one illustrated here. It is arguable that if your information file requires this degree of sophistication, you ought seriously to consider keeping it on computer.

For a small community information service, it may be quite adequate just to note the date when the information was collected, checked or updated.

Updating. By their very nature the entries in your database will be changing continually. Hours of opening, meeting places, officers, membership fees, subscriptions, charges, etc., are all susceptible to frequent change. Therefore, it is important to have a system for regularly updating each entry in the database. There are several ways of achieving this but, whichever method you adopt, it must be regular and ongoing.

Interim updating. All the entries for Organisations should be checked at least once a year to ensure they are still correct. In between times, however, new information will be brought to your attention by various means, including word of mouth, newspaper reports, Organisation newsletters, company reports and by direct contact with the Organisation itself. If the source of information is reliable, it can be substituted immediately for the out-of-date information in the database but, if not, it should be noted and a further check made to verify its accuracy. A simple way to add new information to an entry in a card file is to write it onto self-adhesive labels or slips (obtainable at most stationers) which can be stuck over the original information. Even though an entry has been updated in between times, it should still be checked formally once a year.

Annual updating. Once a year is probably a reasonable time-span for updating your database but a shorter interval may be necessary if the information content changes frequently. You will need to decide how the annual update is to be carried out. Some Organisations like to update the entire file at the same time, so that they can say the file was as accurate as possible at a particular date. However, this does create a tremendous amount of extra work for a period of several weeks and you may feel it necessary to get extra paid, work-experience or volunteer help. Another disadvantage of this method is that it captures a picture of Organisations at a set moment in time. Some Organisations may be just about to make changes, and your records for these would be out of date for almost a year.

Alternatively, you may decide to update on a continuous basis by using either the date the record was added to the database or the Organisation's annual general meeting (AGM) date as a trigger. This is easy to do if your database is kept on a computer, since a date field can be used to produce a subset of records and, by linking the database with a word processing package, a personalized standard letter can be printed out for sending to each Organisation. It is less easy with a card or any other kind of file. You can get little coloured metal tags to clip on to the top edge of cards, a different colour for each month, or you could use an appropriate symbol on the heading of the card, such as a coloured dot, a letter or number. Tags can make the file look a bit messy and are easily knocked off if it is in constant use; symbols require the whole file to be checked through.

It is better to update records shortly before or after each Organisation's AGM, since most Organisations, if they are going to change their officers or constitution, generally do it once a year at the AGM. This is so because many Organisations do not know their AGM date a year in advance, it is enough just to indicate the month in which the AGM is usually held. For those Organisations and services which do not have an AGM, you will need to use the date the information was added as the trigger.

When writing to Organisations to update their information, it is better to send them a copy of their record with a request to indicate any changes, rather than sending a blank questionnaire. This saves the secretary unnecessary time in repeating information that has not altered.

An alternative to writing to each Organisation is to phone, but this is time-consuming and costly, and only feasible if the number of Organisations to contact is fairly small. Avoid sending out updates at times when people are likely to be away, such as during the summer. There are certain times when it is more appropriate to update other kinds of information, e.g. social security benefit rates (which usually change in April and September), adult education classes or school, college and university courses which change term-wise.

When an updated entry is returned it should be checked to see if the subject or place headings still apply. Minor changes can be recorded on the master card and any other cards in subject or place files; major changes may require a new set of cards to be produced. For those with computerized databases the process is simpler as just the one record has to be updated. Don't forget to change the date the information was last checked or updated.

The Hardware

As well as the database, most information services will need a certain amount of 'hard' information to answer enquiries. Short, unrecorded or inadequately recorded items of 'hard' information, as we have already seen, can be incorporated into the database. However, the majority of hard information will usually be found in one or more of the vast range of print forms, starting from locally produced free broadsheets to extremely expensive multi-volumed loose-leaf reference works.

Within the scope of this book, it is not possible to go into detail about the sources of this material, since they will vary considerably according to the type and subject range of the service you are operating. Community information changes rapidly so any printed sources should be treated with care. However, you might find useful a chapter on the sources of community information that I contributed to Printed reference material and related sources of information, 3rd edn, Library Association Publishing, 1990, which concentrated on Organisations and on those items which are regularly updated.

The following framework for collecting community information was originally devised by Grainne Morby, who at the time was working for the Community information Project, with some additions of my own:

In other words, identify the main topics into which the subject scope of your information service naturally divides. Throughout this framework I will take as an example an information service for which the main area of interest is housing. It is sometimes useful to apply a consistent criterion when dividing up a subject, although obviously this would not be so easy for an information service whose scope covers as broad an area as, say, 'community information'.

However, taking housing as our example, you could decide to divide it by type of accommodation, e.g. owner-occupied, private-rented, council-rented, New Town, Housing Association, institutional accommodation, tied accommodation, mobile homes, etc. In most cases you would probably need an additional category for subjects that cut across all or more than one category. In the case of housing, this might be 'squatting' or 'homelessness'.

Since the material you want to collect will usually be written to meet a particular need or needs, it is advisable to collect information around those needs rather than for fitting into a theoretical framework. The kind of broad client groups that might be identified in the field of housing are landlords, tenants, owner-occupiers, squatters, transients, elderly people, people with disabilities, the homeless. Then, one could identify client groups who share a common problem or need associated with their particular type of accommodation, such as eviction, dampness, house repair, renovation, harassment, mortgages, rent arrears, planning permission, redevelopment, etc. Once these subject areas and client needs have been identified, it should give you clearer guidelines when you come to select material from the various sources identified in the next part of the framework.

Print sources

1. Official

(a) National

- *pre-legislation:* political party manifestos and policy documents, speeches by Ministers, the Queen's Speech at opening of Parliament, White Papers, Green Papers.
- *Legislation:* Bills, Hansard reports of debates in both Houses of Parliament, Acts, Statutory Instruments.
- *Guidance to local statutory bodies:* circulars and letters from Ministers, guidance notes, reports of Inspectors.
- *Reference books:* collections of legislation, e.g. Statutes in force, Legal aid handbook.

– *Periodicals:* from government departments and agencies, e.g. Department for Employment gazette.

– *Guidance to the public:* leaflets, posters, videos and other A/V material.

– *Ombudsmen.*

(b) Regional

– Health authorities, British Rail.

– Privatized utilities: gas, water, electricity, telephone.

– Consumer watchdog bodies: Post Office Users' National Council (POUNC), Office of Gas Supply (OFGAS), Office of Electricity Regulation (OFFER), Office of Telecommunications (OfTel), Office Of Water Services (OFWAT).

(c) Local

– *Local authority policies and decisions:* agendas, minutes, standing orders, bylaws and regulations.

– *Guidance to the public:* handbooks, leaflets, etc. from local authorities, area and district health authorities, Community Health Councils, local offices of government agencies.

2. Non-official

(a) National

– Reference books and handbooks from commercial publishers.

– Voluntary Organisations.

– Pressure groups, self-help groups.

– 'Umbrella' Organisations, e.g. National Council for Voluntary Organisations, Federation of Independent Advice Centres.

– Professional bodies, e.g. The Law Society.

– Trade associations, e.g. National Association of Retail Furnishers.

- Educational bodies, e.g. National Extension College, Open University.
- Trade unions.
- The media.
- Practitioners in the field who publish.

(b) Local

- Claimants' unions.
- Law centres, other specialist advice centres.
- Neighbourhood and generalist advice centres, resource centres.
- Local 'umbrella' groups.
- Pressure groups, campaigning groups, action centres. Voluntary Organisations.
- Local media: newspapers, community newspapers, radio, cable television.

(c) New technology

- Video-text systems: Prestel, teletext, private viewdata.
- Online computer databases, e.g. Volnet
- CD-ROM, videodiscs, etc.

This list is not intended to be exhaustive but will give you some idea of the range of sources in which to look for information. Howard Matthews, in his book *Community Information* has drawn up a set of criteria for selecting community information materials. It is aimed particularly at library community information services but may be generally helpful for anyone setting up such a service.

1. Selection should be done by those who know the community best.
2. Material should relate to specific, local, identified needs.
3. All material should be current.

4. All material should be written at a level appropriate to its intended use.

5. Material should be concerned with the practicalities of problem solving.

6. All new material should either fill a gap, offer a new viewpoint, or promise something better.

7. Material should take into account the level of use the client will make of it.

Obtaining publications and other material. Once the material you require has been identified, you will need to obtain it. Some material will be priced, in which case- you will need to order it, and some will be free.

Priced publications. The procedure for obtaining priced publications, particularly in the field of community information, is not as simple as you might suppose. Since a lot of the material may well be fairly cheap and the small or community publishers, booksellers and library suppliers are reluctant to obtain it as the profit margin is likely to be too low for the amount of effort involved. The alternative is to order direct but this also has its difficulties as many small publishers now insist on money with order, and this can cause problems for some Organisations through the need to raise a cheque or limitations on the amount that can be spent from petty cash.

A few national voluntary Organisations, e.g. Age Concern England, operate a standing-order system for their publications-this is one solution, although you may need to accept blanket coverage of the Organisation's output. In the larger cities, you may find a community or alternative bookseller who is prepared to supply this material to order. A directory of alternative bookshops is published annually by the magazine *Radical Bookseller*. Whatever the method of ordering, it is important to keep a record of what has been placed on order and from whom to avoid duplication of titles and as a check on supply. For each title make out an order or slip. This can be either a scrap 5in x 3in card or one specially printed with a standard grid. The following indicates the kinds of information that need to be recorded:

- title of publication-more important than author for this kind of material, since authorship is often unclear;
- author-might be an individual or an Organisation;
- price, date of publication and, if a periodical, frequency;
- supplier-this may be a bookseller, library supplier or the address of the producing body;
- date of order;
- source of information about the item;
- location, if you are ordering for more than one centre.

You may find it helpful to use the order cards later as the basis of a catalogue of the publications in your information centre; in which case., leave space at the top of the card for either a subject heading, classification number or filing code. After an order has been placed with a supplier, the order cards are filed, preferably by title, in one alphabetical sequence known as the 'order file'. When a publication is received, the order card is removed from the file and accompanies the publication to the next stage if it is to be used later as the catalogue card. If not, you may find it useful to file the order card in a 'publications received' file, until such time as the publication is permanently recorded in the system, after which the card can be thrown away.

Periodicals. Publications which arrive at regular intervals – weekly, fortnightly, monthly, quarterly – will not require an order card but you will need to keep a record of each title taken. This should include the following items of information:

- title of periodical;
- frequency;
- supplier;
- when subscription is due for payment;
- a grid to record receipt of each issue;
- instructions for disposal of back copies.

For those using computers, there are software packages available for periodicals management but these are aimed at Organisations who take an extensive range of periodicals and such packages are not cheap. If you have a database management package on your computer, you would do better to devise your own periodicals database.

Free material. This can vary from quite substantial loose-leaf binders plus updates to leaflets, posters and bookmarks and may be required in bulk for clients to take. Since this is likely to be a frequent type of request, it may be quicker and simpler to duplicate a standard letter to send to Organisations, with space left to fill in address, title of item, format (leaflet, booklet, poster, etc.) and number of copies required. It is advisable to keep a record of what is requested, if only as a check on whether it has been received or not.

A lot of the sweat has been taken out of identifying free materials, and addresses from where they can be obtained, through the setting-up of Camden Libraries' Free Leaflets Information Service (FLIS). For an annual fee (E120 in 1992) subscribers receive a copy of the Frills directory of free information leaflet suppliers, a monthly batch of new and updated leaflets and amendments to the Frills directory, and details of a model system for organizing leaflets. Details of this service can be obtained from Community Information Services, Camden Leisure Services Department, St. Pancras Library, 100 Euston Road, London NWI 2AJ. A similar, but not so extensive, service is provided by the NACAB as part of its Information Service, but you would need to have approval to subscribe to the full pack.

Organizing hard information. We have already seen that hard information can be found in a great variety of forms. For the benefit of organizing it, the following categories can be identified:

Material in book form for use by clientele or information workers will be best arranged on shelves in the broad subject groups identified when acquiring the material or according to a classification scheme.

Ephemeral material for use by information workers is best stored in a vertical file using the same subject headings as those in the subject sequence of the information file, though probably with more subdivisions, or using a classification scheme. Alternatively, the material could be kept in file boxes on shelves using broad subject headings.

Ephemeral material for use by clientele on the premises is best kept in file boxes, ring or display binders and ideally interfiled with books. Vertical files are not recommended for public use as they tend to be a deterrent. Another way of dealing with ephemeral materials is to gather them together in packs on particular topics and, for maximum impact, to display them face outwards on sloping shelves.

Ephemeral material for the public to take away can be displayed in special leaflet dispensers, on a sloping surface or on tables. Ideally, they should be displayed in broad subject groups or by originating Organisation, e.g. Benefits Agency, Department for Employment, but this is rarely possible because even within Organisations leaflets are produced in varying sizes.

Beyond Setup

Many Organisations produce printed material in the course of their work or activities. The most common types of material are directories or address lists of members (individuals or constituent groups), newsletters, events sheets or cards, annual reports, constitutions, posters, leaflets, funding appeals, campaigning literature, advertising brochures, balance sheets and commemorative booklets (anniversaries, etc.). All this material is potentially useful as back-up information to the database but there is no sure way of obtaining it. When sending out the original questionnaire to Organisations, you can ask to be put on their mailing list for this type of material, if one is maintained.

Some Organisations that operate on a shoe-string budget may make a small charge for their mailing list facility. Even when you are put on a mailing list, regular receipt of material may depend very much on the enthusiasm or efficiency of the secretary of an Organisation. Often the best solution to obtaining material is to maintain regular contact with Organisations and to pester them continually. When material arrives, it should be dated, so that you know roughly how old it is, and carefully filed for future use. The simplest method is to have an envelope or folder for each Organisation. Write on the outside of the envelope the name of the Organisation as used in your database and arrange envelopes alphabetically in boxes or a vertical file. You should also add to this file any cuttings from newspapers or magazines concerning those Organisations. The file should be checked regularly, at least once a year, to remove out-of-date material. When writing to Organisations for updated information for your database, ask them for any new literature.

Before throwing away the withdrawn material, check to see if it would be of use to some other Organisation or section of your service which collects material on local history.

Classification

It is not my intention to go into any great detail about the classification of community information materials. For most small information services, it will be quite adequate to arrange material by broad subject groups subdivided according to the form in which the clientele's needs and problems are presented. For ease of labelling vertical files, book spines and boxes, a simple notation can be used based on the initial letter or letters of subjects. For example, Cambridgeshire Libraries' community information service covers 21 categories:

Ben	Benefits	Gov	Government
Bus	Business	Hea	Health
Car	Careers	Hou	Housing
Corn	Community	Law	Legal rights
Con	Consumer	Mon	Money
CR	Community relations	SC	Senior citizens
Dis	Disability	Tra	Transport
Edu	Education	Ump	Unemployment

Emp	Employment	Worn	Women
Env	Environment	You	Youth
Fam	Family		

Some libraries also include as separate categories: Death, Equal opportunities, Fuel (or Energy), Gay rights, Leisure, and Trade union rights. These categories can then be broken down into smaller subcategories as necessary. Taking the earlier example of Housing, a possible range of subcategories with a mnemonic notation might be:

A	Agricultural accommodation	Re	Rented accommodation
H	Homelessness	ReC	Council housing
I	Institutional accommodation	ReH	Housing Association housing
M	Mobile homes	ReP	Private rented
O	Owner-occupied	S	Squatting

Numerals could be introduced for more detailed subdivisions, e.g. O1-Buying and selling a house; O2-Home insurance; O3-Planning applications; O4-Development; etc.

An effective method that can be used where you have only a small number of broad categories (no more than ten and preferably less) is colour coding. Allocate a colour to each subject and attach an appropriate coloured sticker or tape to the spine of each book or file box. Colour coding can be used in conjunction with notation to provide more detailed subdivision of a subject. When a community information service grows to a size where broad categories are not adequate to 'contain all the material and allow efficient retrieval, then it may be necessary to consider using a classification scheme.

Two choices are open to you, either using or adapting a ready-made scheme or constructing your own. There are a number of general classification schemes used in libraries, of which the most well known is the Dewey Decimal Classification. These schemes have been constructed to organize the whole of knowledge and subjects are usually arranged on philosophical or logical principles. Consequently, they may not be sufficiently detailed or treat subjects in the way your clientele express their information needs. Most schemes have a degree of flexibility and it might be possible to adapt them. The NACAB has its own scheme for arranging materials in the broad area of community information, but it hardly merits the description of a classification scheme. However, it is sufficiently detailed and client oriented to be worthy of consideration.

8

The Network

The explanation of Organisational structure was left to two main-stream approaches. The first was the economic model whereby the business Organisation was subsumed into the market. Structure was thus defined as an extension to the market. The second was through the Taylorist and management science movements, where Organisations were seen as no more than vehicles for management control. In neither case was sufficient analytical sensitivity provided to appreciate the close-relationship between structure and its technology.

Today, different ideas about Organisation are prolific. The traditional views are still around but there are many others which have greater sophistication and which span a range of academic disciplines. They can be condensed into three major perspectives or metaphors. Scott, for example, identified these as follows. Firstly, Organisations are rational systems, based upon some collective rationale such as profit maximization or growth. This perspective also embraces the two approaches already mentioned above. Secondly, Organisations are natural systems; arising from the behaviourist movement of Elton Mayo whose perspective views Organisations as a living organism. Thirdly, Organisations are open systems which are seen as processes being open to the environment.

Watson, on the other hand, identified 'waves' of Organisation theory. The first sees Organisations as machines, portraying the view that, like machines, they are predictable. The second wave sees Organisations as organisms to demonstrate that they are as complex and unpredictable as a living organism. The final wave sees Organisations as processes, thus highlighting their dependence upon interactive behaviour. Others, such as Gareth Morgan, have gone further in identifying metaphors of Organisation (brain, machine, psychological prison, etc.) that we use to aid our understanding of them. Whichever perspective is supported, they all agree that Organisation structure provides some form of framework.

Mintzberg's book places considerable emphasis on structure and his definition proposes it as the summation of the ways in which a firm's labour is directed and coordinated into tasks. Although this definition's simplicity is appealing, it leads us to view an Organisation in terms of a division of labour and the co-ordination of management control to maintain that. It is an outlook typically portrayed by the firm's Organisation/ management chart, which identifies quite precisely who is responsible for what and to whom. This merely lists a functional relationship, which although important, reveals only part of the Organisation structure. Handy hints that there may be more when he talks 6f linking mechanisms between roles and co-ordinating structures. Although the elements of line control and co-ordination are still present, Handy extends his definition to cover the perceptual domains of an Organisation. This can lead to a more open definition. The concept of linkages increases our awareness of both interdependence and independence between factions; of how resource groupings can either contradict or complement other resource groupings. Linkaging is, therefore, necessary to cement the otherwise contradictory elements to prevent dispersal, or to reaffirm the complementary to prevent them becoming contra-dictory.

The Sphere

Linkaging, therefore, provides the Organisation with its completeness, establishes a boundary (perceptual or physical) which can be identified as being the domain of a particular Organisation. The idea of a boundary is an important aspect of structure since it enables us to determine how integrated the structure is with both its internal and external environments. For managers also, the boundary is useful since it enables them to identify their area of control. However, with the increasing implementation of information technology the issue has taken on greater significance. Boundaries can no longer be so easily identified. Modern technological systems directly link Organisations into other Organisations, thus merging in part their established boundaries. For example, a major retail outlet requires all its suppliers to link into their own stock control network. Those firms have thus become tied into their customer. In this situation it is difficult to determine where the supplier's boundary ends and the customer's begins.

Robbins proposes a traditional view of the relationship between a structure and its boundary. He determines the structure being defined by its boundary in the same way that a human skeleton defines a person. However, by equating boundary with human skeletons he has missed an important point. The body of a person is a finite concept in that it is spatially bounded within the physical domain.

On the other hand, an Organisational structure, although providing a framework, is as much perceptual as physical. That is, it exists because its members perceive it to do so. To someone who does not understand the concept of an Organisation, the distribution of its physical resources has no significance and thus they will not see an Organisation. This problem is not as remote as it may appear. It is common, for example, for small business Organisations to share resources such as office space, equipment and even staff, therefore possessing the same physical structure. There is no suggestion, however, that they are the same Organisation. Their differentiation is thus established by the perception of the actors (employees, suppliers, customers, etc.) and not the physical aspects. Organisations are not like people even though they comprise them. They are not necessarily spatially bounded; their buildings, for example, do not represent their outer edges. Indeed, some Organisations have no formality about them or physical structure, such as some political or religious institutions, but they are just as real as a small business enterprise. Organisations are not bounded by a temporal framework in the same way that people are. Individuals have their historicities which influence their behaviour, but they are creatures of the here and now. Their socialization has made them believe that all there exists is the physical domain which is governed by the present. The operational levels of Organisations are also bounded by time and the physical domain. However, the structure is not. It exists in the minds of its members and therefore is in the present, but it is also equally valid in the past because its existence is just as dependent upon past interaction.

For example, a firm's production process, which forms part of its structure, is physically bounded by time. It can produce only so many items within an hour or a day. This is its operational level—the dimension of doing. But the same process is time independent because how it can produce is and will be determined by decisions taken in the past, the present and the future. Structure, therefore, has to be more than a static framework, of functional and co-ordinative hierarchy, because Organisations themselves are fluid, perceptual entities and as such could not be supported by a rigid framework. Robbins' model of complexity, formalization and centralization does suggest a certain fluidity in structure, but only to the extent of differentiation between particular Organisations and not within the unit itself. In other words, Robbins recognizes an infinite variety of structures befitting the mode of operation, but once set they provide a rigid framework in the short term which can be changed only in the longer term.

Structural Setup

Watson's ideas about an Organisation's structure provide a better match for a considerably more complex form of structure than so far developed. He does not see structure as a given framework but rather as a fluid, abstract entity which is the outcome of ever-changing employee interaction. Such a view can present no definitive solution to the quest for perfection, because the outcome is dependent upon so many variables.

With such a cost comes also a benefit. There is a freeing of structure from the constraints of 'conventional wisdom', by allowing greater flexibility in Organisation design and therefore enabling a more appropriate framework to be established for the analysis of the impact of other forces such as technology. Watson's words reflect a school of thought which considers the only reality of an Organisation is to be found within our minds. The structure we put on that Organisation is also within our minds. It will change as people's actions and perceptions change, and can never be completely controlled. Innovating forces like information technology, for example, can have the greatest impact upon an Organisation's structure through the minds of its participants. Structural change could occur through differing actions/ perceptions of the employees, which may be beyond the control of management.

Structure must be seen to be more than a rigid framework. It may well be that some Organisational structures have become increasingly flexible in the past few years as a consequence of their information technology systems. However, it would also seem likely that structures have never been as rigid as many would suggest. Some are more stable than others within a given period. Others are more responsive to certain situations such as crisis or particular market conditions. They may all have areas of rigidity within them which can subsequently cause problems. Whatever their apparent characteristics they are manifest not because of the way we organize our physical resources but rather as a consequence of the way we relate to those resources. Structure is indeed in our minds. As such any boundaries which are obvious to us are there only because we perceive them to be. If we then introduce a technology with a strong perceptual impact, such as information technology, it is not surprising that a change occurs in the way we view our Organisation. Such changed perception may lead to a changed structure.

The idea that Organisations are perceptual maps has implications for their analysis and design. How we view them, and hence how they manifest themselves, will depend upon the particular Organisational model we use. Thus, in a self-determining way we align our particular Organisation's characteristics, as far as possible, to those found within the model which matches our own opinions. For example, if we believe along with our colleagues that the most realistic metaphor for an Organisation is a machine in terms of formality and controllability, then our behaviour would be governed by that belief. The Organisational structure would then be affected and to a limited extent changed by such perceptions if there is not a match. Problems can occur, of course, if these perceptions are not fully disseminated throughout the Organisation. The models of Organisation we have, therefore, are themselves affecting the environment which they are attempting to analyse. From this aspect alone it is worthwhile determining what these models are. However, we need to also consider them in terms of their suitability for the impact analysis of information technology.

The mechanistic view of Organisation is the first wave of theory, which comprises the metaphor of Organisation as a machine. Like a machine, its characteristics are determinable and controllable. The degree of its formality is not considered because all actions and behaviour within it are considered to be purposeful and co-ordinated. In other words, Organisations are rational processes. Therefore the underlying assumption is one of an Organisation as a formalization of a need to meet certain objectives. Such objectives are seen as rational in that they are based upon an obvious range of criteria suitable for the type of Organisation. Thus, a business Organisation's objectives could be to maximize profits, to grow or to dominate a particular market or industry.

The emphasis is on goal attainment and its management. The profound question presented by this metaphor is, why are some managements better at achieving their objectives than others? This metaphor evolved from the economic model in which Organisations are perceived to be unitary entities pursuing the same collective objective, controlled and driven by market forces. As such, Organisations do not have any analytical value other than as a unit of the market. From this, however, four softer perspectives developed, each a response to the demand of business managements at the time for better understanding.

The first is Taylor's scientific management. The second is administrative principles proposed by people such as Henri Fayol. The third is Weber's theory of bureaucracy, and lastly Simon's discussion on administrative behaviour. There are many books which cover these areas quite adequately. Apart from an introduction below, these will not be dealt with in detail. The emphasis will be placed on examining their approaches to technology.

The founding father of the scientific movement is claimed to be Frederick Taylor and subsequently developed by others such as Lillian Gilbreth. Their perspective is an extension of the economic model by recognizing that Organisations are not determined solely by market forces but can be moulded by management activity. They prescribed a methodology for action through a scientific analysis of tasks in a firm so that formal procedures could be established for optimum efficiency. The approach, in short, is prescriptive in that it presents patterns for management behaviour. Although lacking in fundamental academic support the traditions of scientific management are still reflected in many of our management training programmes.

The 'modern' view is more developed in its recognition of greater uncertainty but nevertheless still portrays a controllable environment. The elements of that environment are also controllable, Thus, the notion of technology is coloured by the certainty of its predictability. Technology in all its forms is a management tool. The original exponents of scientific management thought this, as do their followers. There is no relationship between a structure and its technology because neither is seen as a social process but rather as building blocks for management use. Thus, the impact of innovations such as information technology is not seen to affect the Organisational structure as such, but rather the relationship between management and workers: any impact is regarded as an input to be controlled.

Innovation, therefore, changes only the way in which management operates (although this might have an indirect effect upon the Organisation itself). Impact assessment of information technology is in terms of functional analysis or efficiency criteria (how good or bad its contribution is to management objectives), the assumption being that the technology will always fit into existing Organisational structures with the appropriate implementation strategy. The emphasis, therefore, is on performance measures and the ability of information technology to meet them. There is a range of literature which explores the scientific manage-ment viewpoint of information technology. Its presentation is pres-criptive and consultative.

The remaining three perspectives within this metaphor are dealt with under the one heading. They are the models initiated by Fayol, Weber and Simon. Their collation is not because the themes they support are necessarily in agreement, although they do cover broadly the same principles, but rather because their implications for the analysis of technology are similar. The major difference between these and the previous approaches is that scientific management sought to establish the Organisation as a management phenomenon whereas Fayol, Weber and Simon sought to establish the Organisation as an administrative process.

The immediate implication of this is that, as an administrative process, the Organisation is less controllable and less predictable. It is no longer a tool but a set of administrative interactions. The objective of this group, therefore, was to identify such interactions and then to determine their appropriate control. Fayol was perhaps the first to recognize the importance of the administrative process in understanding Organisation. However, his work was not translated until the late 1940s and thus not widely known.

A sociologist, Max Weber, was also developing an ideological set of administrative principles. He identified bureaucracy as being the ideal form of Organisation. The formal and impersonal structural characteristics allowed for the most appropriate administrative processes and for an efficient achievement of objectives coupled with a certain humanity. Although advances were being made in other areas, it was not until the late 1950s, with the appearance of Herbert Simon's ideas, that advances in this area were made. He sought to portray a more open administrative process in which the actors are not machine-like in their rationality but more human in pursuing their own interests and in many ways ignorant of their total environment. He saw their rationality bounded by the complexity of the environment and thus their decision-making was not perfect or indeed predictable. Simon, along with others such as Cyert and March, perhaps provided the link between this metaphor and the second wave. They viewed people as being less predictable than did their forebears, but still nevertheless determined the Organisation itself to be of machine-like stature.

Perhaps by default, technology is, therefore, more integrated into the administrative mechanisms of the Organisation. There is concern about technological fit, thus the approach is directed away from one of expert handling to one of greater integration. This is particularly evident in this view's handling of information technology. The literature which reflects it concentrates upon the user end: it is here that a controllable interface exists between the administrative process and the machine. A classic example of this view is to be found in a book by Whisler, although it is becoming outdated. In the 1980s, with the increasing power of computer technology, many other books found their way onto the market. They all sought to merge the computer with the work processes of the Organisation rather than to allow it to dominate them, but stopped short of seeing it as a social process.

Peter Blau determined that it is irrational to view an Organisation as rational in the way that the machine metaphor does because it does not take account of the non-rational behaviour of people. Such a perspective summarizes the natural or organismic metaphor, in that Organisations are seen as complex, living entities which do not have machine-like qualities. They are no longer reified, cohesive units which act in harmony and with total rationality towards a common set of goals. In the same way that a living organism is a collection of competing and interacting forces, some living and some not, so too the Organisation comprises individuals and social forces which compete with and contradict each other.

The consequence is that the Organisation cannot be so easily prescribed for management action, being at best a rather fuzzy area for common agreement. Technology, therefore, as an element of Organisation, cannot be so predictable in terms of a resource. Neither is there agreement on how to model the metaphor. With some justification it is claimed that Elton Mayo provided a foundation with his Hawthorne experiments. As social psychologists, their contribution was in recognizing the importance of behaviour in Organisational design. Their work initiated the behaviourist school for the explanation of firms.

The offshoots are many and are still very much in vogue today. Since Weber's work the sociologists have also been major contributors to this metaphor, particularly through the work of Selznick and Parsons. Rather than placing the emphasis upon the people element of an Organisation as the behaviourists did, these and other theorists who followed were interested in the complete entity and how it worked. In true functionalist tradition they identified various component parts and studied interaction between them. Selznick highlighted the relationship between these and the Organisation's employees, whilst Parsons developed a dynamic model in which people were an integrated part. The technological tradition which grew from this metaphorical approach is less prescriptive and more analytical than that of the machine metaphor.

The earlier ideas are typically represented by the works of Gouldner or Wedderburn and Crompton. Theirs is mainly an examination of production technology and its relationship with the workforce. The structure of an Organisation was a consequence of the way its workforce produced, in particular of the relationship existing between workforce and technology. However, a more formalized development of this took place in the late 1950s and early 1960s which was influenced in part by Elton Mayo and also by considerable empirical research. Although not labelled until much later, the approach became known as contingency theory. In contrast to the classical approach (whether the machine or natural metaphor) which sought to achieve a universally best structure for a business Organisation, the contingency theory proposes that there is no one best solution.

Different situations demand different Organisational structures, which are governed by forces of change known as contingencies. Thus, the prevailing contingent would shape the corresponding Organisational structure. For Woodward, after extensive research of over a hundred firms in Essex, the most important contingent is technology. If, for instance, a firm has a mass production technology, then its structure would develop in terms of the other contingents, such as size and culture, which would best suit that. So mass production technology, for example, by its very nature determines that firms generally be large with formal cultures. Quite apparently, therefore, technology is seen by Woodward as a determinant of Organisation. Although others, such as Pugh and the Aston Group, do not agree with her upon the extent of the power of technology to determine structure, there is a general consensus on the nature of technology itself. It is no longer a resource as such, but as much an element of Organisations as structure, people and their culture.

Information technology is perhaps not addressed as positively as it is in the previous metaphor. This is because there is no formal distinction made between general technology and information technology. Both are social processes and therefore to be treated as such. That is not to say there are not writers on the subject. Miles *et al.*, Anderson and Mumford and Zuboff are typical of the works produced. Information technology is analysed in terms of its ability to integrate into society or business. In general, the conclusions seem to be doom-laden, predicting dire consequences if we do not get it right.

Organisational Setup

This metaphor describes the Organisation as a complex conglomerate of interaction which does not necessarily produce a clearly identifiable form. An Organisation exists because people are told it does by management teams, corporate identity, and so on; although, in reality, apart from resource allocation, members/ employees act very much for themselves as individuals or within groups, occasionally forming alliances to get things done. It is the process of doing (production, administration, etc.) which is the major input to Organisation structure, so that the Organisation is a series of different or interlocking processes. Its structure is shaped by those processes because it is the arena in which they are actioned. As with the other two waves there are disagreements, in particular over the identity of the process. Some put forward the decision process as a dynamic which determines the Organisa-tional structure. Others view the Organisation as a political arena in which structural adjustments are made through political mechanisms such as ownership of power. Yet others, such as Johnson *et al.*, regard these processes in terms of their relationships with one another and how open they are to external influence. Contingency theorists Lawrence and Lorsch, on the other hand, determined a particular relationship between the Organisation and its environment as being the important process, whilst Weick highlighted the processes between the individual and their social formation.

In general, Organisations are no longer seen as hierarchical and solid (albeit at times fuzzy) frameworks. Structure is considered not to be as important as the processes themselves because it is a transient thing, created and remoulded by the whim of changing interactions. Watson described this Organisation as being formed in the minds of the employees through their perception of its interactions. The process or open systems metaphor, therefore, shifts the emphasis of analysis from the design of the Organisation to the functioning of its elements. It allows these elements (e.g. technology, politics, decisions) a far greater impact than the previous two metaphors. For technology in particular the approach is significant. In the machine metaphor, technology is not part of the Organisation, whilst in the organismic metaphor technology is part of an Organisation's social process and a determinant of structure. In the process metaphor, technology can be a process in its own right, determining the perceptions of individuals and affecting their behaviour. Its ability to affect the characteristics of an Organisation are thus considerably increased because the mechanisms involved (i.e. employee perception) form the essence of an Organisation. These ideas have been most prevalent in the analysis of information technology. The relationship between the behaviour of people and the technology they use is portrayed by the socio-technical systems theory. This applies a systems methodology to the analysis of information technology and how it affects the way we organize. Its roots can be traced back to Mayo and his Hawthorne experiments in terms of the paradigm's behavioural aspirations. It was Mayo who first formally stated the link between our behaviour and Organisational design. But it was Trist and Bamforth who galvanized those ideas into understanding the impact of technological innovation.

With the growth of computer technology as the dominant innovative technology it was, therefore, not surprising that Trist and Bamforth's methodology was quickly taken up by others to analyse its impact. Burns and Stalker produced an impressive model based upon empirical research describing a close behavioural relationship between our technology and the way we organized. If the structure of the firm did not suit the technology employed then pathological responses evolved on the part of management.

Response Awaited

Just as firms are not merely a collection of resources, human or otherwise, nor are they merely a collection of processes. As with all social entities, they are a combination of physical and perceptual: but it is how the relationship between the two is understood which is important. Quite obviously many Organisations do have buildings which figure strongly in the image they project but also quite obviously the influence of the Organisation does not end at a brick wall. They do comprise physical beings constrained by their physical environment but beyond such environments they have resources which can be both physical (machinery, etc.) and perceptual (knowledge). Any complete model of Organisation must accommodate both domains. Organisations, however, must be more than the summation of individuals, resources and perceptions within them. Unfortunately the metaphors discussed describe no more than this. Yet Organisations tend to develop some sense of being in their own right. This is not in terms of a conscious, spatial positioning, as any individual would have, but is rather a consequence of history.

Continuity of an Organisation, for example, cannot be solely explained as the perception of individuals or the particular allocation of resourcing. There is a logic within it which outlives any temporary input an individual may care to make. It is indeed a process, but one which is at the same time both independent and dependent. For example, previous decisions made by management can constrain and develop the Organisation's structure in future years. Both the physical and perceptual aspects of the decision as real as each other. One could be seen in the production line whilst the other, although not seen, is ingrained within the management culture. Together they form ail inheritance passed onto subsequent management which constrains their action. It is in this sense that an Organisation can be said to be existing independently. Decisions and actions are taken all the time which can then exist beyond their initiators and add to a bank of knowledge within the firm. To a certain extent we are referring to the Organisational culture, but culture's form relates only to the rules for action and does not express the logic of the actions themselves, as does structure. Structure can thus be determined by neither domain alone. More probably, it arises as a consequence of a relationship between the two domains continually interacting with one another through a historical process which in turn feeds the logic of the Organisation. In the same vein, information technology (or technology in general) cannot be treated as either a physical or perceptual phenomenon.

The way in which each of the three metaphors provides analytical tools for the assessment of its impact restricts our being able to see the whole framework. Information technology does have a strong physical impact: it can, for example, turn an inefficient firm into an efficient one. The criteria used to assess such a change are based in the physical domain in that there can be more information output in terms of management reports or invoices billed, and so on. It can also change user behaviour, as we see in socio-technical systems, so that, employee perceptions of their tasks or indeed their firm change. In many models the two domains sit either separately or uncomfortably side by side.

However, it is not so much the consideration of the individual domains that is important (although obviously for line managers it cannot be ignored), it is the relationship between them which must be analysed and the subsequent effects such interaction has upon Organisation design.

9

Students' Domain

A major segment of the market involves entertainment: personal computers offer a growing array of games, music and art far more sophisticated, in terms of speed and capability, than video material based only on television. This advantage results from the ability of computers to store and quickly retrieve large amounts of information. The future will bring many more uses for computers in both business and home. Indeed, the possibilities are virtually endless. A great variety of computers, large and small, are now available. A personal computer is a machine or system meeting all the major qualifications.

The system is designed to accept secondary memory devices to supplement the primary, built-in memory, the user is expected to interact with the system continuously, not only at the beginning and end of a problem, at least one general language (Basic, Fortran, Cobol, Pascal, ADA, or Q is available for this interaction), the system is usable for a wide variety of problems and is not designed for any single application and the computer is distributed through mass-marketing channels, with the marketing emphasis on the first-time computer user.

A typical modern personal computer consists of a circuit board with a silicon chip, microprocessor and one or more memory chips attached. The microprocessor can perform hundreds of thousands of calculations every second, and the memory chips provide the primary storage for instructions and data.

External storage devices, such as cassette tape units or small recording disks (floppy disks), augment the memory capacity and provide a storage medium that can be physically transferred from one personal computer to another. (Typical users begin with cassette units but soon change to disks to gain the advantages of greater speed and capacity.) Input is through a typewriter-like keyboard unit. Output typically takes the form of words and numbers displayed either on a television screen or a similar specialized screen called a monitor. Most monitors are designed to display 24 lines of letters and figures, with each line containing a maximum of 80 characters. Adding a printer unit permits output in the form of a printed paper. A special device, called a "modem" (for modulator/demodulator), permits the computer to receive and transmit data over a conventional telephone line. But the significant factor in defining a personal computer is not its physical features but the characteristics of the operating system.

Designers of personal computers and software attempt to provide a friendly human-machine interface, even at the expense of brute computing power. Optional programs are also available so that the computer can be used for many different purposes. Although word processors and hobby computers have many characteristics of personal computers, they lack this flexibility.

Recent trends in microelectronics, memories, input-output mechanisms, and software suggest that the trend in microprocessors is toward larger "words" and higher circuit speeds. A computer capable of handling larger "words" is able to perform a complete operation in fewer machine cycles and to operate directly with larger memory. Both these assets enhance performance by increasing the speed of operations and the number that can be performed in a sequence without the operator's intervention. In addition to greater speed and memory access, these larger micro-processors have the advantage of greater accuracy.

The first wave of personal computers used 8-bit micro-processors—that is, microprocessors in which 8 binary digits (0 or 1) can be processed in parallel, giving the capacity to process in a single operation any number up to 256, or to address any file up to 256 points in the memory. Processing larger numbers with an 8-bit microprocessor requires multiple operations, which take more time. Newer systems use 16-bit microprocessors, and 32-bit microprocessors are now available.

The primary memory in personal computers is of two different types: read-only memory (ROM) and random-access memory (RAM). In the former information is fixed in the memory at the time of manufacture and is not lost when computer power is switched off. The role of such a ROM is to guide the computer through a fixed procedure, such as calculating square roots and translating a user's program into machine language. In a RAM, information such as special programs and data files can be "written in" or "read out" as frequently as desired, with any storage location directly accessible. RAMs are of two types: dynamic RAMs, which are cheaper but lose their store information unless they are "refreshed" often, and static RAMs, which are costlier but do not need to be "refreshed." If power is lost, both types of RAMs lose their stored information.

Over the past decade, the number of memory circuits per unit of area on a chip has increased by a factor of 64, and cost on a unit basis has been reduced by a factor of 50. Both these trends will continue. So-called 64K dynamic RAMs (each contains 65,536 bits of information [K = 210 = 1024; 64K = 64 x 10241) remained popular until about 1984, when the much larger memory capacity of 256K dynamic RAMs became standard.

Most manufacturers supply system programs on ROMs, and this practice will continue because programs are secure against power failures and users are less able to duplicate programs in this form. Computers' main memories will be supplemented by secondary storage devices that offer larger and relatively inexpensive, though slower, capacity for long-term storage of program and data files. The most popular of these is a so-called "floppy disk"-a disk of mylar coated with magnetic material on one or both sides. Data are stored in a series of spots-either magnetized or demagnetized-along the concentric tracks. Heads for reading or writing data can be moved radially across the disk to reach a specified segment of circular track.

Storage capacity depends on the format used for the stored data, the quality of magnetic surface, and the design of the reading-writing head. Floppy disks in current use typically have capacities of I to 4 million bits, sufficient to store 20,000 to 80,000 words of English text. During the next four years, higher-density floppy disks will be common. Indeed, disks offering capacities of 50 to 100 million bits are already becoming popular, but they are much costlier than floppy disks.

The primary display device used in all personal computer systems is a cathode-ray tube (CRT), either standing alone or as part of a television receiver. This system will continue through the foreseeable future. Output is typically presented in alphanumeric form-letters and numbers. Charts and game boards can be presented, but the memory and software required to display such graphical images is often complex and expensive. The letters and numbers in alphanumeric displays are patterns of dots programmed in special ROMs known as "character generators." The quality of the image depends on the number of points (or pixels) on the screen that can be addressed by the computer—that is, the number of points at which dots can be located. A typical low-resolution screen has a field of 6144 (128 times 48) pixels (picture elements-dots on the screen). High-resolution systems (100,000 pixels or more) allow sophisticated graphics for animation or detailed figures and may provide colour as well.

Access to Computer

The personal computer industry has grown as a direct result of the evolution of the microprocessor. This evolution began when Intel in 1971 packaged a complete, if somewhat limited, processor with a 4-bit word size in a single integrated circuit. The company followed with the first 8-bit processor in 1972 and an improved version in 1974. One year later Micro Instrumentation and Telemetry Systems, Inc. (MITS), an Albuquerque firm, developed the first personal computer around Intel's 8-bit processor. The basic system sold for $395 in kit form and $621 in assembled form, not including accessories (peripherals).

Though the MITS system is no longer manufactured, its method for connecting peripherals and the main computer has become an industry standard. Within three years after it was introduced, Radio Shack, Apple, and Commodore had entered the market.

Now makers of large computers such as IBM and Honeywell, as well as minicomputer leaders such as Digital Equipment Corp. and Data General Corp., are also making personal computers, having observed their traditional markets being eroded by the new low-priced products. The results are rapid development of the market and growing popular interest and faith in personal computers.

The pioneering manufacturers did not survive beyond the initial phase of personal computer development resulting from the preoccupation with the needs of hobbyists. New entrants such as Radio Shack, Commodore, and Apple captured a major share of the market in 1978 by promoting fully assembled, ready-to-operate systems that were easier to use. Though the success of the companies now in the competition will depend at least partly on their financial and technical resources, their products' ease of use (or "user-friendliness," in trade jargon) is a significant competitive feature.

The personal computer market can be divided into four segments in terms of the computer's intended use: business, home, research-technical, and educational. The business segment, by far the largest at present, accounted for 750,000 sales (retail value of $2 billion) in 1982, or 54 per cent of the units sold and 65 per cent of the dollar sales. This segment will continue to be a major factor, with more sales than all other segments put together. No wonder, then, that the leading makers of personal computers are concentrating their sales efforts on the business sector.

The most visible segment of the personal computer "revolution" is in homes, where computers are used for entertainment and education, sending messages, and home finances. The development of appropriate software will soon enable sophisticated users to pay bills, manage bank accounts, compute taxes, and even buy household items without written transactions.

The potential market for personal computers in education has barely been tapped. Computer manufacturers recognize that schools are the logical environment in which to develop computer skills, and they have reason to expect that students will purchase the machine on which they first learn computing. So manufacturers

Mail order firms offering discounts ranging up to 30 per cent appeal to price-sensitive customers, but their total lack of continuing support disenchants users. Price-cutting penalizes the full-service dealers on which manufacturers want to rely as major sales outlets. Accordingly, major companies are trying to discourage sales through mail order firms.

Direct sales staffs are used for large-volume sales to government, educational institutions, and major corporations who prefer dealing directly with the manufacturer. But such direct sales tend to antagonize dealers by depriving them of some of their most profitable opportunities, and profit margins are inadequate to support direct sales to small-volume and individual buyers.

Value-added houses serve specialized users with coordinated hardware and software, such as printing companies that need word-processing and typesetting capabilities but have little or no internal computing expertise.

Though franchised retail outlets are the largest sellers of personal computers in the US, the one compelling characteristic of personal computer distribution today is diversity. No one form of vendor or market approach is dominant.

Computer for Individual

No one should select a personal computer system without taking into account the tasks for which it will be used and the environment in which it will function. Even within a single business, personal computer users come from different areas—personnel, accounting, management, manufacturing, research, sales—and have different computing needs.

Even within these departments there are many possible uses. The personnel department will run personnel files on a regular basis but also may want to study policy questions—the likely benefits in terms of increased revenue from a larger sales force, for example. Furthermore, different users have different strategies for using a computer for adhoc applications. Thus, the person who will use a personal computer should—almost by definition—choose it, partly on the basis of the services it will provide and partly on the basis of its apparent user-friendliness.

Indeed, the machine's responsiveness to its user's needs and style is the critical technological breakthrough. But it is not necessarily so simple. In many Organisations, personal computers create and fill completely new needs that were not originally anticipated. Consider the example of a personal computer acquired to improve one lay worker's access to a main computer facility. While retrieving data from the main computer to run programs locally, this user finds that the personal computer can help evaluate alternative business strategies, answering, "what-if...?" questions instantaneously. The original application for which the personal computer was purchased becomes secondary. Given that the uses and benefits of personal computers are hard to predict, and that a wide range of systems and software are available, how should a potential buyer decide what and when to buy? And should such a buyer postpone action, expecting costs to decline in the future as they have in the past?

There are two arguments against postponing purchase in anticipation of a lower future price. One is the high cost of waiting, based on the computer's great (and often unexpected) uses. The other is that prices are expected to decline less dramatically in the future than in the past: future systems will offer technological improvements that increase performance at unchanged cost. Prices seem likely to stabilize at around $1500 for a full personal computer system.

Future personal computers are likely to offer increased memory size, increased processor power (16-bit and even 32-bit instead of 8-bit microprocessors), improved printers, more powerful programming languages that give the user more compact and natural communication with the computer, improved user access (better keyboards supplemented or replaced by touch screen and voice systems), and greater flexibility (the computer will be able to intermix and manipulate text, numbers, and graphics more easily). Yet today's personal computers may rapidly become obsolete, reflecting the rapid pace of change in semiconductor technology.

Changes in the microprocessor, the heart of any personal computer system, are most likely—and most serious. A computer with a 16-bit microprocessor cannot operate on hardware and software designed for an 8-bit microprocessor. Though many vendors provide add-ons that enable a new microprocessor to support old software, there is never total compatibility.

Software for a personal computer is expensive, and for most users new software development is impractical. So the amount and utility of the software available with a particular system is the key question in the buyer's choice of a personal computer. The variation can be large: 11,000 programs are available for the Apple II and Apple II Plus computers, whereas fewer than 100 widely distributed programs exist for the IBM personal computer, a more recent introduction. Of course, the IBM programs may be just the ones the buyer needs, and more software will be developed for the IBM.

Price is also an important variable, including not only the manufacturer's suggested price but the range of discounts offered by different retail computer sources. But discount alone does not tell the story. The critical factor is the ability of the distributor to provide both routine hardware maintenance, usually at the retail outlet, and software support and maintenance. A company store is likely to offer very good service on that company's product line but not necessarily on any other line, while a retail computer store is likely to offer moderately qualified service and support for many different manufacturers' systems. Mail order sales offer very little service but usually have the highest discounts.

The ultimate question for the purchaser is that of system configuration: what combination of hardware and software is appropriate for a buyer's current and projected needs? Perhaps the most important options are off-the-shelf software. To be sure they buy what they need, buyers should gain some experience with available programs before making the purchase; otherwise they risk having to modify their needs to fit the software they've purchased or embarking on the costly and time-consuming route of software development.

The programming tools on most personal computers are primitive compared with the equivalents available for mainframes, and the widespread dearth of good programmers is a complicating factor. Indeed, trying to develop special programming for a personal computer is inadvisable except under extraordinary circumstances. Memory capacity is another important variable. Most computers based on 8-bit microprocessors have no more than 48 or 64 kilobytes of built-in accessible memory (RAM), while the newer 16-bit processors can have 1, 4, or even 16 megabytes. (One byte is a string of 8 binary digits that represents one alphabetic character.)

Additional memory can be inserted into most personal computers by plugging cards into slots or inserting extra chips directly onto the microprocessor board. Storage capacity of the main memory for programs and instructions can also be supplemented by secondary devices, of which floppy disks are the most popular form. Disks with capacities ranging from 100,000 bytes to several megabytes now come in two standard sizes: 8 inches and 51/4 inches in diameter. But personal computer buyers should be aware that disks designed for one system will not generally operate in another maker's system because of different data-formatting conventions.

The critical performance characteristic of a floppy disk is the response time to a read-write request, which may range from 200 to 500 milliseconds. Though the response time for such a single file request is very short, a single compilation or word-processing command may involve 20 or more accesses to a floppy disk, and access time may account for 80 percent of the total command execution time. Where better performance-and/or capacity are required, "hard" disks in the same format as the 51/4-inch and 8-inch floppy disks are useful. They offer storage capacities ranging from 5 to 50 megabytes and response time averaging 20 to 40 milliseconds, but their high cost (around $2000, including interfaces) can double a buyer's total investment in hardware.

All personal computer systems use cathode-ray tubes as output devices. If "hard copy" is required, buyers have a choice of several printing devices. Thermal printers, costing under $500, create images by applying points of heat to special paper. A dot-matrix printer, costing from $500 to $1500, has a vertical array of 7 to 10 dot-printing elements. These are activated by the computer as the printing head passes across the paper, forming alphanumeric characters and also graphs and drawings.

The limited number of elements result in a somewhat stylized character, but the process is as fast as thermal printing—50 characters per second. If letter-quality printing is required, a printing mechanism with precisely machined character matrices that strike the paper through a ribbon is required. Such printers cost $750 or more and print between 30 and 90 characters per second. Various accessories such as floppy disks and printers or "peripherals" are attached to personal computers through special "slot" receptacles. The IBM personal computer offers five such slots for peripherals such as printer, colour display, dual floppy-disk controller, communications channel, and memory module.

All business-oriented personal computers offer text editing for word processing. Some permit use of a light pen to directly indicate on the screen the word to be edited, and a few check spelling against a mini-dictionary stored in the computer memory. Business data manipulation is facilitated by "spreadsheet" packages such as VISICALC—a very popular package that enables users to see on the CRT the impact of altering one figure (say, retail price) on all other figures (profit margin, corporate profit, return of investment).

Software is now becoming available for generating displays such as those accompanying this article with only a few minutes' effort. For example, ExecuVision permits displays combining information in numbers, text, and pictures. It also provides animation that can add emphasis to presentations. Though personal computers are today viewed primarily as stand-alone work stations for individual users, the ability to transmit and receive data and programs is an important attribute of most contemporary systems. Personal computers are already serving as intelligent terminals for retrieving and manipulating files from large computers. These networking and communication capabilities are important considerations in selecting a personal computer. Unfortunately, no industry standard for communication protocols and interfaces exists. Different vendors use different protocols, so it is difficult to link various personal computers in a single network.

Technological advances in communications are expanding the power of personal computers. For example, owners of personal computers can now receive current stock market quotations by telephone. Personal computers can be connected with nationwide electronic funds transfer systems, so users have access to full banking facilities. They may transfer funds from one account to another and buy and sell financial instruments.

In homes, personal computers are now primarily used for recreational activities such as computer games. But these applications should not be underrated. Computer games test and develop mental capabilities while generating familiarity with computer operations. Home computers are also used for office work at home, and many other applications are, or soon will be possible. For example, a tax return can be prepared with the aid of VISICALC. The user can analyse which forms and deductions to use for paying the minimum taxes. A personal computer can be used to balance check-books and plan investment strategies. And, of course, word-processing capabilities are useful in writing letters and professional papers.

As commercial databases such as Dow Jones News/ Retrieval and the Source are expanded and their subscription costs reduced, personal computers will be useful for locating stores and services, comparing prices, and placing orders. This would be especially appropriate for products or services whose prices fluctuate rapidly, such as those of the airline industry. Computers are being used increasingly for security applications. Traditional home security systems are limited, often failing to distinguish between a natural event and an intrusion by an unwanted visitor. Computer-controlled home security systems can include a variety of routines to analyse the signals from sensors before generating an alarm. Such an analysis can distinguish, for example, between the entry of a cat and the entry of a human being, or between the noise of a telephone ringing and a door opening.

Another home-oriented application is a medical information system that performs some of the diagnostics of a medical doctor.

Perhaps the most useful application of this is a database for poison or first-aid: the user reports what substance the patient has ingested or the nature of an accident, and the computer responds with a step-by-step first aid plan. Children turn out to be heavy users of home computers. They enjoy computer games and seem able to learn computer languages faster than their elders. They find personal computers intriguing for recreation, school assignments, and self-paced courses that are now becoming available. Even though today's personal computers are equivalent in basic computing power to the mainframes of the 1960s and the minicomputers of the 1970s, they should not be used as substitutes for the earlier machines. Rather, users should capitalize on the new technical developments, including the diminishing cost of computing, and the English-like languages that replace the cumbersome digital languages of early machines, to make personal computers supplement, not displace, mainframe computers.

Personal computers should be used to analyse more issues in greater detail than ever before—not to do the more routine work typically assigned to mainframes. In the 1960s and 1970s, computers were used principally for well-structured, periodic jobs such as payroll accounting. Today's personal computers are especially useful for more casual, adhoc analyses and problem solving, such as studies of the impact of cost of living increases, new tax regulations, or alternative hiring and layoff policies.

Consider the stock analyst who uses data from company balance sheets to evaluate investment risks. The balance sheets contain detailed, current information on assets and liabilities. But interest rates fluctuate, markets rise and fall, taxes change, competition falters or gains. Each such change affects a company's current performance and future prospects.

Using a central computing facility is an expensive way to analyse such problems, resulting in time delays and partial answers. But using a personal computer in the interactive mode linked to the central computer and a financial database makes it possible to understand the impact of changes quickly and accurately.

Psychological Approach

Manufacturers, media, and computer scientists have presented the public to computers the way one might have presented Aladdin to his lamp. Here was the genie, the workhorse that we could mount today and ride onto the new millennium. By the end of the 1970s, with the mass manufacture of personal computers, the promises extended into the home. Home computers would teach us French, help us with financial planning, even do our taxes. For many Americans, the first thing that computers brought into their homes was not a more efficient medium for work but new worlds to conquer in play.

"Space Invaders" became a household word for people with home computers or the machines' junior siblings, computerized video games. The experience of the decade has resulted in a widely shared public rhetoric. When people talk about the computer and their futures, they tend to fall back on the two images they know best: the computer as tool and the computer as toy; objective instrumentality and engrossing play. But there is another dimension. What people do with computers weaves itself into the way they see the world. People use a discourse about computers for thinking and talking about other things, about politics, religion, education, and about themselves and other people.

The subjective dimension of the computer presence is not merely a matter of discourse, of using the computer intellectually as a metaphor or model. There is another, and more emotionally charged, aspect which does not engage ideas about computers as much as the immediate quality of an individual's experience when working with them. Working with computers can be a way of "working through" powerful feelings. In this essay we develop this idea by using as a case study a group of computer users for whom issues related to control are particularly salient. For a first generation of computer hobbyists, controlling the computer is a way to deal with frustrations and desires, both personal and political, that have nothing to do with the computer per se.

The subjects of my study are men and women who bought personal computer systems in the four years that followed the

1975 announcement of the "Altair"—the first computer small enough to sit on a desktop, powerful enough to support high-level language programming, and that you could build for only $420. My study began in 1978 with a questionnaire survey answered by 95 New England computer hobbyists (their names had been drawn from the roster of a home computer club and from the subscription list of a personal computer magazine), and continued during 1978 and 1979 with nearly 300 hours of conversation with 50 individuals who owned home computers. What we found can be read historically: a study of the pioneer users of an increasingly ubiquitous technology. But most central to the intent of this essay is to use the story of the early hobbyists as a window into the highly personal ways in which individuals appropriate technologies. It is a case study of the "subjective computer," the computer as a material for thinking, for feeling, for "working through."

It is acknowledged that the subjective is at odds with a widespread ideology that quickly grew up around the emergent computer hobbyist culture. The Altair, aimed at a strictly hobby market, was followed by other small systems—the Pet, the Sol, and, most successfully, the Radio Shack TRS-80 and the Apple, marketed to less specialized audiences of small businessmen and curious householders. With this explosion of hardware came a lot of rhetoric about a personal computer revolution. Most of the talk, both from the companies that marketed the machines and from those who claimed to be the most visionary spokesmen for the people who bought them, was about all of the things that a home computer could do for you.

The utilitarian, "genie in the bottle," ideology is expressed in the content of hobbyist conventions and magazines, filled with articles on how to make your home computer dim your lights, control your thermostat, run an inventory system for your kitchen or tool-room. And it is also found in writing on the personal computer from outside the hobbyist world. The view from the "outside" was well illustrated when, on May 14, 1979, the *Wall Street Journal* reported on its own little "evaluation experiment." The paper had drafted one of its staff reporters, Mitchell Lynch, into the ranks of the "home computer revolution." It presented him with a TRS-80 and asked him to take it home. His assignment was to report back six months later on what it had been like.

The terms of Lynch's evaluation are instrumental: what can the computer do? On these terms it fails, and when he goes to the experts for an explanation of what went wrong, he encounters an official "instrument" ideology from within: "Experts say that people like me have neither the technical training nor technical inclination to make a home computer strut its stuff." The point of having the computer, says the expert, is to make things happen. And, reassures the expert, they will happen with a better operator or a simpler computer. This instrumental view is an important ingredient of the hobbyist ideology but it is not the whole story. In the course of my work I found a very different answer from within.

Most hobbyists do make their computers "strut their stuff," but their sense of engagement and energy are found primarily in the non-instrumental uses of the technology. When asked in a questionnaire "What first attracted you to computers?" more than half the respondents gave reasons that were highly subjective. In response to an open-ended question, 26 per cent said that they were first attracted to computers by an appeal that was intellectual, aesthetic, involved with the fun of what I would call "cognitive play." They wrote of "puzzle solving," of "the elegance of using computer techniques to handle problems," of the "beauty of understanding a system at many levels of complexity." They described what they did with their home computers with metaphors like "mind stretching" and "using the computer's software to understand my wetware."

Another 26 per cent wrote of reasons for getting involved that seemed more emotional than intellectual. They wrote of the "ego boost" or "sense of power" that comes from knowing how to run a computer, of the "prestige of being a pioneer in a developing field," of the "feeling of control when I work in a safe environment of my own creation." The hobbyists who responded to my survey seemed familiar with Lynch's brand of scepticism, with people who ask them what they do with their computers and who won't take "cognitive play" for an answer. David, a 19 year-old undergraduate at a small engineering school, put it this way: "People come over and see my computer and they look at it, then they look at me, then they ask me what useful thing we do with it, like does it wash floors, clean laundry or do my income tax-when we respond no, they lose interest." David said that when he started out, he was attracted to the computer because "we liked the idea of making a pile of hardware do something useful, like doing real time data processing ... like picking up morse code with an amateur radio and transcribing it automatically into text," but in his list of things that he currently does with his computer.

Thirteen percent of those who responded to my questionnaire told a similar story. Like David, they began their relationship with personal computation for instrumental reasons (they had an image of a job to do, a specific task), but they became absorbed by the "holding power" of something else. A full two-thirds of my survey sample either began with or ended up with a primary interest in what I have called the "subjective computer," the computer seen in its relationship to personal meaning. Clearly, to understand what people are doing with their home computers we must go beyond the "performance criteria" shared by the hobbyist magazines and the *Wall Street Journal*. The simplest way of thinking about the subjective computer is through the metaphor of "the computer as Rorschach"-that is, seeing the computer as a projective screen for other concerns. In the Rorschach test, one is presented with a set of ink blots and asked to make some sense of them. Some people see the blots as threatening; others see them as benign. Some focus on small, complex details; others on global form. So too, the computer presents us with an ambiguous stimulus. For example, although most people think of the computer as an object without real intentionality, they accord computers enough autonomy in action to make "blaming the computer" a commonplace of daily life.

The very fact that the computer is a machine that touches on a sphere like intelligence that man has always considered uniquely his, is enough to make many people experience the computer as an object "betwixt and between," hard to classify, hard to pin down. Sometimes people deny the irreducibility of computation by asser-ting that, no matter how complex the computation "product," a move in a chess game for example, "all the computer really does is add." Of course in a certain sense this is correct. But saying that a computer "decided to move the Queen by adding" is a little bit like saying that Picasso "created Guernica by making brush-strokes."

Reducing things to this level of localness gives no satisfying way to grasp the whole. Just as in theoretical psychology there is a tension between the gestalt and the atomic, so too in computation there is a pervasive tension between the local simplicity of the individual acts that comprise a program or a computation, and what one might call the "global complexity" that can emerge when it is run. The elusiveness of computational processes and of simple descriptions of the computer's essential nature, the tension between local simplicity and global complexity, all contribute to making the computer an object of projective processes, and exemplary "constructed object." Different people apprehend it with very different descriptions and invest it with very different attributes. In views of the computer's internal process, individuals project their models of mind.

In descriptions of the computer's powers, people express feelings about their own intellectual, social, and political power, or their lack of it. Looking at the computer as Rorschach, has projected, puts the emphasis on aspects of the individual—from cognitive style to personal fears—that are revealed through behaviour with the machine. But of course the computer is more than a Rorschach. The Rorschach ink blots are evocative, revealing, but they stay on the page. They do not enter the life of the individual. The computer does. It is a constructive as well as a projective medium. For readers who have not had the experience of programming a computer, this idea may be sharpened by an analogy with another technology. In my own studies of people's emotional relationships with technologies, airplanes emerge as startlingly like computers in respect to the issues they raise for their hobbyists. Specifically, both are powerful media for working through the issue of control.

Various Devices

There is always a compelling tension between local simplicity and global complexity in the working of a computer and in the appreciation of a computer program. Locally, each step in a program is easy to understand; its effects are well defined. But the evolution of the global pattern is often not graspable. You are dealing with a system that surprises. This play between simplicity and complexity allows programmers, as pilots do with flying, to make of compu-tation very different experiences that provide a context for working through different needs in relation to issues of personal control. Depending on how the programmer brings the computer's local simplicity and global complexity into focus, he or she will have a particular experience of the machine as completely understandable, under control, or as baffling, even as controlling. By focusing on the local, the line by line, you can feel in control. By focusing on the global, you can feel control slip away. In their style of pro-gramming a computer, people betray different levels of tolerance for temporary losses of control.

Some will avoid it at all costs; but others will seek it out, and enjoy "playing" with sensations of risk and danger. And so different people end up with very different relationships to controls and power in their programming work. To illustrate this point, it is useful to begin with an example at one extreme. We see a first style in Howard, an ex-programmer, now a university professor, who describes himself as "having been a computer hacker." Howard was not in my sample of hobbyists. He has a terminal at home which links to a large timesharing system, but when asked about home computers, he winced in distaste and said that he "wouldn't touch the stuff. It's too simple." His case, in which we see a love of programming for the feeling of "walking near the edge of a cliff," is meant as a contrast for what we found to be a prevalent and more conservative "hobbyist style." Howard described his longtime fantasy that he would walk up to any program, however complex, and "fix it, bend it to my will." As he described his intervention, he imitated the kind of hand gestures that a stage musician makes toward the hat before he pulls out the rabbit.

Wizards use spells, a powerful kind of local magic. Howard's magic was local too. He described his "hacker's approach" to any problem as a search for the "quick' and dirty fix." For Howard, what was most thrilling about the experience of programming was "walking down a narrow line," using the program's flexibility (for him defined as the possibility of making a local fix) in a struggle to keep the whole under control. Weekends at the terminal with little to eat and little or no rest were frequent, as was the experience of not being able to leave the terminal while debugging a program, even when the obvious need was for sleep and looking at the whole in the morning, instead of trying to "fix it" by looking at it line by line all night. For Howard, the urgency of these encounters was tied to his sense that through them he was grappling with a computational essence—the struggle to exert control over global complexity by mastery of local simplicity.

A second programmer, Bob, is a computer professional, a microprocessor engineer who works all day on the development of hardware for a large industrial data system. He has recently built a small computer system for his home and devotes much of his leisure time to programming it. Whereas, for Howard, the excitement of programming is that of a high-risk venture, Bob likes it as a chance to be in complete control. Although Bob works all day with computers, his building and programming them at home is not more of the same.

At work he sees himself as part of a process that he cannot see and over which he feels no mastery or ownership: "Like they say, we are just a cog." At home Bob works on well defined projects of his own choosing, projects whose beginning, middle, and end are all under his control. He describes the home projects as a compensation for the alienation of his job. He works most intensively on his home system when he feels furthest away from any understanding of "how the whole thing fits together at work."

Howard and Bob have very different opinions about what is most satisfying about programming. These translate into different choices of projects, into different choices of programming language and level to program at, and ultimately into what we might call different computational aesthetics. Howard likes to work on large, "almost out of control" projects. Bob likes to work on very precisely defined ones. Howard finds documentation a burdensome and unwelcome constraint; Bob enjoys documentation, he likes to have a clear, unambiguous record of what he has mastered. Indeed, much of his sense of power over the program derives from its precise specifications and from his continual attempts to enlarge the sphere of the program's local simplicity.

Hobbyist programmers mean different things when they say that machine language programming "puts them in control." For some, the reference seems objective. Given the primitive higher-level languages available on the first and second generation of hobby computers, machine-level programming seems to them the best instrumental solution. For others, the issue is more subjective. Many hobbyists who said, they felt Lineasy using systems programs for which they didn't have the source code also admitted never looking at the source code listing which they felt they had to have. Having access to the code was symbolic.

In other cases it was apparent that machine language programming was valued because the experience of doing it was pleasing in itself. It meant that the programmer was writing instructions that acted directly on the machine, no "building on top of" somebody else's interpreter. Most hobbyists have relationships with computation at work which involve sharing the machine with countless and nameless others. In personal computation they see a chance to be independent and alone.

The machine comes to them virgin. They have full possession. Finally, there is the issue of asserting control over an inferior. Bob, like many of the other hobbyists I spoke with, is a middle-level worker in the computer industry. He does not feel very good about the importance of his job. Proving that he is "better than any dumb compiler" gives a sense of importance. Using the computer to assert control was a central theme in my interviews with hobbyists. It was expressed directly, and also wove itself into four other issues that characterize the hobbyists' "subjective computer." These are using the computer to strengthen a sense of identity; to construct a completely intelligible piece of reality that is experienced as "transparent" and safe; to articulate a political ideology; and to experience a sense of wholeness that is absent in one's work life. It is these four issues to which I now turn.

The Valadity

In achieving a sense of mastery over the computer, in learning about the computer's "innards," people are learning to see themselves differently. Among other things, they are learning to see themselves as "the kind of people who can do science and maths." This was most striking among hobbyists who had no technical background. But it also came up among hobbyists who did see themselves as "technical people" but who for one reason or another had gotten "scared out of real science." Barry is 28 years old, an electronics technician at a large research laboratory. He went to college for two years, hoping to be an engineer, then dropped out and went to technical school. He has always loved to tinker with machines and to build things. His current job is to calibrate and repair complex instruments, and he is very happy with it because he gets a chance "to work on a lot of different equipment." But he came to his job with a feeling of having failed, of not being "analytic," "theoretical," of not being capable of "what is really important in science."

Five years ago, Barry bought a programmable calculator and started "fooling around with it and with numbers the way I have never been able to fool around before," and says that "it seemed natural to start working with computers as soon as I could." To hear him tell it, numbers stopped being theoretical, they became concrete, practical and playful, something he could tinker with. I'll pick up the calculator, and if we don't know how to do a problem I'll play with the calculator a few minutes, or a few hours and figure it out. It's not so much that the calculator does a particular calculation, but you do so many, have so much contact with the numbers and the results and how it all comes out that you start to see things differently ... The numbers are in your fingers.

When the calculator and the computer made numbers seem concrete, the numbers became "like him," and Barry felt an access to a kind of thinking that he had always felt "constitutionally" shut out of: "When I write in assembler I feel that mathematics is in my hands ... and I'm good with my hands." Barry claims to have "grown out of" his aspiration to be an engineer. He says he doesn't keep engineering as a pipe-dream or think of his computer skills as something that could make it real. In terms of his career he says that "nothing has changed." But a lot has changed. Barry has always thought of himself as a bundle of aptitudes and inaptitudes that define him as the kind of person who can do certain things and cannot do others.

Working with the computer has made him reconsider his categories. We really couldn't tell you what sort of thing I'm going to be doing with my computer in six months. It used to be that I could tell you exactly what we would be thinking about in six months. But the thing with this, with the computer, is that the deeper you get into it, there's no way an individual can say what he'll be thinking in six months, what we are going to be doing. But we honestly feel that it's going to be great. And that's one hell of a thing. For Barry, the world has always been divided between the people who think they know what they'll be thinking in six months and those who don't.

And in his mind, his home computer has gotten him across that line and "That's one hell of a thing." For Barry, part of what it means to have crossed the line is to start to call the line into question. When he was in school, his inability to do the kind of mathematics he had "respect" for made him lose respect for himself as a learner, The computer put mathematics in a form that he could participate in. Barry has three children, has bought them their own calculators, and encourages them to "mess around with the computer." He feels that they are going through the same problems with maths and science that he had and he wants them to have "a better start." For Barry, the computer holds the promise of a better start, not because it might teach his children a particular subject, but because it "might change their image of themselves. They might think of themselves as learners." Personal computers are certainly not the only hobby that people use to enhance their sense of identity. For my informants, "hobbies" have always been a way of life. Almost 90 per cent of them had been involved in a hobby other than computation, most usually in another "technical" hobby, such as photography, ham radio, or model railroading.

Fifteen percent of the hobbyists surveyed were using their computers to "augment" their participation in another hobby—for example, using the computer to keep an inventory of motorcycle parts, figure out ideal compression ratios for racing cars, interface with amateur radio equipment. For nearly a third of them, their home computer had completely replaced another hobby. People spoke of these abandoned hobbies as "fun" and as "good experiences," but their remarks about past hobbies underscored several ways in which in our day and time a computer hobby can be special. In particular, people spoke about their "switch to the computer" as making them part of something that was growing and that the society at large "really cared about."

Gregory is in his mid-forties, and has been in the electronics industry for all of his working life, as a technician, a programmer, and currently as a products designer. For two years, his computer shared space in his study with an elaborate model railroad system. A year and half before we met him he had bought a new hard copy printer and a graphics plotter. In the overcrowding that followed, the trains had finally found their way to storage in the basement.

We heard many echoes of Gregory's phrase, "it's part of the real world too." Hobbyists spoke about the computer offering them a connection with something beyond the hobby. For some, having a computer and "getting good at it" means crossing a frontier that separates "tinkering" from "real technology." They feel that the world sees their computer hobby as serious (several commented that friends and neighbours hardly even look at it as a hobby, as though the word were reserved for frivolities), and they start to see themselves that way too. Most first-generation hobbyists have technical educations, but many of them, like Barry, feel they have never been part of what is most exciting and important in the scientific and technical cultures. They see themselves as the low men on the totem pole.

Working with computers, even small computers, feels technologically "*avant garde.*" A smaller group of hobbyists (but a group whose numbers are growing as new generations of personal computers become more accessible to the non-specialist) have always felt completely left out of the scientific and technical worlds. For them, owning a computer can mean crossing a "two cultures" divide. Alan, a 29-year-old high school French teacher who describes himself as "having a love affair with a TRS-80," has always felt he wasn't "smart enough to do science."

Alan majored in French ("It was easy for me ... my mother is from Montreal") and took up carpentry as a hobby. And although he was good at it, it only reinforced his sense of not being able to do intellectual things, which in his mind meant not being able to "do anything technical." When Barry began to do mathematics with his calculator, he felt that he started to cross a line to become the kind of person who could expect change and excitement in his intellectual life. For Alan, his TRS-80 led him across a line to become a member of a different culture, a scientific culture, a culture of "powerful people." For Barry, Alan, Gregory, relationships with computation enhanced self-image.

There is another way in which working with a computer can influence an individual's sense of identity. Ideas about computers, about how they work and what they can and cannot do, can be used to assert ideas about people. They can provide metaphors for thinking about oneself. Many hobbyists, fascinated by the idea of someday being able to trace out the complex relationships of electronic events, machine and assembly language instructions, and higher-level language commands within the computer, used the image of these many levels of intelligence to think about how people might work, about how people might, or might not, be like machines.

Some of this epistemology was implicit, for example when people made comments about "using the computer's software to think about my wetware." And sometimes, although less frequently, the issue became quite explicit. Conversations that began with descriptions of household "robotics" projects, such as a plan to build an energy monitoring system, led to reflections on how these projects would require programs that could represent the system's knowledge to itself, and from there into formal epistemological reveries: were these the kind of self-representing programs that ran inside people's heads? Do people have different kinds of self-representation programs for representing different kinds of knowledge, such as the knowledge of a dream and the knowledge of being awake? What kind of self-representation program might be running within people that allows them to remember and then forget their dreams?

Materialising Reality

Hobbyist's descriptions of what it is like to work with their own computers frequently referred to the idea that the computer provides a safe corner of reality. Other hobbies can give a similar sense of security but often exact a price. For example, people can feel safe but limited. Alan, the French major, now "in love with his TRS-80," felt secure in his carpentry hobby, but he experienced it as a safety that came from refusing challenge. "It was an 'arty' hobby. We couldn't see myself any other way." The computer is more likely than most other media to allow the experience of playing worlds (let us call them "microworlds") that are secure and also adventurous enough to allow for mind-stretching explorations. Almost all of the hobbyists we interviewed described some version of a limited, safe, and transparent microworld that was embodied in their personal computer.

For Alan just the fact of working with a computer created such a world. For others, it was more specific: a morse code microworld; a text editor microworld; and, most generally, the assembly language microworld. This use of the computer as a place to build a microworld is particularly salient for children when they are put in computational environments in which they have access to programming. Elsewhere I shall report on mv study of elementary schoolchildren and adolescents who have gone through an experience with a LOGO computer system—a System designed to allow children to work in visually represented microworlds that are sufficiently constrained for a child to be able to understand and control them, yet sufficiently open-ended to give a child a real experience of intellectual power. Here I will mention only briefly one child and what she made of the computer as a medium for world building. Deborah at 11 years old was the baby of her family, the youngest of three children. Her childhood, had been spotted with illnesses which further exaggerated her "baby" position.

The members of her family were always doing things for her, insisting that she was not old enough to do the things that she wanted to do most: take out the laundry, baby-sit, stay over at a friend's house, choose her own hair style and her own clothes. Dependent on others at home, very overweight, and with an image of herself as sick and weak, Deborah had little sense of her own boundaries, her ability to say no, to assert control. Even at 11, she had become involved with a crowd of older kids who were smoking, drinking, using drugs. Towards the end of her eleventh year a LOGO computer came into Deborah's classroom as part of an educational experiment. At first, she found the computer frightening and threatening: until one day she hit upon the idea of confining the designs she made with the computer to ones in which the lines always came together in multiples of 30 degrees. She called it her "30 degrees world."

This restriction defined for her a space in which she felt safe but in which she was able to produce designs of great ingenuity and complexity. When I interviewed her two years later I found that she had used her experience with the "30 degrees world" as a kind of model, an experience-to-think-with. In her mind it represented how you could take control and make things happen by the judicious use of constraint. In Deborah's words, it was the first time that she ever "laid down her own laws." It was a turning point in her ability to take control of other situations. She lost 20 pounds, has given up smoking and drugs, and says that she "only sometimes" has a drink. For Deborah and for many adult hobbyists the sense of safety with the computer derived from the feeling of working in a sphere of intelligibility and transparency, a sphere that is protected, much as the space of a psychotherapeutic or psychoanalytic relationship is set off, bracketed.'

People talked about feeling safe and secure in the world they had built with their home computers, a world where there were few surprises and "things didn't change unless you wanted them to." Of course, there was much talk of problems, of false starts, of frustrations. There are "bugs" in hardware and in programs. Things don't work; things go wrong. But bugs, with time, are either fixed or become "known" bugs. Joe is an insurance salesman in a small North California suburb who owns a second-hand Commo-dore Pet "with a lot of hardware problems." To Joe the bugs in his system "have become almost like friends": "We turn on the machine and we systematically check for my 'old friends,' and we swear, finding them there has a certain reassuring element."

Various Angles

The use of the computer as a medium for building a transparent and intelligible world brings us to how it can be used to think through questions of political ideology. Fred sells components for a large electronics supply house. He narrowly escaped starvation in a prisoner of war camp during World War II, and from that experience he says that he took " a sense of optimism," "we mean, if there is something out there and you want to do it-do it, understand it, act." Fred has tried to live that way. He is active in local politics; he keeps up with the news; he writes letters to the editor of his town newspaper. He bought his TRS80 on an impulse because "it seemed that you wouldn't be able to understand American society any more if you didn't know about computers." When it comes to working with his computer, Fred wants to know "exactly how things work": "There is a big gap in my own mind between the fact that an electrical circuit can be on or off and the binary number system ... and again from there to the BASIC language. I've got to understand all of that."

When hobbyists like Fred spoke about "wanting to know exactly how things work" in their computers, they were usually talking about wanting to know how their systems were built up from level to level, from electrical circuit to high-level language command. Fred, for example, expressed sharp frustration at gaps in his ability to follow the system through: "we can't really follow the continuum. I'm going to a user's group meeting, I'm talking to people and reading books and some of it is helping, but I am really frustrated. We want to be able to follow the whole thing through."

Larry, 35, lives in a Boston suburb. His computer offered him the first way he ever found to challenge the school's judgments of his child's abilities. A year before we met him, Larry had bought an Apple computer for small business use and ended up bringing it home so that his children would be able to play with it. His 12-year-old son Todd had been judged "backward" by his teachers through six years of schooling. His maths scores were low; he could barely read. But Todd picked up the Apple manual, taught himself how to use the game packages, and then taught himself how to program in BASIC. As far as anyone knows, the Apple manual was the first book that Todd had ever read. In three weeks Todd was writing his own games, games that demanded an understanding of variables and a knowledge of geometry that his teachers claimed he didn't have. Larry is starting to demand more from his son's teachers. His experience with Todd has made him optimistic about what computers will mean for politics because "people will get used to understanding things, of being in control of things, and then, will demand more." This optimism is widely shared among hobbyists, part of a distinct style of talking about computers and politics.

Hobbyists, like Fred and Larry, take what is most characteristic about their relationships with the computer—using computers to build safe microworlds of transparent understanding-and turn it into a political metaphor. Hobbyists associate images of computational transparency and of "knowing how the in machine works" with a kind of politics where relations of power will be transparent, where people will control their destinies, where work will facilitate a rich and balanced cognitive life, and where decentralized power will follow from decentralized information resources. For many hobbyists a relationship with their home computer carries longings for a better and simpler life in a more transparent society. *Co-Evolution Quarterly*, *Mother Earth News*, *Runner's World*, and *Byte Magazine* lie together on hobbyists' coffee tables.

Small computers become the focus of hopes of building cottage industries that will allow people to work out of their homes, have more personal autonomy, not have to punch time cards, and be able to spend more time with their family and out of doors. Some see personal computers as a next step in the ecology movement: decentralized technology will mean less waste. Some see personal computers as a way for individuals to assert greater control over their children's education, believing that computerized curricula will soon offer children better education at home than can be offered in today's schools. Some see personal computers as a path to a new populism: personal computer networks will allow citizens to band together to send mail, run decentralized schools, information resources, and local governments. In sum, many of the computer hobbyists I have interviewed talk about the computers in their living-rooms as windows onto a future where relationships with technology will be more direct, where people will understand how things work, and where dependence on big government, big corporations, and big machines will end. They imagine the politics of this computer-rich future by generalizing from their special relationship to the technology, a relationship characterized by simplicity and a sense of control.

Over 40 per cent of those who responded to my survey worked, or had once worked, as computer programmers. The programmer is typically in a situation where he or she is in touch with only a very small part of the problem that is being worked on. Increasingly, programmers work in large teams where each individual has very little sense of the whole, of how it all fits together.

Programmers have watched their opportunities to exercise their skill as a whole activity being taken away (for those who are too young, the story of the process remains alive in the collective mythology of the shop). They have watched their work being routinized, being parcelled out into the well defined modules that make up the tasks of the structured programming team. They mythologize a golden age. This live experience at work made programmers particularly sensitive to the parcellization of knowledge and to the alienation from a sense of wholeness in work. And they bring this sensitivity to their home computer hobbies.

Hannah worked as a programming consultant for a large business system for ten years before starting her own consulting company through which she offers her services to other computer hobbyists. To her, nothing is more depressing than working on a tiny piece of a problem. In her old job, "most of the time we didn't even know what the whole problem was." She likes working with computers at home because she has more control of her time and can spend more time with her family. But she says that what is most important about working with a personal computer is that "we can finally think about a whole problem." Hannah's feelings were widely shared among the hobbyists interviewed, most notably among programmers, ex-programmers, and "team engineers." Images of lack of intellectual balance, of fragmentation, of not being connected, came up often, with the computer at home usually placed in the role of righting what had been wrong at work. As Hannah put it: "With my computer at home we do everything, we see my whole self, all my kinds of thinking."

For these people, having a computer at home meant "thinking experiences" where they could see what their real capacities were, where they had a chance to try things out. Karl, for example, who worked for a long time as a programmer and who is now an engineer in a microprocessor firm, had thought a lot about his mental "ecology."

> In the first half of an engineering project there is literally nothing coming together and that's when we find that we need to go home and put something together. We used to make lamps like those in the living room out of glass bottles. But then towards the middle of an engineering project, things did start to come together and we would lose the need for cutting glass. But if you never or rarely get to finish things at work, if your job is basically to make little pieces and it's somebody else's job to make them fit into a whole, then working with the computer at home can give you an experience of getting it all together. You do the whole thing—building up from machine code to finished project. It makes you feel in balance.

When we spoke with Karl he was at a point where everything at work seemed "pretty disconnected." Or, as Karl put it, if he hadn't had his home computer, it would have been "glass cutting time". Karl saw his current work with the computer as a corrective to fragmentation on the job. During our interview, he spoke to me about his current plans for revamping his computer system.

Computer systems like his which have several components (keyboard, display screen, printer) have to be connected by using devices, usually simple circuits, called "interfaces." Karl's plan called for using a separate microprocessor as an interface for each component. He had conflicts about the "rationality" of his project.

After all, he admitted, it was far from economical if one measures economy in terms of the cost of the hardware. Each interface circuit needed only a few specialized and inexpensive chips. There was no need for a general-purpose microprocessor at each node. Specialized chips could do the job more cheaply, but could not satisfy his desire to experience the system as maximally coherent. By replacing the special-purpose circuits by separate, but identical, general-purpose microprocessors, the whole system, at least in Karl's eyes, became uniform, intelligible, and systematic. Karl could not help concluding: "We guess you could say that my choice of projects is not always rational." But from the perspective of using a relationship with computation as a way of "working through" personal concerns, Karl's rationale was clear. For Karl the "inexpensive" solution., using a collection of opaque, adhoc circuits, felt unintelligible. It felt to him like his work situation. His plans for his multiprocessor system were dictated by the logic of compensation rather than by the logic of material economy.

Mechanical Side

In studying the hobbyist experience we have found people, largely people with technical backgrounds, in intense involvement with machines. They describe their work (or rather their leisure) with the computer as different from what they have done before with other hobbies. They describe it as an involvement with greater personal consequence. Some of the sense of consequence comes from an historical moment: the computer hobby is seen as signifying a place in the "*avant garde*". Although in some circles "computer person" is a term of derision, the hobbyist experiences it with pride.

Some of the sense of consequence comes from experiencing an individualistic and independent relationship with computation that can be mythologized as belonging to a now-past "golden age" of the programmer. But most of the sense of consequence comes from the holding power and intensity of the time spent with the computer. What is there about these people and these machines that makes possible relationships of such power and such intensity? For me, the relationships that hobbyists form with their home computers can be partially captured with a metaphor of the "mind" and the "body" of the machine.

The "mind" of the computer is that side of computation that involves thinking in terms of high-level programs. In this metaphor, relating to the "body" of the computer means not only working on hardware, but also, and indeed especially, working with programs in a way that is as close as possible to the machine code – that is to say, as close as possible to the core of the computer, its central processing unit (CPU). In terms of this metaphor I have found that the prototypical hobbyist is trying to get into a relationship with the body (rather than the mind) of the machine, to assert power and control in the relationship with the computer, and to create safe worlds of transparent understanding. In trying to find concepts for thinking more clearly about what draws the hobbyist to this kind of relationship with the CPU and about what its meaning might be, we find three issues particularly salient. We think, moreover, that, although we formulate them here in terms of computers, they are relevant to understanding relationships with other technologies as well. The first issue goes back to control.

The hobbyist complains of a work situation where everyone suffers from the constant presence of intermediaries. Bureaucracies stand between the programmer and the computer, a bureaucracy that schedules the computer, that decides its up and down time, that apportions the work for its software design and decides on priorities and procedures for access to it. At work, when something goes wrong with the system it is usually the fault of an intermediary person, one of the many "somebody elses" who deal with the machine. Or it may be the fault of a technical intermediary, one of the many elements in the computer system that mediate between the user and the bare machine: a compiler, an interpreter, an operating system, someone else's program. At home, the hobbyists feel themselves as working directly with the CPU, in complete and direct control of the machine's power.

And when something does blow up, the situation has a special immediacy. It is between them and the bare machine. When a FORTRAN program is run on a large IBM machine the events in the machine are far from being in one-to-one correspondence with the steps of code written by the programmer. Two factors contribute. First, it is in the nature of higher-level languages to work in a conceptual space different from that of the machine. FORTRAN works in a "formula" space, COBOL works in a "business" space, both very different from the space of bits and bytes. Second, the sense of indirect relationship is exacerbated when the compiled code is run by an operating system which allocates memory, mediates control of peripheral devices, and even interleaves the program with other programs. At home hobbyists can follow machine-language programs step by step as their instructions pass through the CPU. They can envision the changes in state of the whole system as being produced by specific actions of the CPU.

And if they suspect that there is a bug in the hardware they can pull out an oscilloscope and see whether the CPU is doing what it should in response to a given instruction. They can figure out where the signals should be going, they can collect their own evidence for what is going wrong, trap and fix the bug themselves. Again and again in my interviewing I heard about the pleasures of debugging-of "going in with meters and scopes and tracking it down." The procedure exhilarates. With every successfully tracked bug comes an affirmation of direct control over the machine. The issue of control was often explicitly recognized by the hobbyists we interviewed. But they lacked a language for naming a second issue which has to do with a notion referred to as "syntonicity" within the psychoanalytic tradition.

Syntonicity implies that we should look for "body-to-body" identification in every powerful relationship with a technology – the body of the person and the body of the machine. It implies that we should understand the appeal of machine language in terms of people's ability to identify with what is happening inside the machine. The CPU of the hobbyist computer lends itself to personal identification with its primary action: moving something that is conceptually almost a physical object (a byte of information) in and out of some thing (a register) that is almost a physical place. The metaphor is concrete and spatial. One can imagine finding the bytes, feeling them, doing something very simple to them, and passing them on. For many of the people that we met in the hobbyist culture, getting into this kind of identification feels safe. It makes the machine feel real. There is a third issue raised by the hobbyists' relationship to the CPU. It is an aesthetic one.

The generation of hobby computers that was born in the 1970s are very primitive machines. The hobbyist thinks of much about them as "klugey," a computerist's way of saying that one is dealing with a compromise, a collection of patches whose structure has been dictated by arbitrary corporate decisions, by economic necessities. The corner of the hobbyist machine that seems to them to have the greatest "intellectual integrity," that distills what they feel to be a tradition of some of the best ideas in computer science, that comes closest to being "clean," is the CPU. And so it is natural for the hobbyist to seek the closest possible contact with it. For a culture in which there is a widely shared aesthetic of simplicity, intelligibility, control, and transparency, getting into the "un-klugey" part of the machine and working in machine code seems the most aesthetically satisfying way to use the personal computer as an artistic medium.

10

Golden Rules for Computer Folks

Software—the set of instructions that tell a computer what to do—is becoming more important than the computer itself. The booming software industry is therefore setting the pace of the information technology, revolution and the pace is frantic. This article first appeared in *Business Week,* February 27, 1984. Hardware is no longer where the action is. Computers are becoming remarkably similar—in many cases they are turning into off-the-shelf commodity products. Now the computer wars are being fought on a new battleground: software-the instructions that tell computers how to do everything from processing payrolls to playing video games.

Peak of Popularity

A key reason for the change in emphasis is an overwhelming demand from customers for packaged software that will let them apply computer power to a broad range of new tasks. Increasingly, corporations are finding they do not have the resources to write the programs they need. As a result, most companies have stopped writing their own software and are instead buying standard software packages. So far, producers have been unable to keep up with the need, and there has been a severe shortage of software able to take advantage of the power of the latest machines. "We're getting the hardware we need from the industry, but software has not moved out at the same rate," says Robert J. Metzler, vice-president of First Computer Services, the data processing arm of First Union National Bank in Charlotte, NC. "There's a tremendous cry in the industry [for software]." The flood of personal computers pouring into small businesses and homes has created an even faster-growing new market.

The booming demand for new and better programs has quickly turned software into big business. During the 1970s software was stiff a cottage industry, 'with sales totaling just $2.7 billion annually. This year-according to estimates by Input, a California market research firm-sales are expected to top $10 billion.

With the industry growing that fast, several once-small software companies have become sizable corporations. Management Science America Inc. (MSA), for example, the largest independent software supplier, quadrupled in size during the past three years, topping $145 million in sales in 1983. Trying to capture some of the soaring market, thousands of new companies have entered the software business in recent years; by one count there are more than 3000 software companies now.

While over the long term a shakeout is probably inevitable, the near-term outlook for most of these companies appears extremely bright. "The upside potential has barely been tapped," says Robert M. Freeman, senior analyst at Input. He expects the market to keep growing by a dizzying 32 per cent a year, topping $30 billion in 1988. Software sales of that magnitude would amount to half of the $60 billion hardware business expected for the same year; today, revenue from software is equal to only 27 per cent of the value of all the computer hardware sold.

Software Market

Sales of software for personal computers-the fastest-growing part of the software industry-should rise by an astounding 44 per cent annually over the same five years. "We're finally at the point where software applications are going to be a big moneymaker," says Jack M. Scanlon, vice-president of the Computer Systems Division of AT&T Technologies Inc. But with the promise of such rapid market growth, has come a feverish competition that is beginning to restructure the entire industry.

Until recently, nearly all software companies concentrated on a particular niche and fit neatly into one of three distinct market segments that were divided along the same lines for both mainframe and personal computers.

Family Front

Systems software, which handles basic housekeeping operations such as controlling the printer and memory, was supplied primarily by the computer makers. They were joined by independent software companies in providing utility software, which, among other things, helps programmers write programs. And a host of other independent software companies competed in the third market; applications packages, which tell a computer how to carry out specific tasks such as accounting payroll or word processing.

But those distinctions are blurring:

Consolidation: International Business Machines Corp., to move faster into applications software, placed all its software efforts into a single, entrepreneurial unit—the same type of Organisation it used to launch the highly successful Personal Computer.

Acquisitions: To provide a full complement of software for their computers, makers such as Hewlett-Packard, Burroughs, and Prime Computer are rushing to buy applications software companies. Other manufacturers, including Honey-well, Sperry, and Digital Equipment, are setting up joint ventures with software suppliers. Says Roger T. Hobbs, vice-president for software products and services at Burroughs Corp.: "The demands for software are increasing so rapidly that it is impossible for the manufacturer to keep up."

Expanding Product Lines: Software companies are expanding product lines to maintain their competitive edge. Those that supply programs mostly for large mainframes—MSA, Cullinet Software, and Computer Associates International, for example—are snapping up personal computer software houses. And companies that specialize in systems software for personal computers-among them, AshtonTate, Digital Research, and Microsoft—are adding general-purpose applications software to their product lines. "Today you have to have a broad line," says Terry L. Opdendyk, president of

VisiCorp. Otherwise, "the vendor is increasingly vulnerable to competition."

New Players: To grab a piece of the action, publishers and other communications companies outside the computer business—including CBS, Dow Jones, Dun & Bradstreet, McGraw-Hill, and Simon and Schuster-are licensing programs they then sell through their own distribution channels. "It's a very fragmented industry, but the potential is absolutely huge," says Richard W. Young, president of Houghton Mifflin Co.

Japan's Drive: To catch up with their US rivals, Japanese computer makers are launching major software development efforts. Perhaps the best evidence of just how important software has become is the drive by Japan's Ministry of International Trade & Industry to change the law to boost Japan's fledgling software industry. One result of many of these trends is that mergers and acquisitions in the industry are at an all-time high. In 1983 there were 146 acquisitions, valued at more than $1 billion-up 130 per cent from 1982—reports Broadview Associates, a New Jersey company handling such transactions. And this frantic pace of activity is turning the software business into a hot investment area.

Policies and Programmes

To complete successfully amid all the turmoil, software suppliers are struggling to formulate new strategies. One common focus is advanced design-especially the development of software aimed at making computers easier to use. But just as important to the success of new software as advanced design is marketing. Nowhere is the new attention to marketing more noticeable than in the hotly competitive personal computer business. To reach the millions of personal computer users, software companies are spending huge amounts to introduce and advertise their products. Industry watchers have dubbed this obsession with splashy promotion "the Lotus syndrome—a reference to the more than $1 million that Lotus Development Corp. spent over a three-month period in 1983 to launch its first product, the highly successful 1-2-3 package. "Lotus advertised so much that companies are going to be forced to step up their advertising just to be heard above the noise," says David E. Gold, a San Jose (Calif.) computer consultant.

Advertising, in fact, has grown so important to software success that it has become one of the biggest barriers keeping out new companies. "The cost of technology development is dwarfed by the marketing cost; the ante has really been upped," says Rodney N. Turner, vice-president for sales at Ashton-Tate, a Culver City (Calif.) software company best known for its dBase II package. It takes as much as $8 million to launch a new software product today, he estimates. Ashton-Tate, by contrast, was founded on shoestring-$7,500. Any personal computer program must be carefully packaged and promoted. "It has to look good and has to be well supported. by national advertising," maintains retailer Gregg E. Olson, a salesman at Mr Software in Boulder, Colo. "A company that wants to sell to us has to have all their marketing elements in place to establish credibility with us and our customers."

Even companies that write software for the large minicomputers and mainframes are plowing more money into marketing. While programs for the larger systems, unlike those for personal computers, do not require heavy consumer advertising, says Martin A. Goetz, senior vice-president at Applied Data Research Inc., his company still boosted its 1984 advertising budget by 60 per cent over 1983, to about $2 million.

This emphasis on marketing comes chiefly from the need to reach a different, far broader group of potential customers. "Ten years ago, [our customer] was the data processing department, and if you had a product, you sold it to the technicians," says Robert D. Baskerville, group vice-president for product management at Computer Sciences Corp. in El Segundo, Calif. Today, he notes, a software company has "to sell to end users, and you have to emphasize more than the technical capability—you have to really sell the benefit."

Software marketing now means beginning with detailed product planning, so that a program will better meet the needs of customers. Before Wyly Corp. even began a $20 million program to diversify into applications software, for example, it brought in all its salesmen from the field to tell programmers what customers wanted-something most software companies had never done. "With modern software development techniques, you can produce almost perfect code, but if you don't understand the market, it could still be useless," says Ron W. Brittian, Wyly's vice-president for research and development.

Critical, too, is a reputation for good service and customer support. "To grow from a startup into a large software company is not so easy anymore; it's a question of distribution and of educating the customer in how to use the product," says Anthony W. Wang, executive vice-president at Computer Associates International Inc. Toward this end, his company recently installed a $250,000 television studio—costing $200,000 or more a year to run—to make training videotapes for its software customers.

User's Helping Hand

As competition heightens and customers become more demanding, companies selling personal computer software are providing a level of customer support far greater than anything they offered before. MicroPro International Corp., for example, has plowed $2.5 million into developing computer-aided instruction and retail-support aids for its software, which includes the best-selling WordStar. The company is also hiring journalists and other non-technical writers to produce more readable instructions for today's less sophisticated customers. "A product is not a product until you have computer-aided instructions, it's not a product until you have, video instructions, it's not a product until you have honest-to-God understandable language [in the manual]," says H. Glen Haney, president of MicroPro.

Establishing a marketing presence is especially critical to companies that provide personal computer software, because they must win space on already crowded retail shelves. Computer retailers are reluctant to take on new software without feeling confident it is a winner. "Unless we're absolutely convinced that it's a great program, we'll wait to see how other channels of distribution do with it," says John H. Rollins, national manager for Sears Business Systems Centers, the computer retailing arm of

Sears, Roebuck & Co. One group trying hard to enter the software business may have an edge: the traditional book publishers. Because they already sell books to computer stores, the publishers "provide ready-made distribution channels," says Input's Freeman. Agrees William M. Graves, president of MSA: "There is a tremendous similarity in the microcomputer business and publishing."

Wide Scope

No matter, how they distribute their products, software companies are finding that they must offer a broader range of products than ever before. "The strategy is to offer a complete solution," asserts Robert N. Goldman, president of Cullinet. "If a customer ends up with eight different vendors, none of the software works together." Cullinet, for instance, is augmenting its data base management software with such applications as general ledger accounting and manufacturing control programs.

Broadening a software line also helps a supplier leverage the large amounts of money spent on establishing a reputation and brand recognition. VisiCorp, which gained market fame with its hit program VisiCalc, is trying to expand its applications software with its family of Visi On integrated software. Similarly, Microsoft is plunging into such applications software as word processing and financial analysis to build on its reputation as a supplier of personal computer operating systems.

The trend toward comprehensive offerings will force small companies to target well-defined market niches. There will continue to be demand for specialized packages designed for the needs of a particular industry or profession. "There will be several very large software companies," contends John P. Imlay Jr., chairman of MSA, "but there will be literally hundreds of small companies, with under $100 million [in sales], that have specialized market niches."

Perhaps the most fundamental change in the software industry is the blurring distinctions among the suppliers. No longer can they be neatly divided into companies that make basic systems software and those that write programs for specific applications.

Moreover, the top mainframe software companies are rushing to market with software for personal computers. And vendors serving only the personal computer market are joining with suppliers of mainframe software. VisiCorp, for example, recently teamed up with Informatics General Corp. to offer Visi-Answer, a program that allows a user of an IBM Personal Computer to retrieve information from an IBM mainframe data base. These changes resulted in large part from the growing number of customers linking personal computers to large mainframe systems.

Process of Functioning

As the emphasis in the data processing industry shifts to software and, as software companies strengthen their sales, service, and distribution, the big-system makers, too, are scrambling to do more to provide their customers with software. "In the old days, our customer wrote his own application [software]," notes Jon Tempas, vice-president for software products at Sperry Corp.'s Computer Systems operation.

Today, "there's an increased expectation for hardware suppliers to provide the complete solution." That means the equipment makers will need to provide more of their own software. Sperry, for example, now writes 95 per cent of the software it sells for its computer line.

Most of the big-system companies, however, are turning to software specialists for help, since much of the demand is for applications software finely tuned to specific industries. "I don't think there's any hardware manufacturer that can-or should-provide all the software," says John E. Steuri, general manager of Information Services Business Unit, IBM's new independent software group. "We'll be more and more dependent over time on software developed outside the company." The pressure to team up with independent software companies is especially strong among makers of personal computers.

"Without an adequate software base, a microcomputer dies," says Eugene W. Helms, vice-president for business development at Texas Instruments Inc.'s Data Systems Group. So TI is recruiting software suppliers to adapt their best-selling programs for its

Professional Computer. Perhaps the most extensive effort to sign up independent software companies was made by Apple Computer Inc., which courted more than 100 companies to write software for its new Macintosh computer. The California company was successful in signing up more than 80 of them.

Companies that do not move quickly to develop a broad line of software will have trouble keeping up. Consider Tymshare Inc., a computer timesharing company. As computer prices began to drop precipitously, more and more of Tymshare's customers stopped renting computer time and purchased their own machines. Tymshare did not have any software packages to sell to its former clients. "We used to look at software as simply an in-house tool that we needed to offer time-sharing," says one Tymshare executive. That attitude, he admits, "came back and bit us in the rear end." In 1983 the California company lost $1.7 million while sales fell 3 per cent to $288 million. Now it is engaged in a major effort to expand into applications software, through internal development and by licensing packages developed by other companies.

With most software companies trying hard to move in the same direction, everyone will face stiffer competition. Already, prices for personal computer software are sliding wherever similar programs have proliferated-in electronic spreadsheets and word processors, for example. And a big battle is under way among suppliers of the various "windowing" software packages—software "environments" that permit the users of personal computers to display several tasks at once. VisiCorp has been forced to slash the price of its Visi On environment package from $495 to $95. "The consumer is going to force the prices down simply by demand," asserts Alvin B. Reuben, executive vice-president at Simon & Schuster Inc.'s electronic publishing division.

As prices fall, the opportunity for, newcomers to jump in and grab quick and easy profits will all but disappear. The cost of developing and marketing new programs is mushrooming just when margins are shrinking. VisiCorp successfully launched VisiCalc in 1978 with a $500 budget. But the California company has spent more than $10 million developing its latest product, the

Visi On environment. Product life is also getting shorter as new products come out faster. As a result, says Softsel's Wagman, "the stakes have gotten higher and much riskier from a development point of view."

For many companies, the risks will ultimately prove fatal. "There are companies out there that are already feeling the pinch of increased costs, new product announcements, and a changing marketplace," warns consultant Gold. Industry watchers predict that some big-name failures will occur within the next 18 months. By the end of the decade, many experts expect the software industry to have consolidated its thousands of suppliers into a few major players.

For those that make it, the future is promising. The demand by the growing army of computer users for easier-to-use software to handle an exploding variety of tasks will drive the industry to create software with far more capabilities than anything available today. "They only limit," says Stuart A. Walker, vice-president of marketing at Konware Inc., "is the limit of new ideas."

Software in the Office: One of the main reasons software has become so highly visible is that the computer has moved from the back room into the office.

Programs of the past, buried inside corporate data processing centers, primarily handled clerical and accounting tasks, such as turning out payrolls and keeping track of accounts receivable. Today's computer handles a rapidly increasing variety of management tasks—employing information as a competitive marketing weapon, for example.

That trend, coupled with the explosion in the use of personal computers by executives, has given new prominence and importance to software in us corporations. "The Programs that we install to do our company's business are analogous to the tools an auto maker puts in place to manufacture auto parts," says Jeffry A Alperin, an assistant vice-president in the Information Systems Support Dept at Aetna Life & Casualty Co. "Our plant is our data Processing system." Since the same computer hardware is available to everyone it is the software that often gives a company a competitive edge. At oil companies, software is now helping drive the search for oil and gas," says Michael C. Balay, general manager of information technology at Gulf Oil Corp. "You can have the same [seismic] information, but a unique software package may help you better interpret the data. "

Nowhere is this increasing importance more obvious than in corporate data processing budgets. Belay estimates that Gulf spends about half of its annual data processing budget to write its own software and to buy packages from independent suppliers. At Aetna, half of the 4000 people on the data processing staff are programmers. And Alperin says that 4 per cent of the $237 million that Aetna spent on information processing last year went to purchase packaged software.

Moreover, individual owners of personal computers are no different from large corporations: over the life of a computer, its owner will spend $2 on software for every $1 spent on hardware, according to industry estimates. But users are finding it increasingly difficult to produce their own programs. Writing software is still a time-consuming process, and users find that, while they want to employ their computers to handle more applications they do not have enough programmers, time, or money to write all of the necessary software in-house. In fact, at many companies users must now wait as long as 18 months for new programs to be written. "The end users are demanding faster development of solutions," declares Richard R. Douglas, group vice-president for the US Marketing and Services Group of Honeywell Inc.

To come up with this software faster, computer users are compromising-buying more ready-to-run software packages than ever before. "There has been a turnaround from five or six years ago," says James T. Manion, sales vice-president at ASK Computer Systems Inc. Few computer users write all their own programs anymore, he says. But while users sacrifice some uniqueness by buying a software package, that disadvantage is often outweighed by the time and money saved. A package can cut the time it takes to get a system up and running by more than half, figures Mayford L. Roark, executive director of systems at Ford Motor Co. He also estimates that buying a program from an outside vendor can cut development costs by 30 to 75 per cent. "It's almost impossible to think of a function you might want to do on a computer that you can't find several software packages for," says Roark.

Where a custom solution to a problem is required, companies often find they can save time by modifying a standard software package for their own use. That is what Aetna did when it needed software to offer a new type of life insurance called universal life, which features flexible premiums. That allowed the company to match its competitors' universal life offerings quickly. With such a variety of software available, companies are finding that writing their own programs from scratch makes about as much sense as drawing their own road maps for their salesmen.

US corporations brought more software packages last year than in the previous year, says International Data Corp., a market researcher. Such purchases, along with software services, now account for more than 8 per cent of the average data processing budget, up from 6 per cent in 1980, IDC says. Similarly, purchases of personal computer software packages soared 74 per cent last year to top $1 billion, according to market researchers at California's Input.

New Trends

The customer's new attitude toward software is beginning to alter fundamentally the way that computer systems are sold. "We're selling to a much more sophisticated consumer base than in the past," points out Elizabeth M. R. Hall, product manager at Infor-mation Science Inc., a Montvale (NJ) software company. From now on, adds Honeywell's Douglas, "Software looms as a much more important factor in [a user's purchase] decision than hardware."

Computing used to be the solitary domain of a priesthood of programmers. The arcane languages that they employed to command their giant mainframe systems were shrouded in such complexity that few laymen could understand, much less control, these behemoths. But the inexpensive yet powerful personal computer is changing all that. Millions of nontechnical users are now running computers. These new operators, however, refuse even to read an instruction manual, let alone memorize the cryptic commands of the priesthood. Their aversion, coupled with the dramatic slide in the cost of computer power, has created a revolution in the way software is written.

Today, making a program simple to control and easy to use is just as important as what the program actually does. Says Jeanne M. Baccash, a software engineer at American Telephone & Telegraph Co.'s Bell Laboratories: "There's a whole new thrust to reach a market that doesn't know or care what it means to 'boot a system' [start a computer].

These efforts to make software simpler are crucial if the information processing industry is to continue its fast growth. "Rapidly advancing technology has left consumers, trainers, and computer salesmen behind," says Terry L. Opdendyk, president of VisiCorp. "How to spread the word of how to use the products is the key limiting factor [to the industry's growth]."

Man-machine Communications: To reduce the number of commands that a user must memorize and type into a computer to get it to work, the latest software enables users to communicate with the machine in new ways. Some of these techniques are relatively simple, such as establishing menus to show users what commands are available to choose from. The most elaborate methods, used on such machines as Apple Computer Inc.'s new Macintosh, replace commands with an array of tiny icons or pictures—for example, a file folder to indicate filing. To tell the computer what to do, users point to the appropriate picture on the screen by moving a pointing device called a "mouse" over a desktop.

Data Exchange: Early programs were built to accomplish tasks, such as calculating financial forecasts, with only the data located within the user's own computer. But users have grown more sophisticated and now want to get data stored in other machines—say, the corporation's central mainframe system.

Artificial Intelligence: This embryonic method of programming, which enables software to mimic human thought more closely, might one day be the easiest approach to use. It is starting to show up in programs such as Artificial Intelligence Corp.'s Intellect and Microrim Corp.'s CLIO, which let a user ask a computer for data with English sentences rather than esoteric commands.

Most programmers are ill-equipped to figure out how office workers and other nontechnical users best handle computers. So companies are bringing in professionals from disciplines as far afield as education and psychology to help in the design of man-to-machine communications. AT&T, for example, had a staff of psychologists survey about 400 computer users to help it decide how to add commands to its Unix operating system. Designing easier-to-use software also requires new development techniques. For instance, International Business Machines Corp. now tests its new software in "usability labs." In these labs, volunteers try to use IBM software while researchers with video cameras watch from behind one-way mirrors. "In the long haul, those that have easy-to-understand software will be the successful companies," says John E. Steuri, general manager of IBM's Information Services Business Unit.

A lot of discussion is going on in research circles over how best to use menus, pictograms, and other techniques to help both computer novices and experts. The type of coaching that a neophyte computer user requires becomes annoying once the user has learned to use the software. So designers want "to make sure the user is not presented with extraneous information when he has to decide what to do next," says Brian K. Reid, a Stanford University electrical engineering professor. Micropro International Corp., for one, is trying to solve this problem by using a time-delay activator.

If a user types in a command less than two seconds after being asked for it, the program assumes the user is proficient and skips over the menu listing of options. Users who take longer are given the benefit of directions from a menu. Researchers are also struggling with the problem of how to standardize commands. Each computer program now uses different commands to accomplish the same function. An early attempt to solve this problem is the "environment" or "windowing" software packages for personal computers that are now coming to market. These packages-products such as Microsoft Corp's Windows and VisiCorp's Visi On-divide the computer screen into segments, each of which shows a different task. Common functions are performed the same way in each window. The large amount of this kind of innovative software now being developed to make personal computers easier to use is also forcing the mainframe software companies to follow suit. "Mainframe vendors have been forced to make software easier' because users have been spoiled by micros," says David Ferris, an industry consultant.

Managing the Functions

Information Builders Inc. has developed a version of its Focus data base management software that can run on an IBM Personal Computer. But the PC version, called Pc-Focus, "has more features than the mainframe product because after using a personal computer customers have come to expect more," says Gerald D. Cohen, president of the New York company. One of the Pc-Focus features is called Table Talk. Each time a user moves from one step to another in the course of retrieving information from a data base, the computer automatically presents him with a menu of the appropriate choices.

Another software challenge is to find simpler ways to exchange data between programs. In most cases, swapping data between a large mainframe and a personal computer is difficult because the two units use different formats for storing their data and different commands for retrieving them.

The problem is similar to that of a person who is trying to communicate with 10 people, each of whom speaks a different language, explains Robert J. Spinrad, director of systems technology at Xerox Corp. "I could either learn all nine other languages," he says, "or we could all learn a common one-say, Latin." But software vendors are not waiting until everyone in the industry agrees on what common language all computers should learn. In the past year a host of vendors, including Cullinet Software, Informatics General, and Cincom Systems, have announced products that link personal computers to large mainframes. Such capabilities will be a requisite for any software in the marketplace, says President Frank H. Dodge of McCormack & Dodge Corp. "If mainframe software doesn't allow that link," he adds, "it's going to be pushed aside pretty rapidly."

Some experts think the ultimate mechanism for exchanging data is the use of sophisticated file-management software, often called data base management systems. These large programs index information and then store it in such a way that it can be retrieved using a variety of names-much the way a library card catalog lists the same book by author, subject, and title. By providing this uniform filing structure, a data base system simplifies the exchange of data.

What may soon make computers even easier to use is artificial intelligence (AI) software. Some companies are already working on AI programs that will eventually be able to remember an individual's habits in using the computer. The first AI applications from Microsoft-expected within the next year-will be likely to use these rudimentary pattern-recognition techniques in tutorial programs that teach novices how to operate software. These programs will adjust the level of tutorial difficulty by determining the proficiency of the student running the program. Says Microsoft Chairman William H. Gates: "Just as humans take actions based on past experience without having to be told again, and again, so will software.

As the second-largest group of computer companies in the world-after the US – they exported $2.7 billion worth of computers in 1983. But in their single-minded determination to build and export hardware that is faster and less expensive, the Japanese have given short shrift to software development. "Hardware manufacturers have been lazy about developing software," acknowledges Hisao Ishihara, managing director of the Japan Software Industry Assn. But now, he points out, "that is suddenly changing." Faced with the twin problems of rapidly falling hardware prices and the growing percentage of computer budgets being spent on software, Japanese hardware makers are scrambling to shift their resources into software development.

In 1981, for example, Hitachi Ltd's Computer Division spent just 10 per cent of its research and development budget on software. In 1984, even though software accounted for about 10 per cent of its computer revenues, Hitachi spent 30 per cent of its R&D money on software. "These days, more and more of the value added in information processing comes from the software," says Toshimitsu Kaihatsu, head of Toshiba Corp.'s Software Management Dept.

The Japanese are also keenly aware that to continue to be competitive internationally in computers they must now start developing world-class software. "We have to sell more overseas if we want to recover our software development costs," comments Shoichi Ninomiya, general manager of Fujitsu Ltd.'s Information Processing Group. His company spent close to $100 million a year-more than one-third Of its R&D budget-to develop software for its mainframe computers. But almost all of that software is now sold to Japanese customers. Until now, software has been the biggest handicap the Japanese have had in selling their equipment abroad-especially in the office and personal computer markets. This point was driven home in 1982 when International Business Machines Corp. sued Hitachi, one of the largest Japanese exporters of computers, charging the company with copying IBM software and reselling it with Hitachi's machines.

Hitachi agreed in an out-of-court settlement to pay IBM between $2 million and $4 million a month in software license fees and agreed to let the US computer giant inspect all new Hitachi products before they go on the market to ensure that they do not infringe any IBM copyrights. To avoid a similar lawsuit, Fujitsu has also agreed to pay IBM many millions of dollars and promised not to copy the US company's software, although it would not disclose the details of its agreement. Because of language and cultural differences, software written in Japan is obviously difficult to export. Not only must instruction manuals be translated, but often the programs have to be completely rewritten. Japanese accounting rules, for example, are different from those in the US, so accounting software written in Japan is useless in the US. This shortage of programs has severely limited the export potential of Japanese home and personal computers.

Japan's software industry is also held back by the preference of Japanese buyers for custom software rather than the standard software products that US customers are increasingly buying.

Scene in Japan

As a result, an independent Japanese software industry has been slow to develop. And the computer manufacturers' efforts to develop all the software themselves have been crimped by the large sums they must invest to improve methods of getting information into the computer and processing it, using Japanese *kanji* characters. But it would be dangerous to write off the Japanese as competitors in world-class software. "The Japanese are as dedicated to computers as they were to autos and shipbuilding," says John P. Imlay Jr, chairman of Management Science America Inc. "If US companies do not innovate and supply quality products and customer support, the Japanese could make inroads."

Already, Japan has a big chunk of the US market for the simplest type of software, that written for video games. Cultural differences are not a barrier to the export of such hit games as Pac-Man. The fast-growing software markets for engineering and scientific applications-which manipulate schematic drawings and numbers rather than words-are other areas where Japanese software could be sold overseas with little modification. The Japanese have also demonstrated their technical ability by creating powerful supercomputer software and sophisticated banking and airline reservation systems. "People are misreading the capability of the Japanese when they say Japanese can't build good software," maintains Joseph C. Berston, president of Comstute Inc., a software consulting firm based in Japan.

Indeed, Japanese companies may actually have some advantages over their US rivals. Because of the legendary thoroughness of Japanese workers, "the finished product here is better, more reliable, and easier to maintain," says consultant Berston. Labor costs are also lower for Japanese software makers. Well-educated, highly disciplined Japanese programmers are paid an average of about $10,000 a year. Their US counterparts can expect a starting salary twice that—from $19,000 to $25,000 according to a survey by Robert Half International Inc., a personnel agency.

In addition to that salary differential, the Japanese claim their programmers are 10 to 15 per cent more productive than their US counterparts because of Japanese investments in program development aids. To widen that margin, they are now building software factories that give their programmers access to even more sophisticated tools.

Computer for Industrial Sector

Toshiba recently completed a factory that employs 3000 software engineers to develop industrial software. Now the company is building a second software factory that will employ 2000 more programmers. "To overcome Japan's language problem and compete with the US," says Toshiba's Kaihatsu, "we have to have productivity double that of the US." NEC Corp., which already spends a significant portion of its annual $400 million software budget on productivity tools, says it will use its productivity and quality advantages to crack the US market. It has hired US software engineers to analyze the needs of US computer users. The resulting lists of requirements are then fed into computers at NEC's Japanese software factories, where programmers write the software. In this fashion, NEC has already started developing commonly used business applications, says Yukio Mizuno, an NEC vice-president. Perhaps the best illustration of the importance the Japanese now attach to software is the move by the Ministry of International Trade & Industry (MITI) to back the industry. MITI has set up several research laboratories to work on software, including a lab that is developing the so-called fifth-generation computer and software. That lab is budgeted to receive $23 million in MITI support this year. The ministry is also giving low-interest loans and tax breaks to software developers.

MITI hopes to boost its fledgling software industry further with a proposed revision in the copyright law.

The ministry is pushing to allow Japanese companies to save money and programming time by making it legal for them to copy portions of existing software products without the permission of the original developers.

Industry observers say the law, if passed, would help the Japanese leapfrog US software companies by enabling them to copy popular US programs and incorporate them into Japanese software products. But even with MITI's help, it will be a long time before Japan's software industry catches up with its US competitors-if it ever does. In 1982, software sales in Japan were only $1.4 billion-just one-quarter of the total US software sales that year.

11

Computer for Kids

Instrumental uses of the computer to help people think have been dramatized in science fiction. Many cultural barriers impede children from making scientific knowledge their own. Among these barriers the most visible are the physically brutal effects of deprivation and isolation. Other barriers are more political. Many children who grow up in our cities are surrounded by the artifacts of science but have good reason to see them as belonging to "the others"; in many cases they are perceived as belonging to the social enemy. Still other obstacles are more abstract, though ultimately of the same nature.

Most branches of the most sophisticated modern culture of Europe and the US are so deeply "mathophobic" that many privileged children are as effectively (if more gently) kept from appropriating science as their own. Space-age objects, in the form of small computers, will cross these cultural barriers to enter the private worlds of children everywhere. They will do so not as mere physical objects. This chapter is about how computers can be carriers of powerful ideas and of the seeds of cultural change, how they can help people form new relationships with knowledge that cut across the traditional lines separating humanities from sciences and knowledge of the self from both of these. It is about using computers to challenge current beliefs about who can understand what and at what age. It is about using computers to question standard assumptions in developmental psychology and in the psychology of aptitudes and attitudes. It is about whether personal computers and the cultures in which they are used will continue to be the creatures of "engineers' alone or whether we can construct intellectual environments in which people who today think of themselves as "humanists" will feel part of, not alienated from, the process of constructing computational cultures.

But there is a world of difference between what computers can do and what society will choose to do with them. Society has many ways to resist fundamental and threatening change. Thus, this book is about facing choices that are ultimately political. It looks at some of the forces of change and of reaction to those forces that are called into play as the computer presence begins to enter the politically charged world of education.

In many schools today, the phrase "computer-aided instruction" means making the computer teach the child. One might say the computer is being used to program the child. The child programs the computer and, in doing so, both acquires a sense of mastery over a piece of the most modern and powerful technology and establishes an intimate contact with some of the deepest ideas from science, from mathematics, and from the art of intellectual model-building.

The learning paths have led hundreds of children to becoming quite sophisticated programmers. Once programming is seen in the proper perspective, there is nothing very surprising about the fact that this should happen. Programming a computer means nothing more or less than communicating to it in a language that it and the human user can both "understand." And learning languages is one of the things children do best. Every normal child learns to talk. Why then should a child not learn to "talk" to a computer? There are many reasons why someone might expect it to be difficult. For example, although babies learn to speak their native language with spectacular ease, most children have great difficulty learning foreign languages in schools and, indeed, often learn the written version of their own language none too successfully. Isn't learning a computer language more like the difficult process of learning a foreign written language than the easy one of learning to speak one's own language? And isn't the problem further compounded by all the difficulties most people encounter learning mathematics?

Two fundamental ideas run through this chapter. The first is that it is possible to design computers so that learning to communicate with them can be a natural process, more like learning French by living in France than like trying to learn it through the unnatural process of American foreign-language instruction in classrooms. Second, learning to communicate with a computer may change the way other learning takes place. The computer can be a mathematics-speaking and an alphabetic speaking entity. We are learning how to make computers with which children love to communicate. When this communication occurs, children learn mathematics as a living language.

Moreover, mathematical communication and alphabetic communication are thereby both transformed from the alien and therefore difficult things they are for most children into natural and therefore easy ones. The idea of "talking mathematics" to a computer can be generalized to a view of learning mathematics in "Mathland"; that is to say, in a context which is to learning mathematics what living in France is to learning French.

It is generally assumed that children cannot learn formal geometry until well into their school years and that most cannot learn it too well even then. But we can quickly see that these assumptions are based on extremely weak evidence by asking analogous questions about the ability of children to learn French. If we had to base our opinions on observation of how poorly children learned French in American schools, we would have to conclude that most people were incapable of mastering it. But we know that all normal children would learn it very easily if they lived in France. Much of what we now see as too "formal" or "too mathematical" will be learned just as easily when children grow up in the computer rich world of the very near future. We use the examination of our relationship with mathematics as a thematic example of how technological and social processes interact in the construction of ideas about human capacities. And mathematical examples will also help to describe a theory of how learning works and of how it goes wrong. Take from Jean Piaget a model of children as builders of their own intellectual structures. Children seem to be innately gifted learners, acquiring long before they go to school a vast quantity of knowledge by a process call "Piagetian learning", or "learning without being taught." For example, children learn to speak, learn the intuitive geometry needed to get around in space, and learn enough of logic and rhetorics to get around parents-all this without being "taught". We must ask why some learning takes place so early and spontaneously while some is delayed many years or does not happen at all without deliberately imposed formal instruction.

Kids' Creation

If we really look at the "child as builder" we are on our way to an answer. All builders need materials to build with. Where we are at variance with Piaget is in the role we attribute to the surrounding cultures as a source of these materials. In some cases the culture supplies them in abundance, thus facilitating constructive Piagetian learning. For example, the fact that so many important things (knives and forks, mothers and fathers, shoes and socks) come in pairs is a "material" for the construction of an intuitive sense of number.

But in many cases where Piaget would explain the slower development of a particular concept by its greater complexity or formality, we see the critical factor as the relative poverty of the culture in those materials that would make the concept simple and concrete. In yet other cases the culture may provide materials but block their use. In the case of formal mathematics, there is both a shortage of' formal materials and a cultural block. The matho-phobia endemic in contemporary culture blocks many people from learning anything they recognize as "math," although they may have no trouble with mathematical knowledge they do not perceive as such.

We shall see again and again that the consequences of mathophobia go far beyond obstructing the learning of mathematics and science. They interact with other endemic "cultural toxins," for example, with popular theories of aptitudes, to contaminate people's images of themselves as learners. Difficulty with school math is often the first step of an invasive intellectual process that leads us all to define ourselves as bundles of aptitudes and inaptitudes, as being "mathematical" or "not mathematical," "artistic" or "not artistic," "musical" or "not musical," "profound" or "superficial," "intelligent" or "dumb."

Deficiency becomes identity and learning is transformed from the early child's free exploration of the world to a chore beset by insecurities and self-imposed restrictions. Two major themes—that children can learn to use computers in a masterful way, and that learning to use computers can change the way they learn everything else—have shaped research agenda on computers and education. The metaphor of imitating the way the child learns to talk has been constantly with us in this work and has led to a vision of education and of education research very different from the traditional ones. For people in the teaching professions, the word "education" tends to evoke "teaching," particularly classroom teaching. The goal of education research tends therefore to be focused on how to improve classroom teaching. But if, the model of successful learning is the way a child learns to talk, a process that takes place without deliberate and organized teaching, the goal set is very different.

The classroom as an artificial and inefficient learning environment that society has been forced to invent because its informal environments fail in certain essential learning domains, such as writing or grammar or school math. The computer presence will enable us to so modify the learning environment outside the classrooms that much if not all the knowledge that schools presently try to teach with such pain and expense and such limited success will be learned, as the child learns to talk, painlessly, successfully and without organized instruction. This obviously implies that schools as we know them today will have no place in the future. But it is an open question whether they will adapt by transforming themselves into something new or will wither away and be replaced.

Although technology will play an essential role in the realization of our vision of the future of education, our central focus is not on the machine but on the mind, and particularly on the way in which intellectual movements and cultures define themselves and grow. Indeed, the role we give to the computer is that of a carrier of cultural "germs" or "seeds" whose intellectual products will not need technological support once they take root in an actively growing mind. Many if not all the children who grow up with a love and aptitude for mathematics owe this feeling, at least in part, to the fact that they happened to acquire "germs" of the "math culture" from adults, who, one might say, knew how to speak mathematics, even if only in the way that Moliere had M. Jourdain speak prose without knowing it. These "math-speaking" adults do not necessarily know how to solve equations; rather, they are marked by a turn of mind that shows up in the logic of their arguments and in the fact that for them to play is often to play with such things as puzzles, puns, and paradoxes. Those children who prove recalcitrant to math and science education include many whose environments happened to be relatively poor in math-speaking adults. Such children come to school lacking elements necessary for the easy learning of school math.

School has been unable to supply these missing elements, and, by forcing the children into learning situations doomed in advance, it generates powerful negative feelings about mathematics and perhaps about learning in general. Thus, is set up a vicious self-perpetuating cycle. For these same children will one day be parents and will not only fail to pass on mathematical germs but will almost certainly infect their children with the opposing and intellectually destructive germs of mathophobia. Fortunately, it is sufficient to break the self-perpetuating cycle at one point for it to remain broken forever.

The Turtle is a computer-controlled cybernetic animal. It exists within the cognitive miniculture of the "LOGO environment," LOGO being the computer language in which communication with the Turtle takes place. The Turtle serves no other purpose than of being good to program and good to think with. Some Turtles are abstract objects that live on computer screens. Others, like the floor Turtles shown in the frontispiece, are physical objects that can be picked up like any mechanical toy. A first encounter often begins by showing the child how a Turtle can be made to move by typing commands at a keyboard. FORWARD 100 makes the Turtle move in a straight line a distance of 100 Turtle steps of about a millimetre each. Typing RIGHT 90 causes the Turtle to pivot in place through 90 degrees. Typing PENDOWN causes the Turtle to lower a pen so as to leave a visible trace of its path, while PENUP instructs it to raise the pen. Of course, the child needs to explore a great deal before gaining mastery of what the numbers mean. But the task is engaging enough to carry most children through this learning process.

The idea of programming is introduced through the metaphor of teaching the Turtle a new word. This is simply done, and children often begin their programming experience by programming the Turtle to respond to new commands invented by the child such as SQUARE or TRIANGLE or SQ or TRI or whatever the child wishes, by drawing the appropriate shapes. New commands, once defined, can be used to define others. For example, just as the house is built out of a triangle and a square, the program for drawing it is built out of the commands for drawing a square and a triangle.

There are four steps in the evolution of this program. From these simple drawings the young programmer can go on in many different directions. Some work on more complex drawings, either figural or abstract. Some abandon the use of the Turtle as a drawing instrument and learn to use its touch sensors to program it to seek out or avoid objects. Later children learn that the computer can be programmed to make music as well as move Turtles and combine the two activities by programming Turtles to dance. Or they can move on from floor Turtles to "screen Turtles," which they program to draw moving pictures in bright colours. The examples are infinitely varied, but in each the child is learning how to exercise control over an exceptionally rich and sophisticated "micro-world".

Readers who have never seen an interactive computer display might find it hard to imagine where this can lead. As a mental exercise they might like to imagine an electronic sketchpad, a computer graphics display of the not-too-distant future. This is a television screen that can display moving pictures in colour. You can also "draw" on it, giving it instructions, perhaps by typing, perhaps by speaking, or perhaps by pointing with a wand.

On request, a palette of colours could appear on the screen. You can choose a colour by pointing at it with the wand. Until you change your choice, the wand draws in that colour. Up to this point the distinction from traditional art materials may seem slight, but the distinction becomes very real when you begin to think about editing the drawing. You can "talk to your drawing" in computer language. You can "tell" it to replace this colour with that. Or set a drawing in motion. Or make two copies and set them in counter-rotating motion. Or replace the colour palette with a sound palette and "draw" a piece of music.

You can file your work in computer memory and retrieve it at your pleasure, or have it delivered into the memory of any of the many millions of other computers linked to the central communication network for the pleasure of your friends. That all this would be fun needs no argument. But it is more than fun. Very powerful kinds of learning are taking place. Children working with an electronic sketchpad are learning a language for talking about shapes and fluxes of shapes, about velocities and rates of change, about processes and procedures. They are learning to speak mathematics, and are acquiring a new image of themselves as mathematicians.

Some of the children were highly successful in school, some were diagnosed as emotionally or cognitively disabled. Some of the children were so severely afflicted by cerebral palsy that they had never purposefully manipulated physical objects. Some of them had expressed their talents in "mathematical" forms, some in "verbal" forms, and some in artistically "visual" or in "musical" forms. Of course, these children did not achieve a fluency in programming that came close to matching their use of spoken language. If we take the Mathland metaphor seriously, their computer experience was more like learning French by spending a week or two on vacation in France than like living there. But like children who have spent a vacation with foreign-speaking cousins, they were clearly on their way to "speaking computer."

When we have thought about what these studies mean we are left with two clear impressions. First, that all children will, under the right conditions, acquire a proficiency with programming that will make it one of their more advanced intellectual accomplishments. Second, that the "right conditions" are very different from the kind of access to computers that is now becoming established as the norm in schools.

The conditions necessary for the kind of relationships with a computer that we will be writing about in this book require more and freer access to the computer than educational planners currently anticipate. And they require a kind of computer language and a learning environment around that language very different from those the schools are now providing. They even require a kind of computer rather different from those that the schools are currently buying. It will take most of this chapter to convey some sense of the choices among computers, computer languages, and, more generally, among computer cultures, that influence how well children will learn from working with computation and what benefits they will get from doing so. But the question of the economic feasibility of free access to computers for every child can be dealt with immediately.

Our vision of a new kind of learning environment demands free contact between children and computers. This could happen because the child's family buys one or a child's friends have one. For purposes of discussion here (and to extend our discussion to all social groups) let us assume that it happens because schools give every one of their students his or her own powerful personal computer. Most "practical" people (including parents, teachers, school principals, and foundation administrators) react to this idea in much the same way: "Even if computers could have all the effects, you talk about, it would still be impossible to put your ideas into action. Where would the money come from?" What these people are saying needs to be faced squarely. They are wrong. Let's consider the cohort of children who will enter kindergarten in the coming year, the "Class of 2010," and let's do some arithmetic. The direct public cost of schooling a child for thirteen years, from kindergarten through twelfth grade, is over $20,000 today (and for the class of 2000, it may be closer to $30,000).

A conservatively high estimate of the cost of supplying each of these children with a personal computer with enough power for it to serve the kinds of educational ends described in this book, and of upgrading, repairing, and replacing it when necessary would be about $1000 per student, distributed over 13 years in school. Thus, "computer costs" for the class of 2000 would represent only about 5 per cent of the total public expenditure on education, and this would be the case even if nothing else in the structure of educational costs changed because of the computer presence.

But in fact computers in education stand a good chance of making other aspects of education cheaper. Schools might be able to reduce their cycle from 13 years to 12 years; they might be able to take advantage of the greater autonomy the computer gives the students and increase the size of classes by one or two students without decreasing the personal attention each student is given. Either of these two moves would "recuperate" the computer cost. Our goal is not educational economies: it is not to use computation to save a year off the time a child spends in an otherwise unchanged school or to push an extra child into an elementary school classroom.

General Impact

George Mamunes, 14, a gangling ninth-grader dressed in flannel shirt, blue jeans and hiking boots, knits his thick, dark eyebrows while putting the finishing touches on a computer program, already nearly 300 lines long. For those uninitiated in the special languages of the computer age, it looks like a hopeless mess of numerical gibberish. But when completed, these instructions should produce a computer image of the heart detailed enough to show every major artery and vein, as well as valves and chambers.

The electronic heart is part of a teaching tool George is putting together for eighth-grade biology classes. A few feet away sits Pam Miller, 14, a ninth-grader with long, brown hair draped far down her back. She is operating a computer program or software that simulates the workings of a nuclear reactor. Today she is fine-tuning the section that governs the control rods, those regulators of the reactor's nuclear fires. Tapping away at the keyboard, Pam explains: "You have to maximize the power output without destroying the reactor." Suddenly, flashing numbers burst upon the screen. "There," says Pam, her face lighting up. "Reactor overheated. Power output low. Reactor core damaged. Melt-down!" A disaster that she has brought on intentionally, just to show how it could happen.

Other disciples, seated at terminals scattered around the room, are no less absorbed. Meilin Wong, 15, chic in blue velour blouse, jeans and Bass moccasins, is trying to figure out what went wrong with her business data management program. She is an old hand at such troubleshooting, having spent much of last semester "debugging" a program that, when printed-out, stretches over 30 ft. Jim McGuire, 13, is creating a video game called Spaceship, which will let electronic star warriors zap a boxy- looking orbital intruder.

A more mundane program is emerging from 15 year old Dave McCann's terminal: a verb test for seventh and eighth-grade Spanish classes. Off in a corner two youngsters are putting the impish face of *Mad* magazine's cartoon hero, Alfred E. Neuman, onto the computer screen. Says Muller, as he presides proudly over these after-hours computer converts: "No one told them they have to be here. They're not usually doing assignments. They're experimenting. They're letting their imaginations run free." Muller's disciples are not all math whizzes. Or straight - A students. Or particularly precocious. They are reasonably normal youngsters who have grown up with computers. For them, in ways that few people over 30 can understand, manipulating these complex machines is as natural as riding a bike, playing baseball or even solving Rubik's cube. Like thousands of others across the country, they are part of a revolutionary vanguard: the computer generation. Not only is this generation propelling traditional education down promising avenues, it is tugging at the entire social fabric, foreshadowing changes at least as startling and momentous as those ushered in by a new generation of automobile users more than a half-century ago.

In the classroom, where youngsters are being introduced to the machines as early as kindergarten, they astound-and often outpace-their teachers with their computer skills. After school they gather at the mushrooming number of computer stores (more than 1500 at last count) or join the computer clubs that are becoming a regular part of the youthful landscape. Huddling around any available machine, they argue over their programs, solve computer problems and swap software as intensely as kids once haggled over baseball cards.

In the summer, they may even go off to computer camps, another growth industry, and if they are Boy Scouts, they may try for a computer merit badge. During mischievous moments, they may tinker with one another's programs, writing in steps that will flash an unexpected insult or obscenity across a buddy's video screen. Some try to pick the encoded electronic locks on copyrighted software, taking glee in outwitting their elders, or spin fanciful plots to break into computer networks.

A few turn their skills to profit by showing baffled businessmen how to get idle, new computers to run, or by establishing Delaware based corporations to market their own software creations. To the bafflement of their parents, they talk in a jargon of their own ("Hey, Charlie, you should have POKED instead of PEEKED"). As with so many other changes in contemporary life, the spark for this revolution is technological: a bit of silicon sophistication variously known as the personal, home or microcomputer. No larger than an attache case, apart from its video screen, this mighty mite packs the computing power of machines that two decades ago occupied a full room. Yet the microsi as they are affectionately called, are a relative bargain to buy and are becoming steadily cheaper.

Many models cost under $1000, bringing them within reach of schools, parents or the children themselves. Last week, in the sharpest price break yet, Timex announced it will begin selling a small home computer for a suggested retail price of $99.95. But size and price cannot explain why computers have taken such a strong hold on so many youngsters. Certainly their interest has been stirred by a related rage, video games, whose computer-generated flashes, zaps, and pings have not only all the appeal pinball machines had for their elders but go a significant step further: they pique young minds to learn more about all that electronic prestidigitation. But many experts, and most of the young operatives, agree that the overwhelming attraction of the machines is the lure of control, the pleasure of being able to think out and then make something happen, a satisfaction all too often denied children.

Recognized by students and teachers, alike as his school's best computer programmer, Lewis works afternoons as an instructor for a computer consulting firm, introducing younger children to the machines. Last year his employers sent him to Chicago, where he displayed his special teaching gifts before a meeting of educators. As Lewis told *Time* correspondent Peter Stoler, "we love these machines. I've got all this power at my fingertips. Without computers, we don't know what do be. With them, I'm somebody."

Perhaps because of the faintly macho side of computers, the bug seems to strike many more boys than girls in the pre-adolescent years. Says Steve Siegelbaum, Lewis's teacher: "Maybe it's because boys are pushed more toward math and logic than girls are. Maybe it's because boys are just more aggressive." Paradoxically, the computer passion is often stirred in youngsters who seem least likely to be interested in high tech. Jay Harstad, 12, of Minnetonka, Minn., litters his house with poems and sketches but will do almost anything to avoid doing his math homework. Yet Jay is one of the Gatewood Elementary School's premier computerniks and regu-larly helps teachers introduce fourth-graders to the machines. At West High School in Wausau, Wis., Chris Schumann, 16, a junior, has made a name for himself by translating musical notes into digital form and getting a computer to play Bach and Vivaldi through its loudspeaker. Originally, Chris regarded computers as remote and forbidding, but that changed when he was introduced to his first micro. "It looked real friendly," he says. "It didn't overpower you. It wasn't this ominous thing but something you could get close to."

The closeness can be contagious. Explains Nick Newman, 15, Muller's chief disciple at Ridgewood: "The more you do on the machine, the more enjoyable it gets. It becomes habit-forming." In Alpena, Mich., youngsters who had learned computer skills in junior high were devastated when they got to senior high school and found too few machines to go around. Says Alpena Elementary School principal Burt Wright: "I've got high school kids begging to come in after school and use our machine." The truly addicted-known half scornfully, half admiringly as computer nerds-may drop out almost entirely from the everyday world. In Lexington, Mass., one legendary 16-year-old nerd got so deeply immersed in computers that he talked to no one, headed straight to his terminal after school and barely sat down for meals.

The only way his father could get him away from the terminal was to go down to the cellar and throw the house's main power switch, cutting off all electricity. Barry Porter, 14, of San Francisco, is a computer-age truant, so attached to the machine that he often skips school, rarely reads anything other than computer manuals and hangs out with his pals in the Market Street computer store, often plotting some new electronic scam. Barry (not his real name) currently boasts an illicit library of about 1000 pirated (i.e. illegally copied) programs worth about $50,000 at retail prices, including such software gems as VisiCalc, the popular business management and planning program. Before security was tightened up, he regularly plugged his computer into such distant databanks as the Source (which provides news bulletins, stock prices, etc.) via telephone without paying a cent.

Computer Generation

No one can say exactly when the computer generation began-certainly not earlier than the 1960s, when computers began appearing in schools. But even computer whizzes in their twenties are acutely aware of how soon they are likely to be outstripped by today's grade schoolers. Says Steven Jobs, the multimillionaire co-founder of Apple Computer Inc.: "These kids know more about the new software than we do." New York computer executive Charles Lecht goes further: "If you were born before 1965, boy, you're going to be out of it." Where their parents fear to tread, the microkids plunge right in, no more worried about pushing incorrect buttons or making errors than adults are about dialing a wrong telephone number. Says mathematician Louis Robinson, IBM's resident computer sage: "They know what computers can and cannot do, while adults still regard them as omnipotent." Hughes Aircraft Chairman Allen Puckett, who used to share an Apple with son Jim, 12 said: "A lot of adults grew up in a-slide-rule world and still reject computers. But computers are as natural to kids as milk and cookies."

More and more members of the computer generation are tasting the heady pleasure of teaching their own teachers how to use the machines and, if they are lucky enough to have computers at home, instructing their parents as well. Says Ridgewood's Newman, a regular teacher of teachers: "It's a sort of mutual doorway. The barriers between adult and child, between teacher and student, are broken, and it's person to person. Nobody's looking down on anyone; they're looking each other right in the eye." Often adults find it easier to ask a child how to do something than to ask another adult. Says University of Kansas education professor Mary Kay Corbitt: "One adult student of mine brought her son to computer class, and we discovered that he was doing her assignment while she watched. Two weeks later she overcame her anxieties and was participating fully." Confronted with the strange and unsettling world of the computer, teachers can get a useful perspective on what it is like to be a student again. After taking part in an elementary course in programming, Lois Brown, 54, a Wausau grade-school teacher, is thoroughly chastened. "Now we realize how little kids feel when there's a concept they don't understand. We sat in that course not wanting anyone to know all the things we didn't understand." Despite their obvious wariness of computers, parents are taking the lead in getting them into the schools. In Florida, communities have staged cake and candy sales, carnivals and tree plantings, weekend car washes, even a bike-athon to raise funds to buy computers. Says Marilyn Neff of Miami: "We feel computers will be the new paper and pencil." Of the 250 computers in the schools of Utica, Mich., more than two-thirds have been purchased by parent-sponsored fund drives. Says Utica Principal Paul Yelinsky: "Moms and dads are coming in and telling the counsellors they have to get their kids in computer classes because it's the wave of the future." So important is computer literacy that the Alfred P. Sloan Foundation is beginning a major program to get even such traditional liberal arts schools as

St John's College in Maryland to begin giving courses in it. Though many schools began purchasing computers with federal aid budget cutbacks are drying up that well. Apple's jobs points out that other nations, especially Britain, France and the Soviet Union though surprisingly not the electronics-minded Japanese are paying far more attention to computer education than is the US. Earlier this year, Jobs persuaded California Congressman Pete Stark and Missouri Senator John Danforth to introduce bills in Congress that would allow computer manufacturers to take a hefty tax write-off for any machines they donate to elementary and high schools. Under the present law, full deductions for such scientific equipment are allowed only if it is given to colleges and universities.

Steve Jobs originally spoke of giving an Apple to every public elementary and secondary school in the country, more than 80,000 computers worth as much as $200 million retail. He thought private schools should be included and encouraged other manufacturers to join in the program as well. Meanwhile, Apple's archrival, the Tandy Corp., maker of the Radio Shack computer line, is taking a different tack: it has pledged $500,000 in equipment to spur development of educational programming, or courseware, for the classroom. Many of the approximately 100,000 computers now in US schools-roughly one for every 400 students-are in affluent suburbs like Ridgewood, a national leader in computer education. But the machines are also found in the unlikeliest of places. On a Chippewa Indian reservation in Wisconsin, computers are being used by young members of the tribe to learn their ancient and nearly forgotten language. Alaska's small rural schools have been ordering computers to meet a special need: they allow students of different ages and abilities in the same small classrooms to learn at their own pace. Dubuque, Iowa, the New Yorker founding editor Harold Ross disdainfully located his provincial old lady, has 13 machines and another 20 on order. Bill Holloway, a professor of, computer education at the University of Kansas, calls the spread of small computers in the classroom nothing less than an avalanche. According to various industry studies, there may be from 300,000 to 650,000 computers in the schools by 1985.

So far, the most common, and least interesting, way to use school computers is in direct drill and review. The machine simply quizzes, prods and grades the student, very much like a robot teacher. Hundreds of programs of this type are available for popular computers like the Apple II Plus, Radio Shack's TRS-80 and the Commodore PET. But many of these programs are little more than computerized rehashes of the old classroom flash cards that go back to the days of McGuffey's readers. One notable difference: today when the student answers correctly, the screen will light up with WOWS, HOORAYS or smiling animals. Wrong answers may produce sad or scowling faces, perhaps accompanied by a falling tear. Partly because of teachers' fears of the machines and for their jobs and partly because of the poor quality of software, the frequently heralded electronic revolution in the classroom has been slow to occur. Now, however, it is being pushed along by steady improvements in teaching programs, thanks to imaginative enterprises like the Minnesota Educational Computing Consortium.

One of its more refreshing drills: a program called Wrong Note, which helps teach sight reading of musical scores. As a simple tune emanates from the computer's loudspeaker, matching notes appear on the screen, but sometimes the quiz intentionally errs and obliges students to find the false note. In order to do so, they can order up a repetition of the tune as often as Bogie and company did in Casablanca. Says Kenneth Brumbaugh, director of the consortium's instructional services: "Imagine asking a teacher to play it again and again!" Even very young children can profit from such exercises. At the Nordstom Elementary School in Morgan Hill, Calif., a suburb of San Jose, Colin Devenish, 7, is working with a classmate on the arithmetic drill, honing his skills in addition and subtraction. Unlike youngsters doing such drilling in the past, Colin seems to be enjoying himself enormously. Why? "Because," he replies mischievously within earshot of his teacher, "the computer doesn't yell."

Computers, operated only by touching a few buttons, are also remarkably effective devices for educating the handicapped. At the California School for the Deaf in Fremont, Rhonda Revera, 16, has worked with computers for five years, studying every subject from fractions to spelling. Rhonda offers a paean to the machine in sign language: "Computer makes me remember. It is fast, easy and better than writing on paper." Still another important use of computers is as a remedial tool. One is a spelling drill with a special incentive built into it: if all the answers are correct, a video game pops onto the screen as a reward. When one youngster worked his way through the drill, even classroom hecklers were impressed. Said one: "Hey, Old Wentworth's getting better." More entertaining and demanding are think tank-type strategy games like Geography Search, which launches competing teams on a Columbus-like voyage of exploration. They must make their way across the Atlantic, taking into account currents and winds, finding their longitude and latitude by means of star patterns and the length of a shadow thrown by a stick at high noon (methods that worked for Columbus, after all), and coping with such unforeseen perils as an outbreak of scurvy, an attack by pirates and a tropical storm. Only shrewd planning, wise choices and cooperative action ensure survival. The simulated voyage becomes uncannily real to the participants. Says the game's creator, Thomas Snyder, 31, who heads Computer Learning Connection, Inc., of Cambridge, Mass.: "When they get near the end and the computer finally shows them another ship near by, they act as if they had actually spotted a ship at sea."

Until a few years ago, the few computers available in secondary schools were essentially "dumb" terminals linked by telephone lines to a large, centrally located machine that served a variety of users through an arrangement called time-sharing. All the courseware was stored in the big computer's powerful memory, which could be tapped at will by students and teachers. The most successful example of such a system-and the one still used by Wisconsin's Chippewa Indians-is PLATO (for Programmed Logic for Automatic Teaching Operations).

Developed in the 1960s by the University of Illinois and Control Data Corp., PLATO is an exemplary teacher containing more than 8000 hours of courseware, much of it in a continuous curriculum. Thus, if a youngster forgets a point from an earlier lesson, PLATO will search its prodigious memory and patiently recapitulate. But such time-sharing schemes are extremely expensive, since they require open lines to the central computer. They also can become backed up at peak hours, and do not always lend themselves readily to what is the most intellectually demanding use of the computer: learning how to program it. For this, the inexpensive, easy-to-operate personal computer, entirely self-contained and relying on equipment immediately at the student's side, is an ideal instrument-much more "user-friendly," as manufacturers like to say, than big machines. Yet even with a handy micro, programming can overwhelm the uninitiated. The programmer and computer must "speak" a common language. In the early days of the digital computer, this was, extremely difficult.

The machine reduces all the information it receives, whether it arrives as letters, numbers or graphic symbols, into the simplest possible electronic statements: either a yes or a no, represented by pulses of high or low voltage. To command the machine in its own internal language meant writing out endless strings of ones or zeroes, called bits and bytes, symbolizing those yes or no statements. But scientists soon began creating alternate languages for communicating with the machines that vaguely resemble everyday speech. The most popular of these computer tongues is BASIC (for Beginner's All-purpose Symbolic Instruction Code).

Developed at Dartmouth by mathematician John Kemeny and his colleague Thomas Kurtz to let even the least mathematically gifted student converse with the university's computers, it is "understood" by virtually all of today's personal computers. To show just how easy the language is, Kemeny offers this extremely simple lesson in programming: tell the computer to find the square roots (i.e., the numbers that, when multiplied by themselves, yield the original numbers) of eleven successive values, say 20 through 30.

The entire operation can be accomplished for a program of just four steps:

```
1 FOR N= 20 TO 30

2 PRINT N, SQR(N)

3 NEXT N

4 END
```

Translated into everyday language, the first line tells the computer to let N stand successively for 20 through 30. The second instructs the machine to print the first value of N (that is, the number 20), compute its square root (SQR) and print out the result. The third tells the computer to go on to each of the succeeding values all the way through 30. Finally, the program tells the computer to call it a day, its job having been done. Even the smallest machine can do such calculations in a flash, compared with the hours of work they might require of human computers. To preserve their creativity, the students can readily store their programs on magnetic tape or on a small, 45 rpm-size plastic record called a floppy disc—which is not, as some parents believe, a new form of back injury. Then when the occasion arises for using the program again, the computer operator merely loads the instructions back into the machine and punches in some new values for N.

The same broad principles apply to the creation of all software, even complex simulations like Geography Search. Literal-minded brutes that they are, computers do exactly what they are told. No more and no less. But youngsters of even the most tender age are surprising educators by showing they can master the beasts with startling ease. Computer software expert Leona Schauble of the Children's Television Workshop (producers of Sesame Street) recalls getting an eight-year-old boy at Manhattan's Little Red School House started on a simple computer game.

The game generated an image of a frog that would leap up and catch a butterfly, provided the right buttons were hit. After a few minutes, she checked back and found the frog jumping in slow motion. When she asked the youngster what happened, he replied, "Well, we wanted to make the frog catch more butterflies. So we got a listing of the variables and slowed him down." In other words, the youngster had broken into the game's program and changed it to suit himself.

To instruct very young children, even Kemeny's BASIC is much too mathematical. Instead, more and more schools are turning to an innovative computer language called LOGO (from the Greek word for reason), developed by Seymour Papert and his colleagues at MIT. A mathematician who studied with the Swiss psychologist Jean Piaget, Papert has become something of a guru of the computer generation, predicting that the machines will revolutionize learning by taking much of the mystery out of mathematics, science and technology. Says he: "The computer can make the most abstract things concrete."

With a deceptively simple set of commands, LOGO enables youngsters who know nothing of geometry and algebra, and barely know how to read, to manipulate a triangular figure, dubbed the Turtle, on a computer screen and trace all manner of shapes with it. At the Lamplighter School in Dallas, teachers using LOGO get youngsters of three or four to write simple computer instructions. In one game, they manoeuvre "cars" and "garages" on the computer screen in such a way that the cars are parked inside the garages. While playing with LOGO, the youngsters learn simple words, the difference between left and right, and geometric concepts that they would not ordinarily encounter until junior high.

The machines crop up in the lives of youngsters even before they enter school-and sometimes before they learn to walk or talk-in the guise of such siliconised gadgetry as Little Professor and Speak & Spell. With a few presses of the button, these computerized games produce flashing lights, squealing sounds and disembodied voices that inculcate the rudiments of spelling and calculating. A record of sorts may have been set by Corey Schou, a computer scientist at the University of Central Florida in Orlando: he rigged up a home computer so his five-month-old daughter could operate it by pressing buttons in her crib and changing the designs on a nearby screen. Says the proud papa: "Basically, it's an electronic kaleidoscope, another diversion, another learning device." Whatever it is, it prepares youngsters for all those buttons they will encounter soon enough in and out of school. Parents and teachers may shudder at the thought, but it is only a short hop from skilful operation of a video game to learning fundamentals of programming. Says MIT Sociologist Sherry Turkle, 33, who has been studying the youthful computer culture for five years: "The line between game playing and programming is very thin. Programming takes what is powerful about games this articulation of knowledge, this learning about strategy and carries it to a higher level of power." By the time the youthful programmers reach the eighth or ninth grade, their skills may reach a marketable level. In Chicago, Jonathan Dubman, 14, and Kay Borzsony, 13, have formed a company called Aristotle Software to sell their own computer games and graphics programs. Says Kay: "The nice thing about the computer business is that there is no real bias against children. In the computer magazines, you read articles by 12 and 13 year-olds." Laura Hyatt, 15, of Ridgewood, helps a stymied local insurance office figure out how to use its software. Says she: "It's better than babysitting." And, at $3.50 an hour, somewhat more profitable.

The prodigy of prodigies may be Eugene Volokh, 14, of Los Angeles. A Russian emigre, he earns $480 each week by doing 24 hours of programming for 20th Century-Fox, while carrying a full load of courses as a junior at UCLA. This year Greg Christensen, 18, of Anaheim, Calif., could make $100,000 in royalties from a video game he developed that was bought by Atari. Other youngsters are waiting at the sidelines in hopes of catching up with these young entrepreneurs. Every Tuesday night, Scott Whitfield, 13, and his brother Shawn, 11, appear at the Menlo Park, Calif., public library to get computer instruction. Says Scott: "We'll probably never get a job if we don't learn how to use a computer." Not all youngsters take equally to the machines. In a typical computer class, only about one in five students becomes seriously involved. Says Steven Scott, 16, of Wausau's West High: "Either you get the hang of it or you don't." Even so dedicated a computernik as Ridgewood's Nick Newman finds programming interesting only for a purpose. His own goal is to apply his computer knowledge to a career in science or medicine. Whatever these youngsters make of their computer experiences, they will surely confront the world differently from their parents.

The precise, orderly steps of logic required to use and program the machines promise to shape-and sharpen-the thought processes of the computer generation. Indeed, the youngsters playing all those strategy games are doing precisely what corporations do when they plan to launch a new product, or what military leaders do when they devise strategies to confront a potential foe.

Whether such abilities will change the world for the better is another matter. Princeton psychologist George Miller, for one, has doubts that "a few years of thinking like a computer can change patterns of irrational thought that have persisted throughout recorded history."

Other social critics ask if clear thinking is enough - if, in fact, there might not be a danger in raising a generation to believe that it has the analytical tools to contemplate any problem. Says MIT computer science professor Joseph Weizenbaum: "There's a whole world of real problems, of human problems, which is essentially being ignored." It is still impossible, after all, to reduce a human relationship to a printout or to solve a moral question by bits and bytes.

Some critics predict a future not unlike that portrayed in Isaac Asimov's I, *Robot,* a science fiction novel set in a society so thoroughly computer-dominated that the people cannot do arithmetic. Humanist critic George Steiner acerbically calls the computer generation the advance guard of a breed of "computer-mutants." Says Steiner: "They will be out of touch with certain springs of human identity and creativity, which belong to the full use of language rather than mathematical and symbolical codes."

Many others are much more sanguine. University of Chicago philosopher of science Stephen Toulmin predicts that computers will "re-intellectualize" the television generation. "TV relieved people of the necessity to do anything," says Toulmin. "Computers depend on what you do yourself." Catholic theologian David Tracy argues that "using computers sharpens the mind's ability to deal with our world: the world of technology." The final word may be simpler, and not pronounced by elders who find a devilish soul in the new machine. More so than adults, the young know the computer for what it is. Says a 10-year-old at Manhattan's Bank Street School: "It's dumb. We have to tell it everything." They also know something important is afoot. Says Shawn Whitfield: "When I grow up it's going to be the Computer Age.

12

Manufacturing Computers

In Japan manufacturing productivity is currently growing at the rate of 4.1 per cent a year. France and Germany have manufacturing productivity growth rates of 4.9 and 5.0 per cent a year, respectively. Meanwhile, in the US the rate of growth in manufacturing productivity has fallen sharply. From 1969 to 1973, output per man-hour increased at a compound rate of 2.9 per cent. From 1973 to 1979, the gains dwindled to 1.6 per cent a year. In the US the program to reverse this productivity pattern significantly must rely on the continued development of advanced technology and its application.

Perhaps the most important element in this reliance on innovation is increased factory automation and a growing use of computers and microprocessor technology in manufacturing. Today, we are on the technological and sociological edge of a dramatic increase in the use of computers in our factories. This will have a profound impact on the nation's productivity growth in the next decade. Within the next 10 to 15 years, four evolutionary trends will meet on the factory floor: (1) the increasing power and simplification of computers, (2) a widespread appreciation of the practicality of computerized manufacturing and robotic applications, (3) a new realization of the impact of computers on people and of people on computers, and (4) a growing awareness of the urgent need for manufacturing innovation in our society.

Many computerized factory systems exist today as islands of automation. The immediate task of the scientific and technical communities is to use the increased power and simplicity of computers to link these elements into an integrated system. Making use of low-cost computer hardware to perform more and more jobs will make such an integrated factory system economically viable. Some difficult technical problems remain. We must develop gene-rally accepted, standardized interfaces between computerized design engineering and computerized manufacturing, between individual machines and machining centers, and between computers and the people using them.

We must also refine the present state of application technology and reduce the cost of the factory automated system through the increased use of computers. Advances in factory automation are dependent on advances in computer technology.

Technology on Rise

The technological changes in the computer field during the past several years clearly equal any technological change that has occurred in our society over the past 100 years. The introduction of high-performance, low-cost microprocessor and storage technology has dramatically improved and enhanced the functions and capabilities of computer software and hardware. With today's increased power, manufacturing computer systems can be made more adaptable to the manufacturing environment, thus cutting systems engineering costs and time per installation. The cost of computer hardware itself has been steadily declining. This trend will continue with the introduction of new technologies such as very high-performance microprocessor chips based on very large scale integration (VLSI). On the other hand, the cost of the human and software resources for systems engineering and programming has gone up. In 1955, 85 per cent of the total cost for processing information was hardware; it is estimated that by 1985 hardware will account for only 15 per cent of this total cost. To improve manufacturing productivity we must reverse this trend by optimizing the use of our human resources and taking advantage of the increased computer power and reduced hardware costs. The need to make increased use of available computer power is heightened by the decline in available technical manpower.

The National Science Foundation found the annual growth rate of scientific and R&D personnel between 1954 and 1969 to be

5.9 per cent. Some 5,56,000 employees were involved in technical work in 1969, but the number fell to 5,17,000 in 1973 and then grew to only 6,10,000 by 1980s – a rate of only 2.8 per cent annually. The increased capability of computer technology and broad availability of application software packages, including the expanded use of problem-oriented languages and database software, can reduce the cost of program development and maintenance by a factor of 10.

The graphics capabilities of engineering computers can link integrated design and drafting systems to manufacturing systems. With these "user-friendly" approaches to provide a bridge between man and computer, the user can interact directly with the manufacturing system without traditional interfaces and jargon-heavy manuals. Computers and the applications they support can now be considered for functions or activities that only recently were impractical. The opportunity for the application of this technology, for all practical purposes, is unlimited.

More Effective in Operations

Advances in the two primary elements of factory computerization-computer-aided design (CAD) and computer-aided manufacturing (CAM) will create a new industrial revolution. By integrating design with manufacturing, we can not only turn out new product designs much faster, but also program the computer to make sure the designs provide quality and reliability as well as the lowest possible manufacturing costs. CAD/CAM is the integrated use of advanced computer technology in engineering and manufacturing. It is a common database of part and product geometry and related information which makes it easier to translate a creative idea into a final product at a reduced cost. With CAD, a user can define a part shape, analyse stresses and other factors, check mechanical actions, and automatically produce engineering drawings from a graphics terminal. When CAD is combined with the CAM system, the user can also manipulate nongraphic data such as bills of material, shop information, and cost factors.

The end result is greater design flexibility and what is referred to as designing to cost. The CAD functions can be grouped in four categories: design and geometric modelling, engineering analysis, kinematics, and drafting.

– In *design and geometric* modelling, the designer describes the shape of a structure with a geometric model constructed graphically on a cathode-ray tube. The computer converts this picture into a mathematical model, which is stored in the computer database for later use. Many other design functions depend heavily on the model. It can, for example, be used to create a finite-element model for stress analysis, serve as input for automated drafting to make a drawing, or be used to create numerical control tapes for the factory.

– After the geometric model has been created, the engineer can easily calculate such things as weight, volume, surface area, moment of inertia, or center of gravity of a part. But the most powerful method of analysing a structure is probably finite-element analysis. In this technique, the structure is broken down into a network of simple elements that the computer uses to determine stresses, deflections, and other structural characteristics. The designer can see how the structure will behave before it is built and can modify it without building costly physical models and prototypes. This procedure can be expanded to a complete systems model, and the operation of a product can be simulated.

– With *computer kinematics*, the user can examine the effects of moving parts on other parts of the structure or design and can analyse more complex mechanisms.

– Finally, the CAD system automatically drafts drawings for use in manufacturing.

Computer-aided design is a good example of the transition of expensive, state-of-the-art computer technology to a commercial, economically justifiable system. Recent advances in CAD technology have increased the productivity and effectiveness of design engineering groups. Such systems will be even more common in the next five to ten years. Manufacturing groups can draw on the geometric and numerically coded description produced by CAD to create numerical control tapes, which allow direct computer control of shop machines, determine process plans and scheduling, instruct robots, computerize testing, and in general improve the management of plant operations.

Computer-aided manufacturing has five main functions: tool design, machine control, process and materials planning, robotics, and factory management.

- Manufacturing engineering and *tool design* deals with the machines and fixtures needed to make a new product. In effect, the set of machines, tooling, and fixtures is a new product, and all the techniques of CAD are used in fashioning it. The CAD techniques are then used to simulate plant operation and the integration of machines and materials handling.
- *Machine automation* consists of a chain of increasingly sophisticated control techniques. At the lower end of the spectrum are fixed automation with relays or cams and programmable controllers, where relays have been replaced by electronics. Moving up the spectrum, numerical control (NC) refers to controlling a machine with prerecorded, numerically coded information to fabricate a part. In this case, the machine is hardwired and not readily reprogrammed. In computer numerical control (CNC) the machine is directly controlled by a mini-computer, which stores the machining instructions as software that is relatively easy to reprogram. Because of the computer control, CNC has the advantages of much higher storage capability and increased flexibility. Virtually all numerical control is computer-based, yet only ten years ago CNC was an expensive exception.
- *Process planning* considers the detailed sequence of production steps from start to finish. The process plan describes the state of the workpiece at each work station. An important element in process planning is group technology, in which similar parts are organized into families to allow standardized fabrication steps; this

permits significant savings by avoiding duplicate tooling and systems engineering. Most automated process-planning systems use a retrieval technique based on part families and existing databases for standard tool in and fabrication processes. Materials planning or manufacturing resource planning is concerned with the precise flow and timing of manpower, materials, and processes; it is a detailed look at how everything comes together. The ultimate goal is to have continuous use of all production equipment, no bottlenecks, and a minimum inventory.

– Because they are widely applicable, *robots* have a distinct advantage over specialized, highly engineered manufacturing systems. The economic advantage of a mass-produced, readily adaptable robot over a one-of-a-kind system with a great deal of engineering content is obvious. Robots are now being used to perform materials -handling functions in CAM systems. They can select and position tools and workpieces for NC or CNC tools, operate tools such as drills and welders, or perform test and inspection functions. Through visual or tactile sensors, the robot can manipulate objects. Through its computer intelligence, it can inspect the object and provide the machine with corrective feedback or actually reprogram the machine or change the tooling.

– *Factory management* coordinates the operations of an entire plant. Factory management systems tie together individual machine tools, test stations, robots, and materials-handling systems into manufacturing cells and the cells into an integrated whole. An integrated CAM system of this sort is usually hierarchical, with Microprocessors handling specific machining functions or robot operation, middle-level computers controlling the operation and work scheduling of one or more manufacturing cells, and a large central computer controlling the overall system.

Reliability is greatly improved by structuring the control system correctly. Local, distributed control (with defined responsibilities) reports up to a supervisory control that, in turn, is linked to a managerial computer. This parallels the structure of the typical industrial Organisation.

Ultimately, the digital output from the CAD computer will be simply plugged into the CAM system to reprogram the plant's manufacturing computers. In such an integrated system, the databases will be organized in a way that avoids redundancy and reformatting of information. And any change in one part of the system will automatically revise dependent or related information in other parts of the system. Bridging the CAM and CAD systems will be one of our major jobs in the future. A fundamental difference that has to be reconciled is that CAD makes use of a pictorial, graphics oriented computer database, while CAM involves a great deal of text-oriented information. In other words, we need to find a way for the computer doing the drawing to speak the same language as the computer directing the manufacturing plant. Layering is one way to link these systems.

Layering is a particular technique for structuring the CAD and CAM databases. It enables various people to input data without losing control of the overall design and manufacturing process. Equally important, it enables shop people to see information that is meaningful to them without having to sort through and understand the rest of the information that is normally included in a drawing. To do this, all information is organized in an arrangement resembling layers, or slices, inside the database. The engineer or users in other departments of an Organisation can provide pertinent information or examine any or all layers of information according to their particular needs. As an example, a printed circuit board may have 250 to 300 layers of information.

A manufacturing engineer inputs layers of information that deal with fabrication and assembly. In turn, machine operators concerned with the details of the drilling and cutting configuration may access layers dealing with this part of the drawing. Other layers provide information pertinent to the needs of the purchasing department or component assemblers. Another major effort to integrate computer systems is an Air Force program called ICAM (integrated computer-aided manufacturing). This is a practical attempt to greatly shorten the time span for the implementation of compatible and standardized computer-manufacturing techniques and to provide a unified direction for industry.

The ICAM program provides seed money for the establishment, within private industry, of modular subsystems designed to computerize and tie together various phases of design, fabrication, and distribution processes and their associated management hierarchy. As appropriate, these mutually compatible modules will be combined to demonstrate a comprehensive control and management package capable of continual adjustment as production needs and the state of the art change.

The ICAM program is divided into five major parts.

- Defining the manufacturing architecture. This permits a concentration on problems of generic scope and wide applicability as the basis for later projects in integration, support, and application systems and demonstrations.
- Developing integration methodology. This activity provides a bridge between industry and ICAM for the transfer of ICAM technology for the integrated factory of tomorrow. The projects addressed include establishing factory simulation techniques, ICAM implementation techniques, configuration management, modelling tools, software integration simulation, automated systems engineering methodology, and various system analysis and design capabilities.
- Establishing support systems. This is concerned with the portion of the ICAM system involving computer operations, including both software and hardware and both operational and managerial aspects of computerized manufacturing.
- Establishing application systems. This includes such items as manufacturing cost and design guides, the design manufacturing interface, manufacturing standards, group technology concepts, and scheduling and process planning. Under an ICAM contract, the National Bureau of Standards considered standards in computer communications,

languages, and networks to identify potential conflicts within an integrated manufacturing environment. Other areas of concern include robotics, prototype integrated production cells, integrated materials-handling and storage systems, and integrated manufacturing control and material management.

– Demonstrating the ICAM program. The ultimate goal in ICAM is the use of totally integrated manufacturing systems by industry in the completely automated factory.

Automatic Functioning

The problems encountered in trying to integrate advanced computer concepts, new manufacturing technologies, and the shop floor are clearly evident in the evolution of robotics. Robots are classified according to the way we provide them with information and the amount of self-adaptability they possess. The most *comprehensive categorization of robots* is provided by Japan's Industrial Robot Association:

– Manual manipulators are worked by an operator.

– A fixed-sequence robot has a manipulator that repetitively performs successive steps of an operation according to a predetermined sequence which cannot be easily changed.

– A variable-sequence robot is similar to the fixed sequence robot except that the set information can be easily changed.

– Playback robot reproduces, from its computer memory, operations that were originally executed under human control.

– An NC robot is a manipulator, whose tasks are programmed by using numerical control tapes or cards.

– An intelligent robot, using sensory perception, detects changes in the work environment and proceeds accordingly, using its decision-making capability.

Industry today is focusing on the development of NC and intelligent robots. There has been a growth in the number of firms that manufacture and sell such robots which is reminiscent of the proliferation of minicomputer companies in the 1960s.

Basically, robots are microprocessor-controlled mechanical devices that perform a function or provide an intelligent interface between machines and processes. They can be intelligent enough to make on-the-spot manufacturing "decisions." But for robots to become practical, we must reduce their size, mechanical complexity, and installed cost—primarily through the expanded use of computer and control technology.

Robots can duplicate human manipulative skills with accuracy and precision. Their flexibility and versatility, as opposed to hard automation, make robots ideally suited to the kinds of small batch jobs that constitute the bulk of industry's manufacturing activity. Today, robots, are freeing people from jobs that present serious health hazards, are mundane, or are highly repetitive. In most cases their use is justified for non-economic reasons. In the US, industry has been slow to adopt robotics. This reluctance appears to be due primarily to the large initial investment and the general availability of relatively inexpensive manual labour. Why install a $100,000 or $150,000 robot to perform a $25,000-a-year job? Also, the majority of today's robots are monsters: bulky, unwieldy mixtures of hydraulic and mechanical contraptions with a machine tool heritage.

This situation is changing. Robots are becoming more streamlined, and, when they are manufactured in large quantities, will rapidly decline in cost. Many technologically innovative firms are entering the business. Equally important, system engineering, which represents as much as two-thirds-of the cost of a robotic application, is being greatly reduced. It is not difficult to imagine that in a short time the cost of a typical robotic system will be paid back in one or two years.

In the next decade the cost of a robot is likely to be down to $10,000 to $20,000, while skilled labour costs might easily be $25 or $30 an hour. When this economic threshold is reached, there will be a virtual flood of robotic applications. When this happens, robots will play an important part in the totally integrated factory of the future. Most of our plants will have a direct numerical control supervisory computer that coordinates the activities of several NC and CNC machines or hardwired machining centers and robots and connects all the machines into a system. The robot interface will handle the transfer of material and, with newly developed sensory capabilities, will also perform the in-line inspection of parts. For the near future, however, our factories will be some particular mix of machines, robots, and people that makes the most economic sense. Eventually in a decade or so-robots will fill a void in the supply of skilled labour. There has been a shift in the labour force from blue-collar to white-collar workers and from production jobs to service jobs. Currently, about two-thirds of our work force and 85 per cent of all college graduates are employed in a service- related activity.

The total service-oriented labour force is expected to increase by 20 per cent in the 1980s—to about 85 million people. This shift to a service economy, coupled with the slowdown in the growth of the US population, suggests that many businesses will find factory labour in short supply: this is already the case in Sweden today. At a leading university in Japan, there is a robot with human-type hands and legs, TV-camera eyes, artificial ears and mouth, and touch and joint sensing. These technologies are combined to provide the robot with some of the capabilities of a two or three year old child.

For example, when ordered to fetch an item in the room, the robot looks around the room and finds the article, walks to it, picks it up, and brings it back. If the robot does not understand a command, it speaks up. Such robots are essentially showcase examples: they are not appropriate for the majority of industrial applications. In fact, a universal person-like robot would make little sense except for very limited, specialized applications. At present, the major applications for robotics are in arc welding and material transfer. In the future, the major application will be in assembly. Artificial intelligence is a worthwhile goal,, but for the moment industry has more than enough applications for "dumb" robots. Employment of robots in these applications is actually limited by the extensive engineering required to put them to use.

It is estimated that by 1990 two-thirds of the robots sold to industry will be off-the-shelf, modular units rather than specially designed systems. Looking at automated systems generally, by the end of the decade, 30 per cent of our systems will consist of hard automation, about 20 per cent will be adaptive control, and the remaining 50 per cent will be systems of a universal programmable nature. Respondents to a study conducted by the Society of Manufacturing Engineers ranked the technical and performance barriers constraining the rapid utilization of robots in US industry.

The leading technical barriers were mechanical manipulation, vision systems, tactile systems, sensory systems, programming, and control systems. The primary performance barriers included accuracy, speed, and the ratio of capacity to size. Robots will have a much greater impact in manufacturing when their total installed cost is reduced and they are more easily programmed. As with CAD and CAM systems, the most difficult thing about putting in a robot is interfacing it with the factory—both the machines and the people.

Research today is focused on the development of (1) equipment that will make greater use of computer technology to cut the cost of systems engineering and power electronics, improve servo-motor technology, and rapidly move from hydraulics to electric; and (2) sensors that will enable robots to perform more reliably and with greater precision and adaptability.

A good *overview of sensor types* has been provided by Bejczy:

The nonvisual sensor information is used in controlling the physical contact or near contact of the mechanical arm/hand with objects in the environment. It is obtained from proximity, force-torque, and touch-slip sensors integrated with the mechanical hand. These sensors provide the information needed to perform terminal orientation and dynamic compliance control with fine manipulator motions.

Terminal orientation and dynamic compliance control are essential and intricate elements of manipulation. Soft and adaptive grasp of objects, gentle load transfer in emplacing objects, assembling or disassembling parts with narrow tolerances, and performing geometrically and dynamically constrained motions (like opening or closing a latch or fitting two parts together) are typical examples of manipulator control problems that challenge both sensor and control engineering.

Vision systems close the control loop and allow the robot to interact in a dynamic, changing environment. A second use of vision will be for the critical inspection of the batch-produced parts. The position and orientation of the part can be used in advanced automation systems to direct a robot manipulator to pick up the part for an assembly or transfer operation.

The Robotics Laboratory at Westinghouse is working on state-of-the-art applications in many of these areas. Systems and development engineers are working on the integration of controls, tooling, processes, computer, and other elements of the automated factory. Specialists in robotics are concentrating, on developing and applying high-speed vision systems, tactile and force feedback sensors, high-performance electric servo systems, adaptable programmable assembly techniques and computer control, and artificial intelligence.

One of these projects is called APAS (automated programmable assembly system). Funded in part by the National Science Foundation, APAS is a pilot program in which robots are used to assemble components into the end bells of the Westinghouse line of fractional horsepower motors. It is a development project intended to transfer newly developed technology to the factory. The fractional-horse power motors are currently assembled in batches averaging 600, units at a time. There is a 20-second assembly time per motor to put together 30 different parts, and there are 13 changeovers a day to handle 450 different motor styles. The first section of the line puts parts on the motor end bells. To start the 15-second sub-assembly operation, a vision system in conjunction with a five-axis PUMA (programmable universal machine for assembly) robot inspects the end bells to make sure they are the style currently being assembled.

The end bell is then oriented and placed on a pallet. The next step in the assembly is the insertion of the uppermost components:

a thrust washer, a bearing cap, and a felt washer. An auto-place robot picks up the parts and loads them onto an anvil. The end bell is moved into the station, and the parts are passed on. At the same time a semisolid lubricant is injected. At the next station, four screws, a plastic plug, and a contact point are inserted. Following this there is a complicated assembly procedure. In order to assemble all the different styles of end bells, several styles of certain parts are required. More precisely, six styles of mounting rings and three styles of dust caps are needed. Programmable feeders are used to accomplish the feeding and orienting of all these parts. At this station, a PUMA robot picks up a mounting ring, dust cap, and felt washer on an oil finger from the programmable feeder and places them on an insertion device, where they are fitted onto the end bell.

At the final station, a vision system and a PUMA robot are used to perform the final inspection of the end bell, pick it up from the pallet, and remove it from the system. The computer control arid sensory parts of APAS are the most revolutionary elements of the application. A distributed microprocessor system is needed to handle many simultaneous tasks in the short 15-second assembly time, and a visual sensory system is required to provide orientation and feedback.

One master microprocessor controls the entire system. Under its control are three types of smaller microprocessors for Vision control, local process control, and robot path control. All these controllers work in conjunction with the master computer to coordinate the inspection and assembly procedures. The vision system on this project recognizes randomly oriented parts on an assembly line after a multipass learning cycle controlled by an operator. It can also be used to rotate the part to any given angle.

New Experiments

The technology exists in many parts of the world to achieve significant advances in many areas of factory automation. Many European countries are working on numerical control, process planning, and group technology approaches rather than the graphics approach emphasized in the US. They are well advanced in integrating CAD and CAM systems. In Japan, major advances are achieved through the efforts of the Ministry of International Trade and Industry. (MITI). For example, hundreds of millions of dollars and some of the finest minds in business and universities are being applied to the task of developing a fifth-generation computer.

Another example is a $60 million government funded project to develop a flexible machine system. This system will use high-energy lasers to manufacture small batches of machined parts with assembly line efficiency. The project involves more than 500 engineers from 20 Japanese companies, and it could revolutionize much of manufacturing. MITI makes use of Japan's homogeneity and Organisational milieu. It would be inappropriate for the US to adopt the same methods to foster manufacturing innovation.

However, we must recognize the urgency of the problem. The US is one of the few major industrialized nations in the world without a significant coordinated industry–government-university program directed at improving manufacturing technology. We need a national strategy for productivity improvement that brings toge-ther government, business, labour, and academia in a cooperative, rather than adversary, relationship. We will have to remove many of the disincentives to innovation and find new ways to capitalize on our diversity and our proven creative and inventive abilities. Just as MITI capitalizes on Japan's homogeneity, we must find new ways to foster, encourage, and channel our innovative diversity.

At present, Westinghouse is working with the National Science Foundation and the universities of Rhode Island, Florida, and Wisconsin on technology development programs. Along with the Robotics Institute of Carnegie-Mellon University, we are developing "seeing," "feeling," and "thinking" robotic systems for several of our factories. We are also very interested in the Air Force's ICAM program to coordinate sophisticated design and manufacturing techniques now used by industry on a piecemeal basis. This program attempts to integrate design, analysis, fabrication, materials handling, and inspection and to develop hardware and software demonstration manufacturing cells in selected aerospace plants.

Role in Society

The easier it is for people to use computers, the broader will be their applications in manufacturing. We are moving away from the airplane cockpit approach, with rows of complex devices, to create simple computer tools. Compare the ease with which we use personal computers today with the way we approached computers in the early 1970s.

The same changes will occur in manufacturing. The computer has three language levels: machine language, programming language such as COBOL or FORTRAN, and user interface or problem-oriented language. Designing the computer so that it can be quickly used by someone familiar with a problem-but not with computers-is the most difficult of all programming tasks. Today, computers "converse" with users in pictures, in ladder diagrams, or in the secretarial language of word processing.

Voice recognition systems will free workers' hands to perform other tasks and make it even easier for them to use computers. In the future, when research efforts begin to pay off in systems with some understanding of natural language and with "common sense," communications with computers may become as simple as talking to a three-year-old. An important area of concern in manufacturing is worker safety. Automated systems and robots must be able to work side by side with humans.

Major developments are taking place in the sensor area, particularly with proximity detectors and ultrasonic sensors, to make robots more suitable for inclusion in existing factories. The application of automated systems in manufacturing will have several major affects on the people involved in production. It will make our jobs more interesting and challenging; it will enhance job security; and it will multiply the productivity increases. Workers today are looking for greater job satisfaction through greater involvement and increased sophistication. New technologies provide this added dimension to the workplace. For instance, draftsmen use CAD today to perform work that was normally performed by engineers just five or ten years ago. Engineers, in turn, are freed to delve into even more technically sophisticated areas. As a peripheral advantage, the critical need for technical manpower is partially satisfied.

To manage technological change, we must manage our human resources better. For example, we must commit ourselves to ensuring that none of our workers is laid off because of technological changes, as long as they are willing to be retrained and accept new job assignments. Our experience at Westinghouse has been that employees displaced by robots normally move up to better, more challenging work. We should also rethink who can do what job.

For instance, there is a tremendous potential for productivity improvement if the person who knows the machine better than anyone else also has the skills to program the machine while it is working on another job and the skills to debug the programs on the spot. In Westinghouse, by putting the programs for people first, we expect to multiply the productivity improvements that are gained through technology and capital investments. With partici-pative management, for instance, employees welcome advanced technology because they feel in charge of it. Only when these programs are in place will we emerge from the showcase and token automation phase that manufacturing is presently in.

Today, scientific work in the application of computers to factory automation is in the embryonic stage. We are on the verge of seeing the cost of NC, CNC, and robotics become low enough for these systems to be economically justifiable for many more applications. The cost will continue to decline as application problems are resolved and the computer becomes an understood and respected partner in the manufacturing environment.

First came numerically controlled machine tools, which performed their operations automatically according to coded instructions on paper or Mylar tape. Then came computer-aided manufacturing, or CAD/ CAM, which replaced the drafting board with the CRT screen and the numerical control tape with the computer. The new systems integrate all these elements. They consist of computer-controlled machining centers that sculpt complicated metal parts at high speed and with great reliability, robots that handle the parts, and remotely guided carts that deliver materials.

The components are linked by electronic controls that dictate what will happen at each stage of the manufacturing sequence, even automatically replacing worn-out or broken drill bits and other implements. Measured against some of the machinery they replace, flexible manufacturing systems seem expensive. A full-scale system, encompassing computer controls, five or more machining centers, and the accompanying transfer robots, can cost $25 million. Even a rudimentary system built around a single machine tool-say, a computer-controlled turning center-might cost about $3,25,000, while a conventional numerically-controlled turning tool would cost only about $175,000.

But the direct comparison is a poor guide to the economies flexible automation offers, even taking into account the phenomenal productivity gains and asset utilization rates that come with virtually unmanned round-the-clock operation. Because an FMS can be instantly reprogrammed to make new, parts or products, a single system can replace several different conventional machining lines, yielding huge savings in capital investment and plant size. Flexible automation's greatest potential for radical change lies in its capacity to manufacture goods cheaply in small volumes.

Since the era, of Henry Ford, the unchallenged low cost production system has been Detroitstyle "hard" automation that stamps out look alike parts in huge volume. There is little flexibility in hard automation's transfer lines, which get their name from the transfer of the product being worked on via a conveyor from one metalworking machine to another. But such mass, production is shrinking in importance compared with "batch production" in lots of anywhere from several thousand to one. Seventy-five percent of all machined parts today are produced in batches of 50 or fewer.

Many assembled products too, ranging from airplanes and tractors to office desks and large computers, are made in batches.

Even such stalwarts of inflexible mass I production as the automakers are developing systems to produce more low-volume models for small market segments. In the past, batch manufacturing required machines dedicated to a single task. These machines had to be either rebuilt or replaced at the time of product change. Flexible manufacturing brings a degree of diversity to manufacturing never before available. Different products can be made on the same line at will. General Electric, for instance, uses flexible automation to make 2000 different versions of its basic electric meter at its Somersworth, New Hampshire, plant with total output of more than I million meters a year. The strategic implications for the manufacturer are truly staggering. Under hard automation the greatest economies were realized only at the most massive scales. But flexible automation makes similar economies available at a wide range of scales.

A flexible automation system can turn out a small batch or even a single copy of a product as efficiently as a production line designed to turn out a million identical items. Enthusiasts of flexible automation refer to this capability as "economy of scope." Economy of scope shatters the tenets of conventional manufacturing. There is no long trip down the learning curve on the factory floor, thanks to the unprecedented precision the system brings to each step of the manufacturing process, from machining to inspection.

The manufacturer will be able to meet a far greater array of market needs, including quick-changing ones seeing the needs of markets the company is not in now. He can keep up with changing fashions in the marketplace-or set them himself by updating his product or launching a new one. He has many more options for building a new plant: FMS frees manufacturers from the tyranny of large-scale investments in hard automation, allowing construction of smaller plants closer to markets. Flexible manufacturing is the ultimate entrepreneurial system: it will allow fast-thinking manufacturers to move swiftly into brand-new fields and to leave them just as swiftly if need be-at the expense of less agile older producers. As the new tools come increasingly into use, "some companies will find themselves blind-sided by competitors they never imagined existed," says Joseph D. Romano, a vice-president at A. T. Kearney Inc., management consultants. Flexible manufacturing systems were developed in the US more than ten years ago by Cincinnati Milacron, Kearney and Trecker, and White Consolidated. The US remains a world leader in the technology: the major machine tool builders are being joined by new suppliers with great financial resources and technical abilities, such as GE, Westinghouse, and Bendix.

The joint venture will bring together GM's considerable capabilities in design and software and Fanuc's expertise in building and applying robot systems. GMF plans to start building products next year. However, most of the action in flexible automation is now in Japan, and both American and European manufacturers will soon start feeling the pressure. Like many other manufacturing technologies conceived in the US—among them numerically-controlled machine tools and industrial robots-the FMS was greeted with a yawn by US manufacturers.

The Japanese have become the implementers par excellence of this new type of factory automation, not because they are great technical innovators, which they admit they are not, but because they have moved fast in putting the new systems into their factories. Once again, the path to success in a new manufacturing method leads through those Japanese factories set up as spotless little towns with flower beds and tree-lined streets. A visitor to Japan these days finds the new manufacturing system turning out parts for machine tools in Nagoya, electric motors near Mount Fuji, diesel cylinder blocks in Niigata, and many other products elsewhere. In most cases these plants run on three shifts. During the day skeleton crews work with the machines. At night the robots and the machines work alone.

In Fanuc Ltd's cavernous, bumblebee-yellow buildings in a pipe forest near Mount Fuji, automatic machining centers and robots typically toil unattended through the night, with only subdued blue warning lights flashing as unmanned delivery carts move like ghostly messengers through the eerie semidarkness. This plant, one of two in the Fuji complex, makes parts for robots and machine tools (which are assembled manually, however). The machining operation, occupying 54,000 square feet, is supervised at night by a single controller, who watches the machines on close-circuit TV. If something goes wrong, he can shut down that particular part of the operation and reroute the work around it. Some Americans think that Fanuc's Fuji complex is just a showcase. Some showcase.

The total cost of the plant was about $32 million, including the cost of 30 machining cells, which consist of computer-controlled machine tools loaded and unloaded by robots, along with materials-handling robots, monitors, and a programmable controller to orchestrate the operation. Fanuc estimates that it probably would have needed ten times the capital investment for the same output with conventional manufacturing. It also would have needed ten times its labour force of about 100. In this plant one employee supervised ten machining cells; the others act as maintenance men and perform assembly. All in all, the plant is about five times as productive as its conventional counterpart would be.

Across the street, 60 machining cells and 101 robots toil in a big two-storey facility automatically machining parts and assembling them into 10,000 electric motors a month. There is nothing else like it in the world. Men perform maintenance functions here in the daytime. The robots work through the night, in silence marred only by hydraulic sighs and the sibilance of those automatic carts. The first floor of the plant contains the machining cells and 52 robots. Machining is carried out on about 900 types and sizes of motor parts, in lots ranging from 20 to 1000 units.

Machined parts are temporarily stored in an automatic warehouse; they are automatically retrieved when they are scheduled for assembly on the second floor. Yamazaki Machinery Works Ltd operates a flexible automation plant near Nagoya that makes parts of computerized numerically-controlled lathes and machining centers; the latter combine several metalworking machines and incorporate automatic tool changers. In the daytime 12 workers man the $20 million plant. At night only a lone watchman with a flashlight is on duty while the machines keep on working. A conventional machining system with similar production volume, according to Yamazaki, would require 215 workers and nearly four times as many machines, and would take three months to turn out the parts the new plant makes in three days.

The company estimates that over five years of operation its plant will produce after-tax profits of $12 million, compared with $800,000 for a conventional plant that size. Yamazaki is now transferring this technology to its machine-tool-making plant in Florence, Kentucky, bad news for Yamazaki's American competitors. But the most astonishing Japanese automated factory will be started up by Yamazaki about 20 miles from its headquarters near Nagoya. This will be what Tsunehiko "Tony" Yamazaki, the personable senior executive managing director, describes as his company's twenty- first-century factory. The new plant's 65 computer-controlled machine tools and 34 robots will be linked via a fiber-optic cable with the computerized design center back in headquarters. From there the flexible factory can be directed to manufacture the required types of parts-as well as to make the tools and fixtures to produce the parts-by entering into the computer's memory names of various machine tool models scheduled to be produced and pressing a few buttons to get production going.

The Yamazaki plant will be the world's first automated factory to be run by telephone from corporate headquarters. The plant will have workmen, to be sure: 215 men helping produce what would take 2500 in a conventional factory. At maximum capacity the plant will be able to turn out about $230 million of machine tools a year. But production is so organized that sales can be reduced to $80 million a year, if need be, without laying off workers.

The Yamazaki plant illustrates yet another aspect of economy of scope: with flexible automation, a manufacturer can economically shrink production capacity to match lower market demand. Though Japanese machine tool makers are the most ambitious installer's of flexible automation, they are by no means alone. FMS is spreading throughout Japanese manufacturing, with Panasonic, Mitsubishi, and other consumer and industrial goods producers installing the new systems. So far, nothing even remotely comparable is happening in manufacturing in the US or anywhere else in the world. Disturbingly, all of US industry can boast only about 30 flexible manufacturing systems in place; in Japan one large industrial company, Toyoda Machine Tool Co., has more than 30. Frets David Nitzan, director of industrial robotics at the research and consulting firm SRI International, "We are facing another sputnik-a Japanese sputnik."

The growing Japanese lead underscores frequently heard charges that US managers are too remote from technical disciplines to appreciate the potential of such new technologies, and too engrossed with short-run financial results to invest in them. More often than not, machine tool makers report, executives of US manufacturing companies look at something like a flexible machining system only in relation to the narrowly defined functions of the conventional tools it might replace-not for its potential to provide a different, and far more efficient, Organisation of the manufacturing process. "Cost accounting is a very poor language to communicate new ideas in," observes Paul R. Haas, vice president of Kearney and Trecker's special-products division. One consequence of this myopia is apparent in the ageing of the US machine tool stock. "Many American factories are barrier reefs—one old, tired technology piled on top of another," says James A. Baker, the executive vice president in charge of GE's drive to develop automated systems. "Even when they build new factories, Americans tend to use the same old machines, shipping them from the old plant to the new plant."

Uncle Sam is the Methuselah of machine tools: more than 34 per cent of US tools are 20 or more years old, the highest proportion in any major industrialized nation. Even England is better off; only 24 per cent of its machine tools are similarly ancient. In Japan, only 18 per cent of machine tools are 20 or more years old; 61 per cent are less than 10 years old, against 31 per cent in the US. In fact, fewer than 4 per cent of machine tools installed in the US are numerically controlled—though the concept has been commercially available for a quarter of a century.

The art of managing the factory is no less antiquated. Fixated by the short run, managers have pursued all sorts of piecemeal efforts to hold down costs without stopping to map out systematic ways of organizing the factory floor for more efficiency. Too often production procedures in US factories appear to be little more than accretions of adhoc solutions to problems ranging from space shortages to union-dictated work rules.

Managers focus obsessively on chipping away at direct labour costs rather than exploring better ways to organize the work-force—or investigating the extent to which new technologies are making direct labour costs less important. Japanese corporate leaders, by contrast, tend to be sympathetic with technical disciplines—a far greater proportion of them are engineers—and they have more freedom to incur short-run costs in pursuit of long-run strategic objectives. Perhaps most important of all, a technology like flexible automation is a logical extension of a manufacturing philosophy that views the production of goods as a seamless activity that starts with product design and ends with support in the field a philosophy, as the Japanese put it, of "making the goods flow like water."

"Japanese management takes a holistic view of manufacturing," says James F. Lardner, a Deere and Co. vice-president who supervised a major restructuring of the farm equipment company's manufacturing operation. "They apply logic and common sense to their problems rather than laboratory investigations and discounted cash-flow calculations."

Even before they began to adopt flexible automation, Japanese plants typically employed far fewer people for a given output than American and European plants. The 'Japanese were able to do that by reorganizing production-including the placement of machine tools on factory floors. In the US and Europe, machine tools are usually grouped by type, and parts are directed to them as required.

The Japanese instead place different types of machines together so that each given part can be processed in one place. Much quicker than anyone else, too, the Japanese have taken to such important concepts as "group technology "the grouping of similar parts into families for easier manufacture and better inventory control. Like so many other Japanese manufacturing methods, group technology isn't new; the idea evolved in the 1920s in Germany. A central element of the Japanese manufacturing philosophy is the famous just-in-time concept, the system in which materials and components are delivered as required on the shop floor, not accumulated and stored for future.

Since one-third of factory space is usually employed for storage, the savings are substantial. But there is much more. By reducing inventories to the lowest level at which operations can be sustained, the Japanese force their manufacturing Organisations to deal with problems previously hidden. For example, the Japanese already practised preventive maintenance on their machine tools to a degree unknown in the US. Just-in-time has forced them to do even better, because the flow through of products requires every single machine to function perfectly all the time. Yet the Japanese do nothing that Westerners can't—if they only decide to do it. Marvellously efficient factories using the latest automated equipment exist in the US and Europe, towering like islands of excellence in a sea of stagnation and yielding remarkable benefits to their owners. Take Deere and Co's giant new tractor assembly plant in Waterloo, Iowa, which need not take a back seat to any plant in any industry anywhere. In the past few years, Deere has restructured the Waterloo complex from a gigantic, somewhat chaotic job shop into a world-class producer. Deere has poured $500 million into the complex, $150 million of it into the 2.1 million square foot assembly plant. Chassis and engines received from sister plants are joined with tractor cabs and bodies made at Waterloo into gleaming mechanical behemoths. Almost all the materials handling at Waterloo is under computer control. Each part or sub-assembly-engine, transmission, wheels, and so on is automatically assigned to a specific customized tractor ordered by a dealer; it is retrieved from storage and delivered automatically to the assembly line just when it is needed. Putting just-in-time to work, Deere has cut inventory in some areas by as much as 50 per cent, saving millions of dollars.

Flexible automation allows Deere to build a tractor at least twice as fast as before. And it has given the company a new agility: Deere can now successfully compete not only against other big manufacturers but also against "short-liners" that make only one farm implement in higher volumes. What's more, the company is right now bidding on a defence contract worth hundreds of millions of dollars. If it wins the contract, it will start making bulldozers, graders, and other heavy construction equipment on its new flexible automation lines-putting new pressure on such established manufacturers as Caterpillar and Case.

But if manufacturers think that they have to pour hundreds of millions of dollars into flexible automation to reap its rewards, they are mistaken. They can begin by acquiring smaller machining centers to modernize portions of their operations. Clifford R. Meyer, president and chief operating officer of Cincinnati Milacron, recalls his delight at recently visiting one of his client companies, which occupies a garage at the end of an alley in a Los Angeles suburb. Inside, a father-son entrepreneurial team mans $450,000 worth of the latest computerized machine tools—successfully competing as a parts supplier to aerospace companies against much larger firms with older production equipment. Furthermore, not all plants that install flexible automation have to be started from scratch. GE, Ford, and GM are among the manufacturers that have successfully revitalized old plants by installing new machinery.

Like many other American companies, GE had for years lagged in automating its own factories. Some old GE plants, James Baker notes, "make Santa's workshop look like the factory of the future." Today, however, GE can boast notable successes in converting some of its old plants into what it calls "factories with a future"—a marketing slogan the company uses to impress upon potential customers that they need not build entirely new factories of the future. Its meter plant in New Hampshire, modernized at a cost of $25 million, is the epitome of an antiquated multi-storey mill building.

Another ancient GE plant, the Erie, Pennsylvania, locomotive facility, is being transformed with a $300 million investment into an ultramodern automated factory—inside if not on the outside. Building a batch of locomotive frames formerly took about 70 skilled machine operators 16 days; the newly automated factory will turn out these frames in a day—untouched by human hands. The displaced workers are being retrained for other, more sophisticated jobs. As a general matter, in fact, flexible automation threatens employment less than might be supposed.

The US faces a shortage of skilled machinists for the rest of the decade, and automation of assembly, where semiskilled jobs predominate, will proceed much more slowly than automation of machining. GM is also advancing. Last October it installed its first flexible automation system, an Italian-built Comau system with three machining centers, at the Chevrolet Gear and Axle Division in Detroit. Almost immediately GM discovered just how valuable the new manufacturing flexibility can be. When an outside supplier failed to deliver a front-axle component up to quality standards, GM brought the job in-house. It designed and built the tooling for the component on the FMS in ten weeks—a job that normally would have taken up to a year. As yet, such examples are rare exceptions.

The majority of US manufacturers either do not yet grasp the significance of the new technologies, or do not want to invest while money is still expensive and future markets uncertain. Moreover, there are still no turnkey flexible manufacturing systems available. Installation of big systems requires skilled people not all companies may have on hand. But as GE's Baker argues: "We're running out of time and excuses." The price of delay may be disaster, as the experience of some American machine tool manufacturers show.

During the 1970s the Japanese became the world's first mass producers of computerized machine tools. While the majority of US machine tool makers—small companies, in the main—plodded along using old technologies and methods, the Japanese redesigned their tools for easier manufacturing with flexible automation and equipped these tools with advanced yet simple electronic controls that the humblest job shop could understand. Then, in the late 1970s, the Japanese caught the US tool-makers napping in the midst of the capacity crunch, with delivery times stretched up to two years.

The Japanese, to be sure, played an additional trump. Their machine tool industry had been mobilized by Japan's Ministry of International Trade and Industry (MITI) into a cartel and bolstered with millions of dollars in government funds, as shown in documents obtained in Japan by lawyers for Houdaille Industries, the US machine tool maker that has asked President Reagan to deny investment tax credits for some Japanese tools sold in the US. This double-barrelled assault left US makers of numerically controlled machining centers and lathes in shambles. By the end of last year the agile Japanese had captured more than 50 per cent of the US market for those machines.

The US machine tool industry has lost its erstwhile position as the world's leading producer to competitors not only in Japan but also in Europe and even Taiwan. The National Academy of Engineering, usually not given to alarmist statements, in a report soon to be issued calls the Japanese and other foreign inroads "a very threatening development that could seriously endanger the future economic security of the American industry."

The reason for concern is simple: the machine tool industry is central to the growth of all manufacturing. There will be more Japanese surprises in the years to come. This October, for instance, the Japanese government's mechanical engineering laboratory near Tokyo will unveil a small prototype factory of the future where novel, laser-equipped machine tools will take production automation a big step beyond where it is now. The new machines will perform metalworking processes now done separately—such as turning, drilling, and milling—all at once, cutting batch production time of metal parts in half and reducing the number of production processes by 60 per cent.

13
New Generation

The current supercomputers are only at the threshold of what computer designers think can be achieved; the next generation of advanced supercomputers will make today's machines look like handheld calculators. "We have problems that would take 500 to 1,000 hours to solve [on today's supercomputers]," says David Nowak, division leader for computational physics at Lawrence Livermore National Laboratory, where a cluster of seven supercomputers-known as "Octopus" are used for nuclear weapons research.

Before the end of the twentieth century, computer scientists had developed machines that not only crunched numbers at high speed but also exhibited artificial intelligence– computers that think and reason somewhat like human beings and that could understand information conveyed by sight, speech, and motion. The question was, which nation's scientists would get there first? The Japanese had announced a two-pronged plan to build advanced computer technologies.

One project was the $100 million, eight-year National Superspeed Computer project, which aimed at producing machines 1000 times faster than the earlier Cray-1 supercomputer built by Cray Research of Minneapolis. The other, the $500 million, 10-year Fifth Generation Computer project, was focussing on artificial intelligence. Both were being countered by American efforts, including a Pentagon request for up to $1 billion over the next five years for superspeed and artificial intelligence (AI) technologies. Although behind, Great Britain and France have also launched national supercomputer projects. The great danger for the losers in the race-and the opportunity for the winners was that whoever built the next generation of computers would have a huge technological and commercial advantage: these computers would be used for computer and microelectronics design-to build even smarter, and more powerful machines. They won't be self-replicating machines, but they would be close. "It takes you a long time to catch up," says computer scientist Rai Reddy of Carnegie-Mellon University, one of the top US computer-research centers. "In some of these areas, that is the difference between a first-rate power and a second-rate power-from an economic point of view and from a security point of view. " The losers in the race will fall farther and farther behind. The leading edge of computer science is still a black art; there are no fixed laws, and the field is highly experimental. That is what worries US scientists about Japan's approach—some success is inevitable. "Because the field is experimental, [the Japanese] will come out with something," says Dertouzos. "It may not be what they wanted, but they'll come up with new architectures, new insights, and new design techniques.

To build the computers that dominated the 1990s, both Japan and the US are depending on the onrushing technological advances in microelectronics. Japan's Fifth Generation project will use faster, denser circuitry to create a new class of superintelligent computers.

The 24 projects in the Fifth Generation concentrate on artificial intelligence, a goal of American computer scientists for more than a quarter century. "We are trying to catch up to you, and not the other way around," says Tokyo University Professor Tohru Moto-oka, who organized the project for the Japanese government. Although the Japanese are highly regarded as superb engineers, Japanese computer scientists have often been faulted for failing to develop innovative computer software.

In a break with tradition, Kazuhiro Fuchi, the Fifth Generation project director, has deliberately assembled a young team: "The question was who would adapt most easily to this research," says Fuchi. "Young people have fewer fixed ideas." The project, head-quartered in a downtown Tokyo skyscraper, will focus on computer architectures, software, and the symbolic logic necessary to build thinking computers. In the US, meanwhile, three huge new programs in electronics and computing are getting under way.

Microelectronics and Computer Technology Corp (MCC)

Last year William Norris, the founder and chairman of Control Data Corp., convened a meeting of top computer and semiconductor industry executives at the Grenelefe Golf and Tennis resort in Oriando, Florida, to discuss setting up a hugh research cooperative.

The companies agreed to form a nonprofit joint venture so that they could pool their resources and share the cost of doing long-range research. Twelve major US corporations joined the new Organisation, including Honeywell, Motorola, RCA, and Control Data. MCC is a bold departure from the way research is usually done in American universities and corporations, and it will probe the limits of the nation's antitrust laws. The venture partly follows the Japanese model: the companies will donate scientists and researchers to MCC, loaning them for up to four years.

The corporate co-owners will also put up the money to fund MCC' research, in return for the rights to use the results. Whether the scheme will work is an open question. The 12 companies in MCC are competitors in fast-moving, high-technology markets, and ordinarily they jealously guard any technological edge they gain. In fact, many top US "firms—Cray Research, Texas Instruments, Intel, and others—chose to stay out of MCC. "That's not our style," says John A. Rollwagen, chairman of Cray Research, an 11-year old company proud of its entrepreneurial creed. "We don't want to participate." The biggest market force of all-IBM-reportedly stayed out of MCC because it feared antitrust action against it if it joined. So far, however, the creation of MCC has not provoked any such suits.

San Francisco antitrust lawyer Joseph M. Alioto did write to the chief executives of the companies that were about to form MCC: "In my opinion, your contemplated conduct is an unequivocal combination in violation of the antitrust laws of the United States." But the threat did not deter MCC's co-owners and, for the time being at least, the Justice Department has allowed the MCC plan to stand. To run the new corporation, MCC's directors chose retired Admiral Bobby Ray Inman, former director of the National Security Agency and former deputy director of the CIA. Inman is widely respected for his managerial abilities and is an adept politician besides. "The day they picked Bob Inman to head MCC," says George W. Keywork II, Ronald Reagan's top science adviser, "any concern about its success diminished in my mind."

Over the past five months, Inman orchestrated a competition among 57 cities for the MCC headquarters; the winner was Austin, Texas, after private donors, the state, and universities put together a generous package of incentives.

The consortium will have a budget of about $75 million a year and a staff of 250. Its first projects include programs in semiconductor packaging and interconnect technology, advanced software engineering and computer-aided design and manufacturing (CAD/CAM) for the electronics and computer industries. Most ambitious is a 10-year program aimed at breakthroughs in computer architecture, software, and artificial intelligence.

MCC will own the licenses and patents to the technologies; the manufacturing and marketing will be left to the companies that sponsor the projects. MCC win give them a competitive edge on the market—they will have exclusive rights for three years before the research is published and other firms are allowed to buy licenses.

Semiconductor Research Corp. (SRC)

Over the past few years Japan has captured a vital segment of the world semiconductor industry, the market for so-called RAM (random access memory) chips, a technology invented in America.

Japan now supplies 70 per cent of all 64K RAMS sold, and it appears that, as the next generation of memory chips, the 256K RAMS, is being readied for market, the Japanese semiconductor companies are threatening to take a big share of sales. It makes for a grim reminder: a decade ago, before an all-out government project to build up the industry, Japanese semiconductor firms lagged far behind American and European chip companies. Last year 13 US chip manufacturers and computer companies banded together to form a nonprofit research consortium, the Semiconductor Research Corp. (SRC), to share the spiraling costs of advanced research and development. SRC's founders include Control Data Corp., Digital Equipment Corp., Hewlett-Packard, MM, Intel and Motorola. Unlike MCC, however, SRC, which is headquartered at Research Triangle Park in North Carolina, does not carry out its own research. Instead, it sponsors research at universities. SRC is spending $12 million this year and has allocated $30 million next year. The goal: "To assure long-term survival in the market," says Larry Sumney, SRC's executive director.

DARPA

The Pentagon's Defense Advanced Research Projects Agency (DARPA) is, more than any other single agency in the world, responsible for the shape of advanced computer science today-and for many technologies now in widespread commercial use.

Over the past 20 years, DARPA has poured half a billion dollars into computer research, in the process virtually creating the science of artificial intelligence.

The first supercomputer, built in 1964, was a DARPA project. Computer time sharing, a fundamental advance, came out of work sponsored by DARPA. So did packet-switched networks, the workhorses of today's telecommunications data networks. And computer graphics—now used on desktop computers and video-arcade cockpits—is a DARPA-sponsored invention. DARPA's next priority is a push for advanced supercomputing and artificial intelligence technologies that may cost as much as $1 billion.

DARPA plans to do everything the Japanese have set out to accomplish-and more. Earlier this year DARPA proposed a "Strategic Computing and Survivability" project, which it hopes will lead to a variety of new machines. "We want some architectures that are good for building semantic memories, memories that can hold knowledge," says DARPA's computer director,

Robert Kahn. "Other kinds of systems are good for logic processing. We want architectures that can do very rapid signal processing [and] structures that can handle very, very large amounts of data in communications."

Once they are in place, these technologies will make possible an astonishing new breed of weapons and military hardware. Smart robot weapons—drone aircraft, unmanned submarines, and land vehicles—that combine artificial intelligence and high-powered computing can be sent off to do jobs that now involve human risk. "This is a very sexy area to the military, because you can imagine all kinds of neat, interesting things you could send off on their own little missions around the world or even in local combat," says Kahn.

The Pentagon will also use the technologies to create artificial intelligence machines that can be used as battlefield advisers and superintelligent computers to coordinate complex weapons systems.

An intelligent missile guidance system would have to bring together different technologies-real-time signal processing, numerical calculations, and symbolic processing, all at unimaginably high speeds—in order to make decisions and give advice to human commanders. While the national security needs are driving supercomputing technologies, there is a growing market for commercial spinoffs.

The same technology that can be used to simulate an anti-tank missile smashing into a heavily armored tank can also be put to work on less martial arts. In Los Angeles, Digital Productions, Inc., is using a Cray supercomputer to produce television commercials for Mattel, rock video segments for Turner Broadcasting, and special effects for Lorimar's "Star Fighter" space epic, which will be released next summer. Instead of shooting a commercial the conventional way—a costly photo session—Digital can create the "pictures" it needs in detail so precise that it's impossible to distinguish between the supercomputer's graphic image and the real photo. For inanimate objects, that is: the Cray-1/S can simulate a car right down to the glint of sunlight on the windshield, but not a human being. As the commercial market grows, the Japanese believe that their strategy of building supercomputers for the general-purpose market will pay off.

During the past year Fujitsu, Hitachi, and NEC have each announced supercomputers faster than the most powerful American machines now on the market, the Cray X-MP and Control Data's Cyber 205. Moreover, all three are designed to use the standard Fortran language, lifted from ordinary mainframe computers, but at much faster speeds. "Although supercomputers right now are mainly being used by specialists," says Takamitsu Tsuchimoto, Fujitsu Corp.'s development manager for supercomputers, "we believe that in the next 5 to 10 years they will be used by a lot of ordinary people, so we wanted to design a machine [they could use] without making great efforts." Designing a supercomputer is no easy task. America's premier supercomputer designer is Seymour Cray, 57, who designed the Cray-I and the basic architecture of Control Data's Cyber 205.

The Cray x-mp contains a dense pack of 240,000 silicon chips arranged to shorten the distances the electrical signals must travel, thereby decreasing the time it takes to perform an operation; the new Cray x-mPs will run at 400 million operations per second. And Japan's superspeed goal is 10 billion operations per second. (An Apple IIe computer contains 31 chips and can execute 500,000 operations per second.) Because of the cost of supercomputers—Cray's x-mp will sell for $11 million—the market will remain limited. Japan's Fifth Generation project, however, plans to build "super personal computers."

These huge increases in raw computer power are just the first step. The most profound changes brought by the new technologies will be the development of reasoning computers that will use superspeed symbol manipulation to simulate human thought. "We are about to see the next explosion, which is the application of computers to reasoning," says Stanford University computer scientist Edward A. Feigenbaum, who is a founder of two artificial intelligence companies, Teknowledge Inc. and IntelliGenetics, and co-author of a new book on Japan's challenge, *The Fifth Generation*.

Limited forms of artificial intelligence are already enjoying commercial success. Digital Equipment Corp. the nation's second largest computer firm, uses an AI program called X-CON to make custom designs of its, computer systems.

Using a set of more than 2500 rules programmed into the system, X-CON examines a customer's specifications, determines whether all the necessary components are included, then draws a set of diagrams showing the proper spatial relationships among the components. Scientists studying artificial intelligence have been aided by advances in computer hardware, too. In 1980 a group left MIT's Artificial Intelligence Laboratory to found a company, Sym-bolics Inc., of Cambridge, Mass., to build computers specially designed to run LISP, a language used to develop artificial intelligence programs; and Xerox has begun to sell similar computers. Symbolics has been selling its machines, the Symbolics 3600, to a broad range of university and industrial research labs.

The company has another customer as well: the managers running Japan's Fifth Generation project have bought 10 Symbolics machines—and they have 15 more on order. In exploring the brave new world of artificial intelligence, computer scientists are concentrating on several important problems. "Knowledge engineers" are building the so-called expert systems that can mimic human expertise in a narrowly defined area. The firm of Teknowledge, in Palo Alto, California, for example, has built an expert system for the French Elf Acquitaine Oil Co., a system that will give advice on one of the industry's most costly technical problems—what to do when a drill bit gets stuck thousands of feet below the earth's surface.

To build the system, Teknowledge engineers interviewed Elf Acquitaine's top troubleshooter, Jacques-Marie Courte, and then programmed his answers into a computer. The program is, in effect, a computer replica of Courtes expertise; the computer will ask the drilling-rig foremen questions, just as Courte would.

Once it gathers the information it needs, the computer will make recommendations by drawing images on the screen and giving suggestions on how to retrieve the bit. Because daily drilling costs are high, Elf Acquitaine may well recover the program's development costs the first time it is used successfully. General

Electric is building a software program that will provide expert advice on repairing locomotives.

The Pentagon would like to build artificial intelligence programs that could serve as a pilot's assistant in the cockpit. Stockbrokers and insurance agents may also soon get help: "Some people are beginning to see a gold mine in [building artificial intelligence programs for] financial services," says Patrick Henry Winston, chairman Of MIT's Artificial Intelligence Laboratory. And savvy software designers for the personal computer industry are beginning to look at artificial intelligence as the next big wave that will sweep the market. Despite the successes, there are problems ahead as researchers attempt to move beyond the building of narrowly defined "experts." "There's a lot of hard stuff out there we just don't have the answers to," says Roger Schank, director of Yale University's Artificial Intelligence Laboratory. Computers have always been maddeningly literal machines, subject to the absolute tyranny of the binary codes they use to do their calculations. (The switches are either on or off, simulating ones or zeros, nothing else.)

That literal-mindedness can transform a problem that would seem trivial to humans into a nightmare. Consider the simple statement "Mary had a little lamb."

For a computer to translate the text into another language—a function scientists are now trying to develop-it would have to sort through what is, by one count, 28 possible interpretations (Mary owned the lamb, Mary ate the lamb, Mary had sexual relations with the lamb, Mary gave birth to the lamb, and on and on).

The kind of understanding humans experience as a "flash of recognition" is also difficult to instill in a computer. The statement "Ronald Reagan is president" carries a number of immediate meanings to a flesh-and-blood American, but a computer would have to rummage through its silicon memory chips in search of dozens of facts—what the word "president" means and biographical facts and details that tell who Ronald Reagan is. And the biggest challenge of all—teaching computers to learn to acquire knowledge on their own—is nowhere near being solved.

Mankind has long been enchanted—and frightened—by the prospect of creating machines that think. "I don't see any limitations to artificial intelligence," says Nobel laureate Herbert Simon, professor of computer science and psychology at Carnegie-Mellon. "All the mechanisms for human intelligence are present. Already machines can think just like people—in a limited sense. Man isn't unique in that respect." Moreover, many machines may soon possess sight, touch, hearing (in the form of voice recognition), and speech, thus imitating humans' sensory capacities along with their intellectual ones. But whole areas of the human thought process—volition, emotion, the creative uses of error—still lie well outside a computer's experience. And scientists doing research on artificial intelligence are far from their ultimate goal—a computer-based analog of the human brain.

Still, the race to build superintelligent computers—Japan's challenge to the US—will almost certainly push the technology to new levels. "While at the beginning I was angry at Japan because I felt that they were swiping our best ideas, really, on second thoughts, I couldn't blame them," says Dertouzos of MIT. "And I don't blame them today at all. I think they're doing exactly what they should." And the Japanese challenge has at last spurred the US into action. "If we really wake up, I'm very optimistic," says Dertouzos. "We could beat the daylights out of them." No one knows where the competition will ultimately lead.

14
Future Prospects

A major development in the short- to medium-term future will be a substantial growth in multimedia telecommunications in one form or another. In this way, multimedia information networks will correspond more closely to the experience of communication and information interchange in everyday life, with a flexible mix of sound, picture, and words. The exact nature of this experience, and its effect on information networking in general, remains to be determined.

A major preoccupation of national governments and regional associations is to build the infrastructure for these developments as quickly as possible (and preferably faster than their competitors). In the United States, for example, in an attempt to accelerate the extension of fibre optic cabling to the home and workplace on a massive scale, the Federal Communications Commission (FCC) decided in 1992 to allow the regional Bell holding companies to transmit video programmes over their telecommunications lines, in competition with the cable television companies. This attempt to create a communications infrastructure for the next decade is seen by many Americans as crucial to the continued economic dominance of the United States.

The FCC, for example, places much weight on multimedia devices such as high definition television (HDTV), a digital two-way interactive television set, as the vehicle for this information expansion, aiming at a 15-year deadline for complete HDTV conversion. The technological futurism is the subject of much political controversy and manoeuvring at the current time; it seems likely though, that the new presidential administration will lead out more liberalization to support competition-led innovation and technological advances in communications media, and there is a clear emphasis on the use of technology for economic development in the shaping of public policy statements.

One more immediate result is likely to be the more rapid development of the National Research and Education Network, sponsored for many years by Vice-President Al Gore. The building of NREN services will bring into focus many of the issues on information access and price, and of the emerging adjustments in role of all those involved in the information cycle. In Europe, a similar urgency has fuelled a number of projects sponsored by the European Commission to work towards the creation of integrated broadband communications systems by the latter part of this decade.

The RACE programme, funding research into advanced communications technology and services, indicates by its name some of its underlying objectives, and the ESPRIT programme has initiated the IDOMENEUS project to co-ordinate and improve European efforts in the development of new information environments in the area of interacting open media.

Adopting lessons learned from the French experience in the establishment of the Minitel system, the EC has initiated a number of pilot projects in fields ranging from banking and finance, manufacturing, transport, distribution, and health care; other projects include distributed multimedia publishing, and a broadband network based library for the petroleum and chemical industries, with a 1995 target date for the introduction of commercial services.

Telephone with Picture

The existence of a technology, however, does not always guarantee its success. It is worth remembering that the Picture Phone was launched by AT&T at the World Fair of 1964. This was a first example of the videophone; in 1992, almost 30 years later, British Telecom launched a low-cost consumer videophone, which can be connected directly to the normal telephone socket; this has yet to make any substantial impact in the market-place.

A development which is likely to be of more significance, though, is the planned availability of audio-visual workstations based on the standard PC. Such a device will make the full integration of data and voice networks within the workplace a reality, and will open up a wider market for multimedia information services. Many of these exist in prototype form within the existing infrastructure, Multimedia electronic mail, for example, is now possible even in a limited text-based medium such as the Internet.

The multimedia information mail extensions (MIME) to the standard Internet mail protocol permit the inclusion of still images, group III fax images, compressed full motion video, and multipart playback sequences of mixed information types. Desktop videoconferencing, the ability to conduct meetings with a geographically remote person each at their own desk, has been established as a feasible communications technology, although so far finding only a niche rather than global market. The experience of this videoconferencing raises some key issues since it is clear that, as with most other information technologies, the technical issues are much less important than the social and organisational ones. Technical advances which have made the idea more feasible include the emergence of high bandwidth ISDN networks, video compression techniques, accepted standards, and powerful graphics-based workstations.

The degree of success in implementing this technology is determined rather by the extent to which it supports the way people work. This involves an understanding of the communication patterns between individuals and groups, and of their information needs and the uses to which information is put; of the way in which contacts with individuals and formal information sources assists the innovative process, and an appreciation of the interdependent balance between formal and informal communication.

Technology has often been used to support formal communication patterns, rather than the informal, and sometimes is intended to replace rather than support either. Multimedia communi-cations systems cannot replace face-to-face contact any more than the telephone (although a similar argument was made against the telephone at its introduction). Thoughtful design may, however, be used to appropriately support existing human communication patterns. The Cruiser Videoconferencing System designed by Bellcore, for example, uses the metaphor of a 'virtual hallway'—floor plan representing the groups of participants—along which a user may navigate, 'cruise' and interact with others in the process. For multimedia multi-user systems such as this, the interface must include some form of social protocol which enables decisions about the nature and style of desired interaction to be taken.

Many issues which will effectively delineate the shape of multimedia networking in the future remain as yet poorly understood and little explored. In some areas, however, there is more immediacy on concerns which are being raised by the substantial growth in network traffic and users, and the potential changes which can be perceived in the near future.

Digital Revolution

The growing importance of digital information and its availability over networks which demand physical and technical access create barriers, which are increasingly insurmountable for many groups of potential users. While there is no space here to discuss the social role of information systems, there are a few examples of attempts to bypass these barriers in recent develop-ments. The Cleveland FreeNet experiment, for example, is an attempt to increase access to Internet information to a wider audience. The vast amounts of information, and the worldwide nature of the Internet, also bring to the fore issues of intellectual property and copyright surrounding electronic information. Much of the information held on this network is freely available, as long as it is used for non-commercial purposes.

The subsequent use of information taken from computer networks cannot be controlled, however, once it has been down-loaded from the origina' source, it may appear in many diverse guises, be re-partitioned, amalgamated, and reused, taking on a life of its own. Print-based copyright legislation does not translate easily to the electronic environment. A feature of the legislation to found the advanced NREN network requires the provision of charging mechanisms to be put in place, suggesting a trend towards more control over use and users.

The characteristics which make electronic information difficult to define and 'freeze' at one point in time also raise questions on the nature of bibliographic control and mapping of information resources. Electronic documents and journals which can be updated immediately, replacing the original copy, are difficult to define as a bibliographic entity which has a declared and fixed content, which can be cited for later use. The identi-fication of various versions of a logical item becomes a complex (or perhaps impossible) task, as does preservation and archiving as a permanent record of publication. These problems also rebound upon ethical issues involving the quality and accuracy of the document content. Electronic documents may easily be changed, or 'falsified' with changing intellectual fashions in a way that print being fixed at one point in time cannot.

The unstructured and fluid process which allows a network user to make information available without recourse to formal publisher or refereeing process has great advantages in stimulating an innovative and creative dialectic, but at the cost of a large proportion of false, misleading, or incorrect information which must also be sorted through and rejected. Whilst the research community, in which much of this type of activity takes place at present, has evolved a fairly sophisticated code of practical ethics for network co-operation and exchange, it is doubtful that this will survive a broadening of access and the introduction of commercial interests.

The increasing ubiquity of the networking environment is raising questions about the relative responsibilities of those involved in the information transfer process. Traditionally, this process could be described in terms of five distinct roles: the information provider, who provides the original source material; the information host, who makes it available and accessible, 'publishing' in a print or electronic sense; the carrier or distributor, providing a channel for the information; the intermediary, traditional role for the information service professional; and the information user, the final consumer. This model has long ago begun to break down when applied to the networking environment.

The information provider is often the same as the information host; the common carrier, the telecommunications authority, provides information services in its own right; and the information user more often wishes to find and retrieve the information directly. Many people have begun to question the role of the publisher in the electronic environment: since the author can mount a document in its electronic form on a local computer (quite probably the format it was originally composed in) and the network facilities act as a distribution mechanism, it becomes harder to gauge the function of a traditional publisher. Although this is clearly not appropriate for many types of publishing, in some areas it is possible to see advantages.

For instance, the traditional venue for reporting research has been through a journal article in some summarized form; network publishing would allow a reader to optionally download original datasets and intermediate analysis, as well as authorial commentary, directly and without a time delay. The development of network publishing is likely to involve identifiable changing characteristics compared to the traditional activities:

- a growth in publishing, with one source file producing a variety of complementary versions in different formats;
- multimedia electronic publishing, integrating database, text, image, sound, and video;
- the use of information tools to skim, navigate, browse, and utilize these new media products;
- selective and customized publishing targeted at particular groups;
- a linking with the concept of a 'virtual library', where access and materials are not constrained by physical barriers.

The information user and the information provider potentially have a much more direct and interactive relationship, possibly to the extent that the information exchange cannot be completely separated from the communication process itself. This raises a question mark against the received role of the intermediary, as a filter between originator, distributor, and recipient.

As the growth in electronic information begins to demand a new philosophy of the nature and function of information, so also the activities of the information professional must, in this setting at least, change and adapt. No longer able to adopt a custodial role in managing and organizing the materials and artefacts of information, the librarian or information scientist must adopt a facilitating strategy, aimed at creating the conditions for a user to negotiate the information sphere successfully. The librarian no longer 'owns' the information since it is not contained within any physical institution; and it cannot therefore be 'managed' in the same physical sense. The information user, however, must still negotiate an information space, now across a digital network as much as before within the confines of a library, in order to achieve a successful resolution to the information transfer process.

15

Further Possibilities

Japan's Next Generation project will use faster, denser circuitry to create a new class of super intelligent computers. The 24 projects in the Fifth Generation concentrate on artificial intelligence, a goal of American computer scientists for more than a quarter century. Although the Japanese are highly regarded as superb engineers, Japanese computer scientists have often been faulted' for failing to develop innovative computer software. But in a break with tradition, Kazuhiro Fuchi, the Fifth Generation project director, has deliberately assembled a young team: "The question was who would adapt most easily to this research," says Fuchi. "Young people have fewer fixed ideas." The project, headquartered in a downtown Tokyo skyscraper, will focus on computer architectures, software, and the symbolic logic necessary to build thinking computers. The Microelectronics and Computer Technology Corp (MCC). Last year William Norris, the founder and chairman of Control Data Corp., convened a meeting of top computer and semiconductor industry executives at the Grenelefe Golf and Tennis resort in Orlando, Florida, to discuss setting up a huge research cooperative.

The companies agreed to form a non-profit joint venture so that they could pool their resources and share the cost of doing long-range research. Twelve major US corporations joined the new organisation, including Honeywell, Motorola, RCA, and Control Data. MCC is a bold departure from the way research is usually done in American universities and corporations, and it will probe the limits of the nation's antitrust laws. The venture partly follows the Japanese model: the companies will donate scientists and researchers to MCC, loaning them for up to four years. The corporate co-owners will also put up the money to fund MCC' research, in return for the rights to use the results. Whether the scheme will work is an open question. The 12 companies in MCC are competitors in fast-moving, high-technology markets, and ordinarily they jealously guard any technological edge they gain. In fact, many top US firms—Cray Research, Texas Instruments, Intel, and others—chose to stay out of MCC.

MCC's directors chose retired Admiral Bobby Ray Inman, former director of the National Security Agency and former deputy director of the CIA. Inman is widely respected for his managerial abilities and is an adept politician besides. Over the past five months, Inman orchestrated a competition among 57 cities for the MCC headquarters; the winner was Austin, Texas, after private donors, the state, and universities put together a generous package of incentives.

The consortium will have a budget of about $ 75 million a year and a staff of 250. Its first projects include programs in semiconductor packaging and interconnect technology, advanced software engineering and computer-aided design and manufacturing (CAD/CAM) for the electronics and computer industries. Most ambitious is a 10-year program aimed at breakthroughs in computer architecture, software, and artificial intelligence.

MCC will own the licenses and patents to the technologies; the manufacturing and marketing will be left to the companies that sponsor the projects. MCC will give them a competitive edge on the market—they will have exclusive rights for three years before the research is published and other firms are allowed to buy licenses.

Over the past three years Japan has captured a vital segment of the world semiconductor industry, the market for so-called RAM (random access memory) chips, a technology invented in America. Japan now supplies 70 per cent of all 64K RAMS sold, and it appears that, as the next generation of memory chips, the

256K RAMS, is being readied for market, the Japanese semiconductor companies are threatening to take a big share of sales.

Over the past 20 years, DARPA has poured half a billion dollars into computer research, in the process virtually creating the science of artificial intelligence. The first supercomputer, built in 1964, was a DARPA project. Computer time sharing, a fundamental advance, came out of work sponsored by DARPA. So did packet switched networks, the workhorses of today's telecommunications data networks. And computer graphics—now used on desktop computers and video arcade cockpits—is a DARPA—sponsored invention.

DARPA plans to do everything the Japanese have set out to accomplish and more. Earlier this year DARPA proposed a "Strategic Computing and Survivability" project, which it hopes will lead to a variety of new machines. "Other kinds of systems are good for logic processing. We want architectures that can do very rapid signal processing [and] structures that can handle very, very large amounts of data in communications." Smart robot weapons-drone aircraft, unmanned submarines, and land vehicles-that combine artificial intelligence and high-powered computing can be sent off to do jobs that now involve human risk. "This is a very sexy area to the military, because you can imagine all kinds of neat, interesting things you could send off on their own little missions around the world or even in local comba. The Pentagon will also use the technologies to create artificial intelligence machines that can be used as battlefield advisers and super intelligent computers to coordinate complex weapons systems. An intelligent missile guidance system would have to bring together different technologies-real—time signal processing, numerical calculations, and symbolic processing, all at unimaginably high speeds—in order to make decisions and give advice to human commanders.

The same technology that can be used to simulate an antitank missile smashing into a heavily armoured tank can also be put to work on less martial arts. Instead of shooting a commercial the conventional way, a costly photo session, Digital can create the "pictures" it needs in detail so precise that it's impossible to distinguish between the supercomputer's graphic image and the real photo. As the commercial market grows, the Japanese believe that their strategy of building super-computers for the general-purpose market will pay off. The Cray X-MP contains a dense pack of 240,000 silicon chips arranged to shorten the distances the electrical signals must travel, thereby decreasing the time it takes to perform an operation; the new Cray X-MPs will run at 400 million operations per second. And Japan's super speed goal is 10 billion operations per second. Because of the cost of super-computers, Cray's X-MP will sell for $ 11 million, the market will remain limited. Japan's Fifth Generation project, however, plans to build "super personal computers." These huge increases in raw computer power are just the first step.

The most profound changes brought by the new technologies will be the development of reasoning computers that will use super speed symbol manipulation to simulate human thought. The Fifth Generation field is not new: scientists in the US have been studying artificial intelligence for more than 25 years, struggling to understand the nature of knowledge and how to represent it in forms adaptable to computer usage.

Digital Equipment Corp the nation's second largest computer firm, uses an AI program called X-CON to make custom designs of its, computer systems. Using a set of more than 2500 rules programmed into the system, X-CON examines a customer's specifications, determines whether all the necessary components are included, then draws a set of diagrams showing the proper spatial relationships among the components. Scientists studying artificial intelligence have been aided by advances in computer hardware too. In 1980 a group left MIT's Artificial Intelligence Laboratory to found a company, Symbolics Inc., of Cambridge, Mass., to build computers specially designed to run LISP, a language used to develop artificial intelligence programs; and Xerox has begun to sell similar computers. Symbolics has been selling its machines, the Symbolics 3600, to a broad range of university and industrial research labs. The company has another customer as well: the managers running Japan's Fifth Generation project have bought 10 Symbolics machines and they have 15 more on order in exploring the brave new world of artificial intelligence, computer scientists are concentrating on several important problems. "Knowledge engineers" are building so-called expert systems that can mimic human expertise in a narrowly defined area.

The program is, in effect, a computer replica of Courtes expertise; the computer will ask the drilling-rig foremen questions, just as Courte would. Once it gathers the information it needs, the computer will make recommendations by drawing images on the screen and giving suggestions on how to retrieve the bit. Because daily drilling costs are high, Elf Acquitaine may well recover the program's development costs the first time it is used successfully. General Electric is building a software program that will provide expert advice on repairing locomotives.

The Pentagon would like to build artificial intelligence programs that could serve as a pilot's assistant in the cockpit. Stockbrokers and insurance agents may also soon get help: "Some people are beginning to see a gold mine in financial services," says Patrick Henry Winston, chairman of MIT's Artificial Intelligence Laboratory. And savvy software designers for the personal computer industry are beginning to look at artificial intelligence as the next big wave that will sweep the market. Despite the successes, there are problems ahead as researchers attempt to move beyond the building of narrowly defined "experts."

Computers have always been maddeningly literal machines, subject to the absolute tyranny of the binary codes they use to do their calculations. (The switches are either on or off, simulating ones or zeros, nothing else.) That literal-mindedness can transform a problem that would seem trivial to humans, into a nightmare. Consider the simple statement "Mary had a little lamb." For a computer to translate the text into another language-a function scientists are now trying to develop-it would have to sort through what is, by one count, 28 possible interpretations.

The statement "Ronald Reagan is president" carries a number of immediate meanings to a flesh-and-blood American, but a computer would have to rummage through its silicon memory chips in search of dozens of facts-what the word "president" means and biographical facts and details that tell who Ronald Reagan is. And the biggest challenge of all-teaching computers to learn to acquire knowledge on their own-is nowhere near being solved.

Mankind has long been enchanted and frightened by the prospect of creating machines that think. All the mechanisms for human intelligence are present. Already machines can think just like people, in a limited sense. Man isn't unique in that respect. Moreover, many machines may soon possess sight, touch, hearing (in the form of voice recognition), and speech, thus imitating humans' sensory capacities along with their intellectual ones. But whole areas of the human thought process volition, emotion, the creative uses of error-still lie well outside a computer's experience.

Japanese planners view the computer industry as vital to their nation's economic future and have audaciously made it a national goal to become number one in this industry by the latter half of the 1990s. They aim not only to dominate the traditional forms of the computer industry, but to establish a "knowledge industry" in which knowledge itself will be a saleable commodity like food and oil.

The Japanese plan is bold and dramatically forward looking. It is unlikely to be completely successful in the ten-year period. But to view it therefore as "a lot of smoke," as some American industry leaders have done, is a serious mistake. Even partially realised concepts that are superbly engineered can have great economic value, pre-empt the market, and give the Japanese the dominant position they seek.

Aims and Objectives

The Japanese Fifth Generation project aims to design and produce computer hardware and software for knowledge engineering in a wide range of applications-including expert systems, natural language understanding by machines, and robotics. To accomplish these goals, the Japanese must improve present computing capabilities dramatically, but they must also make major innovations in existing technology that will enable Fifth Generation computers to support very large knowledge bases, allow very fast associative retrievals, perform logical inference operations as fast as current computers perform arithmetic operations, utilise parallelism in program structure and hardware to achieve high speed, and develop a machine-user interface that allows significant use of natural speech and images.

All experts systems built by knowledge engineers to date consist of three main parts. First, is the subsystem that "manages" the knowledge base needed for problem solving and understanding. Secondly, is the problem-solving and inference subsystem, which discovers what knowledge is useful and relevant to the problem at hand, and with it constructs, step by step, a line of reasoning leading to the problem solution, the plausible interpretation, or the best hypothesis. Thirdly, are the methods of interaction between human and machine, in modes and languages that are "natural" and comfortable for the user. Ordinary human natural language is often preferred, but the stylised notations of some fields like chemistry are also desirable for specific groups of users. Knowledge—based management, problem solving and inference, and human interaction-these have all been approached in our present expert systems via software innovations, innovations that have pressed traditional von Neumann hardware architectures to their limits.

The Fifth Generation plan organises its work around these three subsystems, but with a critical added dimension: for each component subsystem there is a hardware level and a software level. And between the levels the Japanese designers must define a "language" with which the software and hardware interact. The knowledge in the knowledge base must first be represented in symbolic form, and in memory structures, that can be used efficiently by the problem-solving and inference subsystem. This representation can take many forms.

A typical kind of associative network is the taxonomy, known as "The... is-a (hierarchy)." For example, "The sparrow is-a kind of bird." In this case, both sparrow and bird are objects within the knowledge base. If the knowledge base is informed that "The bird is-a kind of animal that can fly," the knowledge base management system must automatically propagate the deduction that sparrows can fly.

A rule consists of a collection of statements called the "if" part, and a conclusion or action to be taken called the "then" part. For example, "If the fog ceiling is below 700 feet and the official weather forecast calls for no clearing within the hour, THEN landing is dangerous, will violate air traffic regulations, and diversion to a neighbouring airfield is recommended." To find out if a rule is relevant to the reasoning task at hand, the problem-solving program must scan over the store of "ifs" in the knowledge base. That search can be immense in the size of knowledge base the Japanese plan to make possible. Here again, the knowledge-base management subsystem will be designed to organise the memory in ways that will reduce the amount of processing to be done.

Parallel processing capabilities in both the software and hardware levels of the system will also speed associative retrievals. In the Fifth Generation plan, knowledge will be stored electronically in a large file known as a relational data base. The job of automatically updating the knowledge in the file, and of organising appropriate searches for relevant knowledge, will be performed by the knowledge-base management software. The Fifth Generation prototype knowledge-base subsystem will handle a modest knowledge base thousands of rules and thousands of objects-about the size needed for current expert system applications. Each object will be allotted 1000 characters of file storage space. Within the ten-year trajectory of their plan, the Japanese goal is to develop knowledge-base capacity in their systems that will be able to handle tens of thousands of interference rules and one hundred million objects! What could so much knowledge encompass?

Since the Fifth Generation is so farreaching, it demands dramatic improvements in other technologies that support the main-line knowledge information processing systems (KIPS) goals. Essential to the future of the enterprise, for example, are extremely high-speed processors, capable of processing by orders of magnitude faster than anything now available. Artificial intelligence made its debut on first generation machines and has been implemented subsequently on second- and third generation-machines, but not yet on fourth generation super-computers.

The Japanese aim for chips with 10 million transistors. Chips in current production carry a few hundred thousand transistors at most. Such processors are being developed in the course of another MITI effort, the SuperSpeed Computing Project, and will be adapted into the Fifth Generation machines. In addition, the Fifth Generation depends on access to knowledge bases in many locations, so its technology will ultimately be fused with the most advanced communications technologies.

The whole area of intelligent interfaces—the ability the machines will have to listen, see, understand, and reply to human users—will require extensive R&D in natural language processing in speech understanding, and in graphics and image understanding. All these have been concerns of artificial intelligence research from virtually its beginning some 25 years ago, and basic research in each of these fields has made reasonable progress. Because non-experts will be the largest group of users, natural language processing is one of the most important research goals of the Fifth Generation.

Research here will cover speech wave analysis, phonetic and syntactic analysis, semantic analysis, and pragmatic analysis, which derives understanding by extracting themes or foci in a given sentence, detecting focus shifts, and so on. For speech output, sentence generation will also be studied. Text analysis is also considered a part of natural language processing by the Japanese, although they are quite aware that the techniques used for large-scale text analysis are different from the techniques needed to smooth the way for an individual user to talk to his machine.

The Japanese see knowledge systems as a potential solution to the steadily increasing amount of text and documents that must be handled by computer. "Our research on intelligent man-machine interface will help to solve this problem," reported a group of Japanese scientists at a Fifth Generation project meeting. Present artificial intelligence research suggests this can be done in a prototype system, intelligent automatic analysis has been successfully applied to a wire news service in the US, for instance-but the sheer scale of the automatic analysis planned by the Japanese dwarfs any existing systems.

All this research in natural language processing will proceed in three stages, beginning with an experimental system, followed by a pilot model implementation stage that is connected with the inference and knowledge base machines, and concluding with prototype implementations. At that point the machines will be expected to understand continuous human speech with a vocabulary of 50,000 words from a few hundred or more speakers with 95 per cent accuracy. The speech understanding system is also expected to be capable of running a voice-activated typewriter and of conducting a dialogue with users by means of synthesised speech in Japanese or English.

The machine's capacity to respond intelligently to users, known as its question-answering system, will first be designed to handle queries in the computing field, but it is expected to be a prototype for such systems in many professional fields: in addition to the query system's 5000 or more words of vocabulary, it will have 10,000 or more inference rules.

Planning

Picture and image processing are considered almost as important as language processing, especially as they contribute to computer-aided design and manufacture (CAD/CAM) and to the effective analysis of aerial and satellite images, medical images, and the like. Here again the research will take place in three phases, beginning with an experimental phase to tackle ' such topics as the hardware architecture of "feature extractors "for example, to distinguish the boundaries of objects – display generators, and the image data base.

The second phase will produce a pilot model, and in the third and final phase a prototype will be built, integrated into the Fifth Generation machine, and applications will be studied. One obvious use is in constructing robots that can see, understand, and act under novel circumstances. The bulk of robotics R&D, however, will be done in a Robotics National Project. Eventually, the image understanding system is expected to store about 100,000 images.

There are both positive and negative sides the Japanese project. First, its flaws. The science upon which the audacious Fifth Generation plans are laid lies at the outermost edge and beyond what computer science presently knows. The plan is risky; it contains several "scheduled breakthroughs." There are major scientific and engineering challenges in every aspect, from artificial intelligence through parallel architectures and distributed functions to VLSI design and fabrication. The project demands early successes to maintain its momentum and funding, and that could be a problem.

Conversely, meeting or exceeding the goals of the first three-year periods might well propel the Japanese ahead of their timetable, bringing increased support from the participating companies. Central to the success of the project are the Japanese managers, both governmental and industrial. Generally conservative and risk-averse, they are now to be charged with managing a very ambitious, high-risk project based on technology they hardly understand. Most of the breakthroughs the Fifth Generation project must achieve are basically innovations in software concepts.

The key ideas in the approach to knowledge information processing systems came out of the software world—ideas about the creation, maintenance, and modification of large and complex symbolic data structures in computer memories and the discovery of symbolic lines of reasoning. A quick fix to the problem is to work on the intermediate territory of the so-called firmware—intricate and detailed "programming" of the hardware-switching functions that sit at the bottom of the computing process. This is not a desirable final solution, however, since interpreting and executing the "firmware program" consumes time and slows down the machine.

Japanese computer specialists and managers are not, and never have been, comfortable with software—it's intangible to them, and its production is notoriously difficult to manage "on schedule and on budget." The Japanese lack the experience base in knowledge engineering and expert systems from which to draw as they begin to work out the details of what to build. In addition, the Japanese lack a large corps of university

Finally, from the AI viewpoint, two elements of the plan are questionable. First, the priority given to the highspeed logic processor. Are all those millions Of Lips needed? Second, is PROLOG the best choice for the machine language of the logic processor? In the American engineering experience, few applications have been limited by the number of inference steps per second that could be performed. Rather, limitations in performance arise from limitations in the quantity and quality of knowledge available to the machine (too little and not well defined); the facility with which it can be managed and updated; and the speed with which it can be searched and accessed.

A second plus for PROLOG is that it solves problems by proving theorems in first-order predicate calculus using computationally fast methods. The user never has to be concerned with the details of the problem-solving process. But PROLOG detractors see this as a serious flaw. The major successes of AI have come from mastering the methods by which knowledge can be used to control the search for solutions in complex problems.

The last thing a knowledge engineer wants to do is abdicate control to an "automatic" theorem-proving process that conducts massive searches without step-by step control exerted by the knowledge base. Such uncontrolled searches can be extremely time-consuming. The parallelism that can be brought to bear is a mere palliative, because the searches become exponentially more time-consuming as the problem complexity increases. One can't keep up with exponential growth simply by lining up a hundred or a thousand more parallel processors.

Creating the knowledge industry, with hardware, software, and knowledge system applications, is a great bet. Indeed, it is one of the few great bets sitting out there now in the information processing industry, ready for a major push toward exploitation.

Of course the traditional modes of numerical calculation and data processing will continue to develop and prosper. But these will see steady incremental growth, not explosive growth.

The exponential growth will be seen in symbolic computation and knowledge-based, reasoning by computer. MITI's key economic insight is correct. For an island trading nation, exports create wealth and in the knowledge industry the value of exports is enhanced by indigenous resources-the intelligence, education, and skill of people. Further, knowledge information processing systems will significantly enhance the productivity of many other industries, thereby indirectly contributing to the value added.

The creating of ICOT, the pooling of talent in a cooperative endeavor, plus the well-coordinated transfer of technology between ICOT and the parallel labs of the firms, seem inspired. The ten-year planning horizon is excellent. Ten years is a long time in the information processing industry. Ten years ago pocket calculators cost hundreds of dollars, video games were primitive laboratory toys, and the Japanese had yet to produce their first viable micro-electronic chip. As we live through it, we tend to underestimate the speed of technological change. MITI's concern for nurturing the innovative talents of Japanese computer scientists appears well placed. The US and the advanced European nations have become wary of providing the leading technologies upon which Japanese technical achievements have hitherto relied.

Trade wars are under way, and blockades are inevitable. Though solutions to the technological problems posed by the Fifth Generation plan may be hard to achieve, paths to possible solutions abound. The Japanese are rich with excellent engineering talent and have an adequate supply of cutting-edge computer scientists. The mix of talents enables (but does not guarantee) a good chance of success.

Hard Facts

Managers of the Fifth Generation project have said that it would not disturb them if only 10 per cent of the project goals were achieved; others have remarked that the ten year planning horizon should not be taken too seriously; that the project goals are so important that an extension over another half or full decade would not be unreasonable. Partially realised concepts that are superbly engineered can have great utility and be of great economic benefit. At the very least, a partial success can pre-empt the area and make it not worthwhile for others to enter playing catch up.

The first 20 per cent of the technical achievement may skim off 80 per cent of the potential economic gain. If true, firms in the American industry might never find it in their economic interest to enter the arena. Being late might put them out of the contest. Consider this: though video-taping was invented in the US, the lengthy and expensive R&D process for the consumer-oriented video cassette recorder led to an all-or-none market share result, with American industry getting the "none." No matter how partial its success may be, the Fifth Generation project will provide a decade-long learning experience for a new generation of Japanese computer scientists.

They will be called upon to confront and perhaps solve the most, challenging problems facing the future of information processing, rather than re-engineering traditional systems. They will be learning advanced software concepts in a way that has never been done before in Japan and has never been widely done in the US or Europe. The Fifth Generation project, in its short life, has emplaced the technology transfer mechanisms necessary for Japanese industry to move effectively to bring its developments to market. Right now, the US has a substantial lead in virtually every area of Fifth Generation work.

Of course, the answer depends on what one substitutes for "XXX." Readers who filled in, say, "national socialism" could have supposed that these words were spoken, as a warning to German intellectuals who had not yet appreciated the glory of the Nazi revolution, by Josef Goebbels on the occasion of the book burning in Berlin on May 10, 1933. Readers could substitute "the ideas of the great leader and teacher" for "XXX" and leave open what particular revolution is being talked about. Leaders who come to mind, and whose names would render the quoted paragraph plausible, are, to name just a few: Karl Marx, General Pinochet, Stalin.

The Germans, by the way, had a word for what intellectuals are here being warned to do: Gleickschalffing, which is translated as "bringing into line" or "coordination." But, implausible as it may seem at first glance, "XXX" in the quoted passage stands for "this new instrument," meaning the computer. The authors of The Fifth Generation maintain that intellectuality, the creative use of the mind engaged in study and in reflection, will soon become inevitably and necessarily dependent on the computer. They are astounded that American intellectuals aren't rushing to enlist in their revolution.

A professor of computer science at Stanford University and a co-founder of two commercial companies that market artificial intelligence software systems, and Pamela McCorduck, a science writer, give the reader an idea of what's happening in the world of computers. They make the following claims. First, certain American computer scientists have discovered that, if computers are expected to intervene in some activity in the real world, then it would help, to say the least, if they had some knowledge of the domain of the activity in question. For example, computer systems designed to help make medical diagnoses had better know about diseases and their signs and symptoms.

Second, other American computer scientists have described designs of computers, "computer architectures," that depart radically from the industry's traditional design principles originally laid down by the pioneer computer scientist. The new architectures allow computational chains to be decomposed into steps which can be executed as soon as the data for executing them are ready. They then don't have to wait their turn, so to speak. Indeed, many steps can be executed simultaneously. Computation time is in a sense "folded" in such machines, which are consequently very much faster than their orthodox predecessors.

Third, still other computer scientists, mainly French and British, have created a computer language which they believe to be well suited for representing knowledge in computers in a form that lends itself to powerful logical manipulation. The Japanese hope that the conjunction of this computer language with the new architecture will allow ultra rapid computation of "inferences" from masses of stored knowledge. Fourth, these developments have taken place at a time of continuing dramatic progress in making computers physically smaller, functionally faster, and with increasing storage capacities.

Finally, the Japanese, who already dominate the world market in consumer electronics, have seized on the resulting opportunity and decided to create entirely new and enormously powerful computer systems, the "Fifth Generation," based on the developments described above. These systems, as the book jacket puts it, will be "artificially intelligent machines that can reason, draw conclusions, make judgments, and even understand the written and spoken word." This appears to be a very ambitious claim. But not to seasoned observers of the computer scene, who have long since learned to penetrate the foggy language of the computer enthusiasts.

In other words, the most recent ambitions of the Japanese were already close to being realised according to leaders of the American artificial intelligence community a quarter of a century ago! All that remained to be done-and it would be done within the "visible future"-was to extend the range of the problems such machines would solve to the whole range of the problems to which the human mind has been applied. That ambition remains as absurd today as it was twenty-five years ago. In the meanwhile, however, much progress has been made in getting computers to "understand" the written word and even some words spoken in very highly controlled contexts. Is the Japanese project then really not very ambitious?

A geriatric robot that frees old people from the murderous instincts of their children and is programmed to lie to them systematically, telling them that it understands their petty stories and enjoys "listening" to them. Mechanical doctors we can be utterly candid with and which won't disapprove of us, as human doctors often do. Technical devices in our own homes that gather information about us and determine to what group we ought to belong and which ones we should hate.

Technical systems that permit us to exchange knowledge "engagingly" with our fellow creatures while avoiding the horror of having to look at them or be looked at let alone touched. This is the world Feigenbaum and McCorduck are recommending. In fact, they haven't told us the whole story. Professor Tohru Moto-oka of Tokyo University and titular head of the Japanese Fifth Generation project promises even more:

> ... first, Fifth Generation computers will take the place of man in the area of physical labor, and, through the intellectualisation of these advanced computers, totally new applied fields will be developed, social productivity will be increased, and distortions in values will be eliminated [emphasis added].

We are well on our way to the kind of world sketched here. Already, we are told, and it is undoubtedly true, many people prefer to "interact" with computers. Schoolchildren prefer them to teachers, and many patients to doctors. No one seems to ask what it may be about today's doctors and teachers, or with the situations in which they work, that causes them to come off second-best in competition with computers.

The computer has long been a solution looking for problems —the ultimate technological fix which insulates us from having to look at problems. Our schools, for example, tend to produce students with mediocre abilities to read, write, and reason; the main thing we are doing about that is to sit kids down at computer consoles in the classrooms. Perhaps they'll manage to become "computer- literate"-whatever that means even if, in their mother tongue, they remain functionally illiterate. We now have factories so highly computerised that they can operate virtually unmanned.

Devices that shield us from having to come in contact with fellow human beings are rapidly taking over much of our daily lives. Voices synthesised by computers tell us what to do next when we place calls on the telephone. The same voices thank us when we have done what they ask. But what does "the same voices" mean in this context? Individuality, identity, everything that has to do with the uniqueness of persons—or of anything else!-simply disappears. No wonder the architects of, and apologists for, worlds in which work becomes better and more engaging to the extent that it can be carried out without face-to-face interaction, and in which people prefer machines that listen to them to people, come to the conclusion that intellectuals are irrelevant figures. There is no place in their scheme of things for creative minds, for independent study and reflection, for independent anything.

Aside from whatever advantages are to be gained by living our lives in an electronic isolation ward, and aside also from the loss to "them" of a market "we" now dominate, what good reasons are there for mounting our own Fifth generation project on a scale, as Feigenbaum and McCorduck recommend, of the program that landed our man on the moon? -if you can think of a good defense application.

One chapter of their book is devoted to "AI and the National Defense." However, the chapter is only six pages long, and is mainly a song of praise-perhaps gratitude is a more apt word-for the Pentagon's 11 enlightened scientific leadership." Laid on thick, the praise tends to betray its own absurdity:

> Since the Pentagon is often perceived as the national villain, especially by intellectuals, it's a pleasure to report that in one enlightened corner of it, human beings were betting taxpayers' money on projects that would have major benefits for the whole human race.

The corner mentioned is the Defense Department's Advance Research Projects Agency, DARPA, also often called just ARPA. Well, there is reason for workers in Al to be grateful to this agency. It has spent in the order of $ 500 million on computer research, and that certainly benefited the AT community (the artificial intelligentsia) enormously. But "major benefits for the whole human race".

The military, however, has good reason to continue, just as generously as ever, to provide funds for work on the fifth generation, as Feigenbaum and McCorduck make clear: The so-called smart weapons of 1992, for all their sophisticated modern electronics, are really just extremely complex wind-tip toys compared to the weapon systems that will be possible in a decade if intelligent information processing systems are applied to the defense problems of the 1990s.

The authors make five points. First, they believe we should look "with awe at the peculiar nature of modern electronic warfare," particularly at the fact that the Israelis recently shot down 79 Syrian airplanes with no losses to themselves. "This amazing result was achieved," they write, "largely by intelligent human electronic battle management. In the future, it can and will be done by computer.

Second, we cannot afford to allow the "technology of the intelligent computer systems of the future . . . to slip away to the Japanese or to anyone else.... Japan, as a nation, has a long-standing casual attitude toward secrecy when it comes to technological matters." Third, with the ever-increasing cost of military hardware, "the economic impact of an intelligent armaments system that can strike targets with extreme precision should be apparent . . . fewer weapons used selectively for maximum strike capability."

Fourth, "it is essential that the newest technological developments be made available to the Defense Department." Finally, "the Defense Department needs the ability to shape technology to conform to its needs in military systems. Here, perhaps more than in any other argument of the book, we are close to what it's "all about." A much shorter, and better, account of the Japanese Fifth Generation project appeared recently as a cover story of *Newsweek magazine*.. People generally should know the end use of their labor.

Students coming to study at the artificial intelligence laboratories of MIT, my university, or Stanford, Edward Feigenbaum's, or the other such laboratories in the US should decide what they want to do with their talents without being befuddled by euphemisms. They should be clear that, upon graduation, most of the companies they will work for, and especially those that will recruit them more energetically, are the most deeply engaged in feverish activity to find still faster, more reliable ways to kill ever more people-Feigenbaum and McCorduck speak of the objective of creating smart weapons systems with "zero probability of error" (their emphasis). Whatever euphemisms are used to describe students' AI laboratory projects, the probability is overwhelming that the end of their research will serve this or similar military objectives. To underline the importance of the computer as the "main artifact of the age of information," Feigenbaum and McCorduck instruct us just wherein the importance of the computer lies: [The computer's] purpose is certainly to process information-to transform, amplify, distribute, and otherwise modify it. But more important, the computer produces information. The essence of the computer revolution is that the burden of producing the future knowledge of the world will be transferred from human heads to machine artifacts [emphasis in the original].

How are we to understand the assertion that the computer "produces information"? In the same way, presumably, as the statement that a coal-fired electric power station produces energy. But that would be a simple and naive falsehood. Coal-fired power stations, transform energy, they do not produce it. Computers similarly transform information, generally using information-losing operations. For example, when a computer executes an instruction to add 2 and 5, it computes.

Role in Society

Since then, it has had some notable successes, enabling computers to perform-albeit in a very limited way some of the tasks normally done by our minds. Some AI workers see AI as a way of helping us understand human psychology; they try to write programs that tackle their tasks in the sort of way in which we do. Others see it as an approach to a theory of intelligence in general, human (and animal) intelligence being a special case. Still others simply want to write programs to do something (to understand language, to describe visible objects, or to solve problems, of various kinds), irrespective of how we do it.

And most of these hope that what their programs do will be not only interesting, but useful. The technological aspects of AI have suddenly become more visible. Public interest in AI, and media coverage of it, have increased enormously over the last two years. More and more people view it as an incipient technology of great potential power and social significance. The public interest dates from the announcement in 1981 of Japan's ten-year national plan for developing "Fifth Generation" computers. These are defined as incorporating AI techniques (as well as large-scale parallel processing).

Since then, large sums of money for AI-research have been made available also by governments and industry in the Western industrialised nations.

Gradual Development

Several core research areas are likely to make solid progress within the next decade. Each of these is already being worked on in various countries, and progress does not depend upon the success of Japan's ambitious "Fifth Generation" project. One is low-level vision, based on techniques using parallel hardware and cooperative processing.

Current "connectionist" research in this area differs in its approach from work on two-dimensional pattern recognition by "property lists," and from-the-top-down /Iscene analysis" of three-dimensional scenes. Based on detailed studies of image formation, it is able to extract from the ambient light information about three-dimensional features (such as shape, depth, texture, and surface orientation) which in previous approaches could have been computed only, if at all, by way of high-level knowledge of the expected scene. Some of this work is being done in the context of human psychology and neurophysiology, some in a more technological context.

Dedicated (massively parallel) machines are being designed for this research, and major advances depend upon such hardware. A second area in which we can expect significant progress is robotics. This includes problems of movement control, trajectory planning, and visuomotor coordination (and will take advantage of advances in low-level vision). As in the case of vision, some projects will rely on "artificial" means to ensure success (such as light stripes for automatic welding machines, capable of recognising different sorts of weld joint and guiding the welder accordingly), while others will relate more closely to psycho-physiological theories of motor control and visuornotor coordination in living organisms. Knowledge-based "expert" systems will multiply enormously in the next decade, not least because there is considerable commercial interest in them. Different domains of human expertise may require different approaches to knowledge engineering. In domains less fully covered by an explicit scientific theory. It may be easier to extract knowledge from human experts who are competent but who have not yet achieved the "intuitive" mastery of the domain that top-flight experts enjoy.

The latter give the right answer more often, but cannot easily introspect their reasoning processes, which happen very fast and are not consciously accessible. The former take time to come to a decision, after consciously weighing distinct considerations against each other and verbally identifying areas of unclarity. Domains (such as medical radiology) that depend on the comparison and interpretation of complex visual images are especially difficult to automate, since low-level visual processes are not open to voluntary inspection or control.

Indeed, experts often give highly misleading advice about how they may be carrying out the relevant comparisons. (Eye movement studies show, for instance, that expert radiologists do not scan x-ray photographs in the way they say that they do.) In tandem with the increasing experience of AI-trained knowledge engineers, further psychological studies of the organisation of knowledge in different domains should be useful. Research on expert systems will also focus on the computational architecture required to deal with large, complex knowledge bases.

Current systems are relatively simple and inflexible, and are restricted to very narrow domains. They can be incrementally improved, but only up to a point. Eventually, the interactions between the increasing number of independently added rules become too difficult to control, and the system's reliability and intelligibility are jeopardised. Current systems have no access to higher-level representations of the knowledge domain and their own problem-solving activity. Special problems arise if a system has to work in real-time, where unexpected events can require quick switching from the current activity to some other.

The next ten years will see some general work on powerful (IKBs) architectures (as well as the production of more examples of specific commercially useful systems), including parallel-processing devices. Progress can be expected also in natural language processing, both of individual sentences and of texts. Key issues include syntactic parsing, the integration of syntax with semantics, and the understanding of connected text.

Machine translation could in principle benefit from advances both in single-sentence parsing and in text analysis. Current work on parsing is motivated both by theoretical (linguistic) interests and by the hope of improving the man-machine interface so as to make it possible for nonspecialist users to communicate with programs in (some reasonable subset of) natural language. Where a program is used for some specific purpose, semantic factors can be more readily used to help in the parsing and disambiguation of queries and instructions input by the user.

Verbal interchanges about lunar geology, or about airline reservations, are already reasonably "natural" because of the exploitation of semantic constraints, and further domain-specific semantics will be developed over the next decade. More generally applicable (theoretical) research will continue into the best point at which to use semantics in parsing: from the beginning of the sentence, or spreading out from the middle, or only after an initial parse of the entire sentence? Text-analysis programs can already give a precis of most short news stories about specific topics (such as earthquakes, hijackings, and road accidents). But they rely on rigid, preprogrammed schemata, which provide the semantic skeleton of the types of stories concerned.

Some recent research is aimed at enabling a text analysis program to learn new schemata for itself, to integrate one schema with another so as to understand a story combining both, and to use a given schema to reason analogically in an unfamiliar context. A high degree of success cannot be expected within the next ten years, but our understanding of the relevant problems should be advanced. A variety of educational applications is already receiving attention.

Some are focused on particular curricular subjects, and require both a model of the theory of that subject and a model of the student's knowledge of it (which varies in level and in organisation, from person to person and from time to time). Others are less specific, and aim to use AI-based techniques to improve the pupil's attitude to intelligence in general. There is some evidence that both normal and handicapped students can attain greater self-confidence and intellectual achievement by experience with these specially designed programming environments. Controlled research into the classroom effects of AI-based systems has recently been initiated, and this can be expected to bear fruit within the next decade. An extremely important area, which is increasingly being studied because of recent hardware developments, concerns the computa-tional properties of large parallel systems. At present, we under-stand very little of the potential and limitations of such systems. Some of the connectionist work mentioned above suggests that cooperative processing may have some highly surprising pro-perties.

For example, the number of individual processors required to make the "human" range of visual shape discrimination appears to be markedly less than one would naturally assume. Again, making a connectionist system stochastic rather than deterministic improves its chance of finding an optimal solution. The computational properties of parallel machines will not be well understood for a long time, but experience with these new systems in the near future will doubtless lead to some advance.

Different Streams

The impacts of AI on other technologies will include many different examples of applications to individual problems. For example, an olfactory chip is being designed using AI techniques of pattern recognition. Given advances in very large-scale integration (VLSI), instruments and products of many different kinds will come to include chips whose design makes use of AI methods. Any commercial-industrial task that could benefit from even a limited degree of intelligence could in principle be performed better with the help of AI, so the technological applications of AI will be extremely diverse. AI will influence other sciences in their general philosophical approach as well as their specific theoretical content. Indeed, psychology and (to a lesser degree) biology have already been affected by computational ideas. And, contrary to what most people assume, AI has had a humanising effect in psychology. AI's influence will be especially strong in the psychology of vision and language, and, as noted above, it is likely that robotics will engage with the psychophysiology of movement. Psychological research will feed back into AI; for example, insofar as psychologists arrive at a better understanding of the organisation of knowledge, their work may be useful in designing computerised expert systems.

Social impacts will be of various types. First, there will be effects on individuals and institutions brought about by specific applications of AI, such as expert systems for medical diagnosis, legal and financial advice, or educational help. These programs will not merely provide a service (whose adequacy should be very carefully monitored), but will very likely change the social relations of the profession or institution concerned.

For example, if general practitioners, or nurses, can use an AI program to aid in various aspects of patient care, the social image of the specialist physician may be profoundly affected. (And legal responsibilities for medical decisions may be assigned in a way very different from today.) Likewise, legal programs may undermine the status of lawyers, and alter the nature of their work.

In both cases, while the mystique, of the human experts may be lessened, their opportunity for exercising their specifically human powers may be increased. The general public might come to be less dependent on human experts than they are today. Reducing the power of professionals such as doctors, lawyers, and teachers would certainly have advantages. But replacing human professional advice by computer programs is dangerous to the extent that AI systems in public use are inadequate-and/or ill-understood. Systems that have taken several man-years to develop (and whose original programmers may be retired, or dead) are often very difficult to evaluate or alter, because even computer scientists do not fully understand how they work.

A second type of social impact concerns general social trends brought about by applications of AI and information technology (IT). These include changes in the proportion of the workforce in service and leisure industries, changes in the division of labour and sexual roles, and changes in general lifestyles and patterns of interaction.

But other potential consequences of AI point in the opposite direction. The widespread use of home terminals, for instance, threatens to have an isolating influence even more powerful than that of television. If people are encouraged to work, and to shop, from their sitting-rooms, there may be unfortunate psychological effects in terms of personal stress and loneliness. Community computer centres could offset these effects to some extent, providing a social meeting place outside the confines of the home and nuclear family.

Some writers even predict that commercially available (and highly profitable) AI systems will be heavily used not only in task-oriented ways, but as surrogates for human contact. On this view, the strong tendency to anthropomorphism that most of us share will result in patterns of interaction being skewed away from human beings, and towards quasi-human computer systems (with naturalistic, "voices," and sometimes even "bodies").

A Continual Process

There will be "more of the same," in that the areas mentioned above will provide perplexing problems for many years to come. Especially hard problems include learning, high-level vision, naive physics, and abstract work in computational logic.

For instance, expert systems are at present unable to "plain their reasoning except by "backwards-chaining": giving a resume of the chain of inferences (rules) that led up to their conclusion. They cannot relate their conclusion to the domain in general, or rely on an overview of the problem to assess the relative theoretical reliability of different hypotheses.

Nor can they monitor and adjust the structure of their own problem-solving, for they have no high-level representation of it. They are unable, too, to integrate different knowledge domains, and to use concepts and patterns of inference taken from one domain to reason (analogically) in another. Nor can current systems explain their conclusions differently to different users, taking account of the specific user's knowledge.

The user can ask for a "deeper" explanation (a more detailed inference resume) but the program has no user model in terms of which to adjust its explanations to the human's particular range and level of knowledge. For this reason also, the pattern of interaction between user and system is at present very limited. The user cannot offer his own conclusions for comment and criticism, for example, as students can do with human teachers. A special case of human knowledge is "naive physics," one's everyday knowledge of the properties and behaviour of different sorts of physical substances, and the nature of the causal relations between them. This knowledge enters into vision and motor control, and also into natural language.

For example, a language-using program would have to understand the differences in meaning between verbs such as pour, flow, spill, drop, and the like, if it were to give instructions or understand texts about activities dealing with liquids. Similarly, a robot capable of seeing that a container was just about to spill its contents onto the object below, and of adjusting its movements accordingly, would need some representation of the behaviour of fluids. Very little work has been done on these issues so far, and they are likely to provide a challenge for many years.

"Computer-aided design" is typically thought of as involving the graphical display of precise three dimensional specifications of various products (from machine tools through cars to buildings), taking into account a wide range of values of many parameters. But a recent form of computer-aided design involves suggestion rather than specification, in the sense that the design program originates novel ideas—ideas that are not merely quantitatively different from previous specifications.

For example, heuristic programs are already being used to suggest novel experiments (described at the intramolecular level) in genetic engineering, or to help design new sorts of three-dimensional silicon chips. The potential of systems like these should be further explored. The computer modelling of creative thinking will require long-term research, especially with respect to domains whose crucial concepts cannot be so readily defined as the concepts of molecular biology, chip circuitry, or set theory. Machine learning is a pressing problem for the future. If a program cannot learn for itself, its development is limited by the time and ability of the programmer to provide it with new information and ideas.

Additional Reading

Bhaskara Rao, Digumarti (1994). *Scientific Aptitude,* New Delhi: Ashish Publishing House. ISBN 81-7024-658-X.

Bhaskara Rao, Digumarti (1995). *Animal Kingdom*. New Delhi: Discovery Publishing House. ISBN 81-7141-274-2.

Bhaskara Rao, Digumarti (1995). *Batracology*. New Delhi: Discovery Publishing House. ISBN 81-7141-279-3.

Bhaskara Rao, Digumarti (1997), *Scientific Attitude*. New Delhi: Discovery Publishing House. ISBN 81-7141-308-0.

Bhaskara Rao, Digumarti (1996). *Scientific Attitude vis-à-vis Scientific Aptitude*. New Delhi: Discovery Publishing House. ISBN 81-7141-308-0.

Bhaskara Rao, Digumarti, Editor (1996). *Encyclopaedia of Education for All,* 5 Volumes. New Delhi: APH Publishing Corporation. ISBN 81-7024-759-4 (set).

Vol. I *Education for All: The World Conference*. ISBN 81-7024-760-8.

Vol. II *Education for All: The EPA-9 Summit*. ISBN 81-7024-761-6.

Vol. III *Education for All: Quality Education for All*. ISBN 81-7024-762-6.

Vol. IV *Education for All: Planning and Monitoring*. ISBN 81-7024-763-4.

Vol. V *Education for All: The Indian Scenario*. ISBN 81-7024-764-0.

Bhaskara Rao, Digumarti, Editor (1996). *Global Perceptions on Peace Education,* 3 Volumes. New Delhi: Discovery Publishing House. ISBN 81-7141-319-6.

Bhaskara Rao, Digumarti, Editor (1996). *National Policy on Education*. 2 Volumes. New Delhi: Anmol Publications Pvt. Ltd. ISBN 81-7488-323-1.

Bhaskara Rao, Digumarti, Editor (1997). *Care the Child*, 2 Volumes. New Delhi: Discovery Publishing House. ISBN 81-7141-394-3.

Bhaskara Rao, Digumarti, Editor (1997). *Education for the 21st Century*. New Delhi: Discovery Publishing House. ISBN 81-7141-389-7.

Bhaskara Rao, Digumarti, Editor (1997). *Reflections on Scientific Attitude*. New Delhi: Discovery Publishing House, ISBN 81-7141-319-6.

Bhaskara Rao, Digumarti, Editor (1997). *Success Story of a Primary Education Project*. New Delhi: APH Publishing Corporation. ISBN 81-7024-850-7.

Bhaskara Rao, Digumarti, Editor (1997). *World Food Summit*. New Delhi: Discovery Publishing House. ISBN 81-7141-386-2.

Bhaskara Rao, Digumarti, Editor (1998). *Adolescence Education*. New Delhi: Discovery Publishing House. ISBN 81-7141-432-X.

Bhaskara Rao, Digumarti, Editor (1998). *Community and School Nutrition Education*. New Delhi: Discovery Publishing House. ISBN 81-7141-435-4.

Bhaskara Rao, Digumarti, Editor (1998). *District Primary Education Programme*. New Delhi: Discovery Publishing House. ISBN 81-7141-396-X.

Bhaskara Rao, Digumarti, Editor (1998). *Earth Summit*, 2 Volumes. New Delhi: Discovery Publishing House. ISBN 81-7141-435-4.

Bhaskara Rao, Digumarti, Editor (1998). *National Policy on Education: Towards an Enlightened and Humane Society*, New Delhi: Discovery Publishing House. ISBN 81-7141-426-5.

Bhaskara Rao, Digumarti, Editor (1998). *Reforming School Education*. New Delhi: Discovery Publishing House. ISBN 81-7141-403-6.

Bhaskara Rao, Digumarti, Editor (1998). *Teacher Education in India*. New Delhi: Discovery Publishing House. ISBN 81-7141-406-0.

Bhaskara Rao, Digumarti, Editor (1998). *World Summit for Social Development*. New Delhi: Discovery Publishing House. ISBN 81-7141-420-6.

Bhaskara Rao, Digumarti, Editor (2000). *Education for All: Achieving the Goal*, 3 Volumes, New Delhi: APH Publishing Corporation. ISBN 81-7648-152-1.

Vol. I *The Global Consensus*. ISBN 81-7648-155-6.

Vol. II *Mid-Decade Review Reports of Regional Seminars*. ISBN 81-7648-154-8.

Vol. III *Issues and Trends*. ISBN 81-7648-155-6.

Bhaskara Rao, Digumarti, Editor (2000), *International Encyclopaedia of AIDS*, 11 Volumes in 13 Parts. New Delhi: Discovery Publishing House. ISBN 81-7141-6 (Set).

Vol. 1 *Introduction to HIV/AIDS*. ISBN 81-7141-523-7.

Vol. 2 *HIV/AIDS—Issues and Challenges*, 2 Parts. ISBN 81-7141-524-5.

Vol. 3 *HIV/AIDS—Socio Economic Realities*. ISBN 81-7141-524-3.

Vol. 4 *HIV/AIDS—Law Ethics and Human Rights*, 2 Parts. ISBN 81-7141-526-1.

Vol. 5 *AIDS and NGOs*. ISBN 81-7141-527-X.

Vol. 6 *AIDS and Home Care*. ISBN 81-7141-528-8.

Vol. 7 *STD Case Management*. ISBN 81-7141-529-6.

Vol. 8 *HIV/AIDS Prevention and Care—Teaching Modules for Nurses and Midwives*. ISBN 81-7141-530-X.

Vol. 9 *HIV Prevention Education for Education for Educational Institutions*. ISBN 81-7141-531-8.

Vol. 10 *Instructional Modules for AIDS Education*. ISBN 81-7141-532-6.

Vol. 11 *School Health Education to Prevent AIDS and STD—A Package for Curriculum Planners*. ISBN 81-7141-5338-4.

Bhaskara Rao, Digumarti, Editor (2000). *International Encyclopaedia of Science and Technology Education*, 11 Volumes. New Delhi: Discovery Publishing House. ISBN 81-7141-548-2 (Set).

Vol. 1 *Science and Technology Education*. ISBN 81-7141-568-7.

Vol. 2 *Science Education in Developing Countries*. ISBN 81-7141-570-9.

Vol. 3 *Organisational Structure of Science*. ISBN 81-7141-570-9.

Vol. 4 *Science Education in Asia and the Pacific*. ISBN 81-7141-571-7.

Vol. 5 *Science and Technology Education for All*. ISBN 81-7141-572-5.

Vol. 6 *Values, Ethics, Talent and Girls in Science and Technology Education*. ISBN 81-7141-573-3.

Vol. 7 *Popularization of Science and Technology Education*. ISBN 81-7141-574-1.

Vol. 8 *Science, Power and Society*. ISBN 81-7141-575-X.

Vol. 9 *Information Technology*. ISBN 81-7141-576-8.

Vol. 10 *Teacher Training in Science and Technology Education*. ISBN 81-7141-577-6.

Vol. 11 *Teacher Training in Science and Technology: A Curriculum Framework*. ISBN 81-7141-578-4.

Bhaskara Rao, Digumarti, Editor (2001). *Distance Education in Different Countries*. New Delhi: APH Publishing Corporation. ISBN 81-7648-229-3.

Bhaskara Rao, Digumarti, Editor (2001). *Decentralised Management of Education (Management of Education in Panchayati Raj and Municipal Bodies)*. New Delhi: Discovery Publishing House. ISBN 81-7141-617-9.

Bhaskara Rao, Digumarti, Editor (2001). *Electrochemistry for Environmental Protection*. New Delhi: Discovery Publishing House. ISBN 81-7141-619-5.

Bhaskara Rao, Digumarti, Editor (2001). *Global Educational Studies*. New Delhi: Discovery Publishing House. ISBN 81-7141-616-0.

Bhaskara Rao, Digumarti, Editor (2001). *Global Synthesis of Educational Assessment*. New Delhi: Discovery Publishing House. ISBN 81-7141-613-6.

Bhaskara Rao, Digumarti, Editor (2000). *International Encyclopaedia of Human Rights*. 7 Volumes in 13 Parts. New Delhi: Discovery Publishing House. (Royal Size). ISBN 81-7141-567-9 (Set).

Vol. 1 *International Instruments of Human Rights*, 2 Parts. ISBN 81-7141-595-4.

Vol. 2 *Regional Instruments of Human Rights*. ISBN 81-7141-604-7.

Vol. 3 *Human Rights and the United Nations*, 2 Parts. ISBN 81-7141-605-5.

Vol. 4 *Fact Files of Human Rights*, 3 Parts. ISBN 81-7141-605-3.

Vol. 5 *Study Stories of Human Rights*, 3 Parts. ISBN 81-7141-607-3.

Vol. 6 *International Meetings on Human Rights*, 2 Parts. ISBN 81-7141-608-X.

Vol. 7 *Professional Training in Human Rights*. ISBN 81-7141-609-8.

Bhaskara Rao, Digumarti, Editor (2001). *Jomtein Decade of Education*. New Delhi: Discovery Publishing House. ISBN 81-7141-618-7.

Bhaskara Rao, Digumarti, Editor (2001). *Nuclear Materials: Issues and Concerns*, 2 Volumes. New Delhi: Discovery Publishing House. ISBN 81-7141-611-X.

Bhaskara Rao, Digumarti, Editor (2001). *World Conference on Education for All*. New Delhi: APH Publishing Corporation. ISBN 81-7141-274-9.

Bhaskara Rao, Digumarti, Editor (2001). *World Conference on Higher Education*, New Delhi: Discovery Publishing House. ISBN 81-7141-610-1.

Bhaskara Rao, Digumarti, Editor (2001). *World Conference on Science*. New Delhi: Discovery Publishing House. ISBN 81-7141-612-8.

Bhaskara Rao, Digumarti, Editor (2003). *Inspiring Experience in Teacher Education*. New Delhi: Discovery Publishing House. ISBN 81-7141-656-X.

Bhaskara Rao, Digumarti, Editor (2003). *International Studies in Education*, 3 Volumes, New Delhi: Discovery Publishing House. ISBN 81-7141-647-0.

Bhaskara Rao, Digumarti, Editor (2003). *Military Conversion: Impact on Science and Technology*, New Delhi: Discovery Publishing House. ISBN 81-7141-578-4.

Bhaskara Rao, Digumarti, Editor (2003). *United Nations Millennium Summit*. New Delhi: Discovery Publishing House. ISBN 81-7141-632-2.

Bhaskara Rao, Digumarti, Editor (2003). *World Assembly on Aging*. New Delhi: Discovery Publishing House. ISBN 81-7141-637-3.

Bhaskara Rao, Digumarti, Editor (2004). *World Conference on Human Rights*. New Delhi: Discovery Publishing House. ISBN 81-7141-661-6.

Bhaskara Rao, Digumarti, Editor (2003). *World Education Forum*. New Delhi: Discovery Publishing House. ISBN 81-7141-639-X.

Bhaskara Rao, Digumarti, Editor (2004). *Education Employment and Human Resource Development*. New Delhi: Discovery Publishing House. ISBN 81-7141-681-0.

Bhaskara Rao, Digumarti, Editor (2004). *Successfully Schooling*. New Delhi: Discovery Publishing House. ISBN 81-7141-677-2.

Bhaskara Rao, Digumarti, Editor (2004). *European Education and Teachers*. New Delhi: Discovery Publishing House. ISBN 81-7141-702-7.

Bhaskara Rao, Digumarti, Editor (2004). *Teachers in a Changing World*. New Delhi: Discovery Publishing House. ISBN 81-7141-694-2.

Bhaskara Rao, Digumarti, Editor (2004). *Learning to Live Together*, 4 Volumes. New Delhi: Discovery Publishing House.

Vol. 1 *International Conference on Learning to Live Together.*

Vol. 2 *Globalisation and Living Together.*

Vol. 3 *Curriculum for Learning to Live Together.*

Vol. 4 *Science Education for the Contemporary Society.*

Bhaskara Rao, Digumarti (2004). *International Guidelines on Open and Distance Education*, New Delhi: Discovery Publishing House.

Bhaskara Rao, Digumarti, Editor (2004). *Adult Learning in the 21st Century*. New Delhi: Discovery Publishing House.

Bhaskara Rao, Digumarti, Editor (2004). *Educational Practices: Research and Recommendations*. New Delhi: Discovery Publishing House.

Bhaskara Rao, Digumarti, Editor (2004). *Chernobyl: Never Again*. New Delhi: APH Publishing Corporation.

Bhaskara Rao, Digumarti, Editor (2004). *Virology and Immunology*. New Delhi: APH Publishing Corporation.

Bhaskara Rao, Digumarti, C.A.P. Swami and B.S.V. Dutt (1997). *Self-Evaluation in Student Teaching*. New Delhi: Discovery Publishing House. ISBN 81-7141-374-9.

Bhaskara Rao, Digumarti and B.S.V. Dutt, Editors (2003). *Education: Programmes and Policies*. New Delhi: APH Publishing Corporation. ISBN 81-7648-470-9.

Bhaskara Rao, Digumarti and D. Naresh Kumar (2004). *School Teacher Effectiveness*. New Delhi: Discovery Publishing House.

Bhaskara Rao, Digumarti and D. Sridhar (2002). *Job Satisfaction of School Teachers*. New Delhi: Discovery Publishing House. ISBN 81-7141-652-7.

Bhaskara Rao, Digumarti and Digumarti Pushpa Latha (1994). *Achievement in Biology*. New Delhi: Discovery Publishing House. ISBN 81-7141-264-5.

Bhaskara Rao, Digumarti, C. Sridevi and K. Vijaya (1995). *Achievement in Social Studies*. New Delhi: Discovery Publishing House. ISBN 81-7141-281-5.

Bhaskara Rao, Digumarti and Digumarti Pushpa Latha (1995). *Achievement in English*. New Delhi: Discovery Publishing House. ISBN 81-7141-283-1.

Bhaskara Rao, Digumarti and Digumarti Pushpa Latha (1994). *Achievement in Science*. New Delhi: Discovery Publishing House. ISBN 81-7141-280-70.

Bhaskara Rao, Digumarti and Digumarti Pushpa Latha (1995). *Achievement in Mathematics*. New Delhi: Discovery Publishing House. ISBN 81-7141-278-5.

Bhaskara Rao, Digumarti and Digumarti Pushpa Latha, Editors (1998). *International Encyclopaedia of Women*. 5 Volumes. New Delhi: Discovery Publishing House. ISBN 81-7141-410-9.

Vol. 1 *Status of World's Women*. ISBN 81-7141-494-X.

Vol. 2 *Women, Education and Empowerment*. ISBN 81-7141-498-1.

Vol. 3 *Women Challenges and Advancement*. ISBN 81-7141-497-4.

Vol. 4 *Women and Family Health*. ISBN 81-7141-497-4.

Vol. 5 *Women and International Action*. ISBN 81-7141-498-2.

Bhaskara Rao, Digumarti, Digumarti Pushpa Latha and Digumarti Harshitha, Editors (2001). *Biological Warfare*. New Delhi: Discovery Publishing House. ISBN 81-7141-597-0.

Bhaskara Rao, Digumarti, Digumarti Pushpa Latha and Digumarti Harshitha, Editors (2001). *Women as Educators*. New Delhi: Discovery Publishing House. ISBN 81-7141-602-0.

Bhaskara Rao, Digumarti and Digumarti Harshitha, Editors (2001). *Education in India*. New Delhi: APH Publishing Corporation. ISBN 81-7141-207-2.

Bhaskara Rao, Digumarti, Digumarti Pushpa Latha and Digumarti Harshitha, Editors (2001). *Assessing Learning Achievement*. New Delhi: Discovery Publishing House. ISBN 81-7141-601-2.

Bhaskara Rao, Digumarti, Digumarti Pushpa Latha and Digumarti Harshitha, Editors (2001). *Energy Security*. New Delhi: Discovery Publishing House. ISBN 81-7141-598-9.

Bhaskara Rao, Digumarti, Digumarti Harshitha and K.R.S.S. Rao, Editors (1999). *Advanced Biotechnology*. New Delhi: Discovery Publishing House. ISBN 81-7141-516-4.

Bhaskara Rao, Digumarti and K.R.S. Sambhasiva Rao, Editors (1996). *Current Trends in Indian Education*. New Delhi: Discovery Publishing House. ISBN 81-7141-311-0.

Bhaskara Rao, Digumarti and K. Vijaya (1995). *A Text Book of Evaluation*. Ambala Cantt: The Associated Publishers.

Bhaskara Rao, Digumarti and N.V.M. Mohana Rao (2002). *Problems of Mentally Handicapped Children*. New Delhi: Discovery Publishing House. ISBN 81-7141-645-4.

Bhaskara Rao, Digumarti and S. Chandra Mohan (2002). *Sports Management*. New Delhi: APH Publishing Corporation. ISBN 81-7648-467-9.

Bhaskara Rao, Digumarti and Sk. Johni Basha (2004). *Teachers' Population Education Awareness*. New Delhi: APH Publishing Corporation.

Bhaskara Rao, Digumarti, V.V. Rao, V.V. Lakshmi and V.V. Krishna, Editors (1999). *Status and Advancement of Women*. New Delhi: APH Publishing Corporation. ISBN 81-7648-169-6.

Babu, P.C., Author and Digumarti Bhaskara Rao, Editor (2004). *Flowers of Wisdom*. New Delhi: Discovery Publishing House. ISBN 81-7141-695-0.

Bhagya Lakshmi, Lingineni, Author and Digumarti Bhaskara Rao, Editor (2000). *Reading and Comprehension*. New Delhi: Discovery Publishing House. ISBN 81-7141-543-1.

Bhuvaneswara Lakshmi, Gadde, Author and Digumarti Bhaskara Rao, Editor (2000). *Attitude Towards Science*. New Delhi: Discovery Publishing House. ISBN 81-7141-541-6.

Devraj, T.A.S., Author and Digumarti Bhaskara Rao, Editor (1997). *Trace Analysis of Uranium and Thorium*. New Delhi: Discovery Publishing House. ISBN 81-7141-375-7.

Durga Rani, K., Author and Digumarti Bhaskara Rao, Editor (2000). *Educational Aspirations and Scientific Attitudes*. New Delhi: Discovery Publishing House. ISBN 81-7141-555-55.

Dutt, B.S.V. and Digumarti Bhaskara Rao (2001). *Empowering Primary Teachers*. New Delhi: Discovery Publishing House. ISBN 81-7141-615.2.

Ediger, Marlow and Digumarti Bhaskara Rao (1996). *Science Curriculum*. New Delhi: Discovery Publishing House. ISBN 81-7141-321-8.

Ediger, Marlow and Digumarti Bhaskara Rao (2000). *Teaching Mathematics Successfully*. New Delhi: Discovery Publishing House. ISBN 81-7141-552-0.

Ediger, Marlow and Digumarti Bhaskara Rao (2001). *Teaching Science Successfully*. New Delhi: Discovery Publishing House. ISBN 81-7141-600-4.

Ediger, Marlow and Digumarti Bhaskara Rao (2001). *Teaching Social Studies Successfully*. New Delhi: Discovery Publishing House. ISBN 81-7141-596-2.

Ediger, Marlow and Digumarti Bhaskara Rao (2002). *Philosophy and Curriculum*. New Delhi: Discovery Publishing House. ISBN 81-7141-631-4.

Ediger, Marlow and Digumarti Bhaskara Rao (2002). *Improving School Administration*. New Delhi: Discovery Publishing House. ISBN 81-7141-633-0.

Ediger, Marlow and Digumarti Bhaskara Rao (2002). *Elementary Curriculum*. New Delhi: Discovery Publishing House. ISBN 81-7141-658-6.

Ediger, Marlow and Digumarti Bhaskara Rao (2003). *Language Arts Curriculum*. New Delhi: Discovery Publishing House. ISBN 81-7141-657-8.

Ediger, Marlow and Digumarti Bhaskara Rao (2004). *Teaching Language Arts Successfully*. New Delhi: Discovery Publishing House. ISBN 81-7141-678-0.

Ediger, Marlow and Digumarti Bhaskara Rao (2004). *Teaching Mathematics in Elementary Schools*. New Delhi: Discovery Publishing House. ISBN 81-7141-687-X.

Ediger, Marlow and Digumarti Bhaskara Rao (2004). *Teaching Science in Elementary Schools*. New Delhi: Discovery Publishing House. ISBN 81-7141-709-4.

Ediger, Marlow and Digumarti Bhaskara Rao (2004). *School Curriculum and Administration*. New Delhi: Discovery Publishing House. ISBN 81-7141-709-4.

Ediger, Marlow and Digumarti Bhaskara Rao (2004). *Modern Elementary School*. New Delhi: Discovery Publishing House.

Ediger, Marlow and Digumarti Bhaskara Rao (2004): *Relevancy in Elementary Curriculum*. New Delhi: Discovery Publishing House. ISBN 81-7141-751-5.

Ediger, Marlow and Digumarti Bhaskara Rao, (2004). *Teaching Social Studies in Elementary Schools*. New Delhi: Discovery Publishing House.

Ediger Marlow, B.S.V. Dutt and Digumarti Bhaskara Rao (2004). *Teaching English Successfully*. New Delhi: Discovery Publishing House. ISBN 81-7141-707-8.

Harshitha, Digumarti and Digumarti Bhaskara Rao, Editors (2004). *Educational Innovations*. New Delhi: Discovery Publishing House.

Indira Devi, Author and J. Prasanth Kumar and Digumarti Bhaskara Rao, Editors (2004). *Values in Language Text Books*. New Delhi: Discovery Publishing House.

Jayasree, Kandi, Author and Digumarti Bhaskara Rao, Editor (1999). *Correlates of Socialisation*. New Delhi: Discovery Publishing House. ISBN 81-7141-517-2.

John Babu, Chikati, Author and T.J.R. Prasad, G.M. Madhukar and Digumarti Bhaskara Rao, Editors (1996). *Problem Solving in Mathematics*. New Delhi: APH Publishing Corporation. ISBN 81-7648-273-0.

Lalitha, T., Author and K.S. Prabhakaram, D.S.N. Sastry and Digumarti Bhaskara Rao, Editors (2004). *Educational Philosophic Beliefs*. New Delhi: Discovery Publishing House. ISBN 81-7141-765-5.

Madhu Bala, Jampala, Author and Digumarti Bhaskara Rao, Editor (2004). *Adjustment Problems of Hearing Impaired*. New Delhi: Discovery Publishing House.

Marja, Talvi and Digumarti Bhaskara Rao, Editors (1996). *Educational Leadership and Social Changes*. New Delhi: Discovery Publishing House. ISBN 81-7141-320-X.

Nirmala Jyothi, M., Author and Digumarti Bhaskara Rao, Editor (2003). *Non-detention Systems in School Education*. New Delhi: Discovery Publishing House. ISBN 81-7141-654-3.

Prabhakaram, K.S., Author and Digumarti Bhaskara Rao, Editor (1998). *Concept Attainment Model in Mathematics Teaching*. New Delhi: Discovery Publishing House. ISBN 81-7141-424-9.

Prasanth Kumar, J., Author and Digumarti Bhaskara Rao, Editor (1998). *Effectiveness of Distance Education System*. New Delhi: Discovery Publishing House. ISBN 81-7141-437-0.

Prasanth Kumar, J., Author and G. Sundara Rao and Digumarti Bhaskara Rao, Editors (2000). *Open University Student Support Services*. New Delhi: Discovery Publishing House. ISBN 81-7141-550-4.

Ramatulasamma, K., Author and Digumarti Bhaskara Rao, Editor (2002). *Job Satisfaction of Teacher Educators*, New Delhi: Discovery Publishing House. ISBN 81-7141-655-1.

Rama Krishnaiah, D., Author and Digumarti Bhaskara Rao, Editor (1998). *Job Satisfaction of College Teachers*, New Delhi: Discovery Publishing House. ISBN 81-7141-438-9.

Rama Kumar Ratnam, M., Author and Digumarti Bhaskara Rao, Editor (1998). *Dukka: Suffering in Early Buddhism*. New Delhi: Discovery Publishing House. ISBN 81-7141-653-5.

Rathaiah, Lavu and Digumarti Bhaskara Rao, Editors (1996). *International Innovations in Education*. New Delhi: Discovery Publishing House. ISBN 81-7141-359-5.

Ramesh, Ganta and Digumarti Bhaskara Rao, Editors (1998). *Environmental Education: Problems and Prospects*. New Delhi: Discovery Publishing House. ISBN 81-7141-423-0.

Rathaiah, Lavu and Digumarti Bhaskara Rao (1997). *Achievement Correlates*. New Delhi: Discovery Publishing House. ISBN 81-7141-385-4.

Reddy, Sudhakar Y., Author, and Digumarti Bhaskara Rao, Editor (2003). *Creativity in Adolescents*. New Delhi: Discovery Publishing House. ISBN 81-7141-659-4.

Reddy, M.S., Author and Digumarti Bhaskara Rao, Editor (2004). *Creativity in College Students*. New Delhi: Discovery Publishing House. ISBN 81-7141-697-7.

Radramamba, B., Author and Digumarti Bhaskara Rao, Editor (2003). *Problems of Teaching*. New Delhi: APH Publishing Corporation. ISBN 81-7648-462-8.

Sanjeeva Rao, P.C., Author and Digumarti Bhaskara Rao, Editor (1996). *A Text Book of Geology*. New Delhi: Discovery Publishing House. ISBN 81-7141-313-7.

Satya Narayana V., Author and Digumarti Bhaskara Rao, Editor (2001). *Physical Education, Social Attitudes and Leadership Qualities*. New Delhi: Discovery Publishing House. ISBN 81-7141-593-8.

Srinivasulu Reddy, M., and K.R.S. Sambasiva Rao, Authors and Digumarti Bhaskara Rao, Editor (1999). *A Text Book of Aquaculture*. New Delhi: Discovery Publishing House. ISBN 81-7141-482-6.

Srinivasa Rao, Mandalapu, Author and Digumarti Bhaskara Rao, Editor (2004). *Achievement Motivation and Achievement in Mathematics*. New Delhi: Discovery Publishing House. ISBN 81-7141-674-8.

Vanaja, M. Author and Digumarti Bhaskara Rao, Editor (1999). *Inquiry Training Model*. New Delhi: Discovery Publishing House. ISBN 81-7141-515-6.

Vanaja. M. and N. Sneha Latha, Authors and Digumarti Bhaskara Rao, Editor (2004). *Student Shyness*. New Delhi: APH Publishing Corporation.

Valeri V. Koustiouk, Author and Digumarti Bhaskara Rao, Editor (2002). *A Text Book of Cryogenics*. New Delhi: Discovery Publishing House. ISBN 81-7141-642-X.

Valeri V. Koustiouk, Author and Digumarti Bhaskara Rao, Editor (2004). *Refrigeration and Environment*. New Delhi: APH Publishing Corporation.

Veena Kumari, Balusu and Digumarti Bhaskara Rao (1996). *Operation Black Board*. New Delhi: Ashish Publishing Corporation. ISBN 81-7024-711-X.

Veena Kumari, Balusu, Author and Digumarti Bhaskara Rao, Editor (2000). *Psycho-Social Correlates of Achievement*, New Delhi: Discovery Publishing House. ISBN 81-7141-547-4.

Vanaja, M., Author and Digumarti Bhaskara Rao, Editor (1999). *Inquiry Training Model*. New Delhi: Discovery Publishing House. ISBN 81-7141-515-6.

Venkata Rao, P. and Digumarti Bhaskara Rao (1989). *A Text Book of Zoology—Junior Intermediate*. Guntur: Vignan Publishers.

Venkata Rao, P. and Digumarti Bhaskara Rao (1989). *A Text Book of Zoology—Senior Intermediate*. Guntur: Vignan Publishers.

Venugopala Rao, K., Author and Digumarti Bhaskara Rao, Editor (2000). *Teacher Morale in Secondary Schools*. New Delhi: Discovery Publishing House. ISBN 81-7141-551-2.

Vidya, C., Author and Digumarti Bhaskara Rao. Editor (1996). *A Text Book of Nutrition*. New Delhi: Discovery Publishing House. ISBN 81-7141-309-9.

Vidya Bharathi, D., Author and Digumarti Bhaskara Rao, Editor (2000). *Educational Philosophies of Swami Vivekananda and John Dewey*. New Delhi: APH Publishing Corporation. ISBN 81-7648-309-9.

Books in Telugu Language

Bhaskara Rao, Digumarti (1986). *Dhrushya Sravana Bodhanapakaranalu* (Audio Visual Teaching Aids). Guntur: Nagarjuna Publishers.

Bhaskara Rao, Digumarti (1993). *Jeevasashtra Bodhana* (Teaching of Biology). Guntur: Nagarjuna Publishers.

Bhaskara Rao, Digumarti (1995). *Vignanasasthra Bodhana* (Teaching of Science) Guntur: Nagarjuna Publishers.

Bhaskara Rao, Digumarti (1997). *Vidya Manovignana Seshtram* (Educational Psychology). Guntur: Creative Press.

Bhaskara Rao, Digumarti (1998). *DSC Study Material*. Guntur: Nagarjuna Publishers.

Bhaskara Rao, Digumarti (1998). *Upadhyayudu Vidya*. (Teacher and Education). Guntur: Nagarjuna Publishers.

Bhaskara Rao, Digumarti (1998). *Vidya Drukpadalu* (Prespectives of Education). Guntur: Nagarjuna Publishers.

Bhaskara Rao, Digumarti (1999). *EdCET Teaching Aptitude*. Guntur: Nagarjuna Publishers.

Bhaskara Rao, Digumarti (2001). *Bharata Samajamulo Upadyayudu Vidya* (Teacher and Education in Emerging Indian Society). Guntur: Nagarjuna Publishers.

Bhaskara Rao, Digumarti (2001). *Bhoutika Sastra Bodhana Paddathulu* (Methods of Teaching Physical Science). Guntur: Nagarjuna Publishers.

Bhaskara Rao, Digumarti (2001). *Jeeva Sastra Bodhana Padhathulu* (Methods of Teaching Biology). Guntur: Nagarjuna Publishers.

Bhaskara Rao, Digumarti (2001). *Vidya Manovignana Sastram* (Educational Psychology). Guntur: Nagarjuna Publishers.

Bhaskara Rao, Digumarti (2003). *Patsala Yajamanyam/Paripalana* (School Management and Administration). Guntur: Nagarjuna Publishers.

Bhaskara Rao, Digumarti (2004). *Vidya Sanketika Sastram mariyu Computer Vidya* (Educational Technology and Computer Education). Guntur: Nagarjuna Publishers.